Assessing Technology

Assessing Technology

International trends in curriculum and assessment
UK • Germany • USA • Taiwan • Australia

Richard Kimbell

Open University Press
Buckingham • Philadelphia

Open University Press
Celtic Court
22 Ballmoor
Buckingham
MK18 1XW

and
1900 Frost Road, Suite 101
Bristol, PA 19007, USA

First Published 1997

A catalogue record of this book is available from the British Library

ISBN   0 335 197825 (hb)   0 335 197817 (pb)

Library of Congress Cataloging-in-Publication Data
Kimbell, Richard.
    Assessing technology: international trends in curriculum &
assessment: UK, Germany, USA, Taiwan, Australia / Richard Kimbell.
      p.   cm.
    Includes bibliographical references and index.
    ISBN 0–335–19782–5   ISBN 0–335–19781–7 (pbk.)
    1. Technology—Study and teaching.   I. Title.
T65.K492   1997
607'.41—dc21   97–19356
                                                              CIP

Typeset by Graphicraft Typesetters Limited, Hong Kong
Printed in Great Britain by St Edmundsbury Press Ltd,
Bury St Edmunds, Suffolk

For Ben, Andrew and Harriet
who were very tolerant of my absences when I was
collecting data for Chapters 7–10

Contents

Acknowledgements

I am indebted to many people for their support and assistance in this project. In early 1996 Goldsmiths College granted me a six-month sabbatical period in which to collect the overseas data, and without that the whole project would not have been feasible. In planning and conducting these overseas investigations I am particularly indebted to the following people: to Mike Hacker at the New York State Department of Education; to John Williams at Edith Cowan University in Perth and Anne Fritz at Sydney University, Australia; to Dietrich Blandow and the late Horst Wengel at the World Council of Associations for Technology Education (WOCATE) office in Erfurt, Germany; and to Dr Chang-Shan Sun in Kaohsiung Normal University, Taiwan. I am also indebted to Sue Miller at the TERU offices at Goldsmiths for managing so effectively the resultant organisational and communications challenges.

In each country I was treated with great patience as I attempted to piece together an adequate account of the technology curriculum and its assessment. Many people gave generously of their time and expertise, and I am particularly grateful to the following:

In Taiwan

Dr Chang-Shan Sun (Associate Professor of Technology Education), Kaohsiung Normal University

Dr Rong-Jyue Fang (President), Taitung Teachers College

Yuh-Shan Chang and Tsu-Yin Wang (Associate Professors of Industrial Arts Education), Hualien Teachers College

Dr Kuo-hung Tseng (Chair of Industrial Education), Kaohsiung Normal University

Dr Hsi-Chi Hsiao (Professor and Chair of Industrial Education), National Changhua University of Education

Dr Ruey-Gwo Chung (Dept of Industrial Education), National Changhua University of Education

Dr Liang-Chih Huang (Associate Professor of Industrial Management), Kaohsiung Polytechnic Institute

Dr Teh-Tsang Tsai, Taiwan Central Area Vocational Technology Centre, Taichung

Shyr-Kai King and Yuang-Shaing Fu, Taichung Senior Vocational High School

Dr Ying-Hau Chen (Commissioner of Education), Taiwan Provincial Government

Archin Cheng (Programme Manager), Taiwan Semiconductor Manufacturing Co. Ltd

Dr Chung-Ta Yeh, Centre of Educational Evaluation, Tsin Chu Teachers College

Shih-Shion Liou (Dean of Studies) and Chin-Sheng Yang (Principal), Ta-An Technical High School

Dr Kun-Tion Chen (Senior Research Fellow), College Entrance Examination Centre, Taipei

Dr Lung-Sheng Lee (Chair of Industrial Technology Education), National Taiwan Normal University

Dr David Lee (Dean of Faculty of Arts), National Taiwan Normal University

In New York State, USA

Mr Michael Hacker (Supervisor for Technology)

Dr David Bower (Office of State Assessment)

Mrs Virginia Hammer (Curriculum Development)

Dr Richard Mills (Commissioner of Education), all at the New York State Department of Education

Mr Tom Venezio (Coordinator for Technology), Shaker High School, Albany

Dr Bruce Tulloch (District Coordinator for Science), Bethlehem High School

Mr Glen Botto (Maths/Science/Technology teacher), Arlington High School

Dr Annette Saturnelli (District Science Coordinator) and Mr Richard Sgroi (District Mathematics Coordinator), Newburgh City Schools

Ms Lucile Lewis (Maths/Science/Technology Coordinator), Brooklyn Middle School

Mr Barry Borakove (Technology teacher), Syosset High School

In Erfurt, Germany

Prof. Dr Dietrich Blandow and the late Horst Wengel, WOCATE

Dr Egon Schmuck, Dr Berndt Hill and Prof Dr Manfred Leutherdt, Pädagogische Hochschule (Teacher Education University College) Erfurt

Dr Marion Malz (Head teacher) and Dr Fothe (*Landesfachberater* for Informatics), Albert Schweitzer Gymnasium (Grammar School) Erfurt

Prof. Dr Mathias Scharlach (Director), Vocational Training Centre for Economy and Administration; Erfurt
Dr Ungewiss (Director), Erfurt Technikzentrum
Jaqueline Truckenbrodt (Teacher i/c Technics), Neuhaus-Schierschnitz Regelschule (Secondary School)

In Australia

Dr John Williams (Technology specialist, Faculty of Education) and Dr Jack Banna (Acting Dean), Edith Cowan University, Perth, W. Australia
Dr Anne Fritz (Associate Dean, Faculty of Education), University of Sydney, NSW
Kathy Melsom (Technology and Enterprise specialist), Dept of Education, W. Australia
Dr Michael Partis (Director) and Valerie Gould (Senior Education Officer, Vocational Education), Secondary Education Authority, W. Australia
Bernie Dierks (Head of Technology), Mount Lawley High School, Perth, W. Australia
Les Nunn (Head of Technology), Hale School, Perth, W. Australia
Dr Kevin Morgan (President, Australian Council for Education through Technology (ACET)), Griffith University, Queensland
Susan McGirr (Head of Technology), Leeming Senior High School, Perth, W. Australia
Peter Cavanagh (Curriculum Consultant), Department of Education, W. Australia
Lyndall Foster (Chief Education Officer, Technology), New South Wales Department of School Education, Sydney
Bob Staples (Board Inspector, Technology), Board of Studies, New South Wales, Sydney
Stephen Keirl, University of South Australia, Adelaide

In developing my understanding of our UK technology curriculum and its assessment I am grateful to so many people, too numerous to mention individually. I would, however, like to thank two in particular who – over ten years of research at Goldsmiths College – have consistently provided me with insights that have enriched my understanding. To Kay Stables and to John Saxton I am deeply indebted; may we long continue to argue.

Introduction

Technology: a new discipline with new problems for assessment

The technology curriculum in the UK has evolved in the last thirty years. In the mid-1960s there was nothing in schools that even vaguely resembled the technology curriculum that is now a mandatory part of every child's schooling. And thirty years is an astonishingly short time for this evolution to have taken place. I have explored elsewhere some of the major landmarks in this evolution and the justifications for its development as a curriculum activity (see Kimbell *et al*. 1996, esp. Chapters 2–3).

In this book I intend to explore the thorny issues of assessment that have been raised by the emergence of the technology curriculum. The heart of this problem lies in the fact that the technology curriculum has consistently been defined as a *process* of design and development rather than just a body of knowledge and skills. The process is influenced and enriched by knowledge and practical skills – but assessing pupils' *capability* in the process of design and development is a far more complex matter than simply assessing their knowledge and skills. Technology has been ahead of the game here. Whilst science, language, maths and the rest of the curriculum are now recognised as having important process elements that need to be assessed, it is in technology that we have been trail-blazing models of process-centred assessment for the last twenty years. It is with these innovations that I am principally concerned in this book.

Ten testing years

The last ten years in particular have been years of dramatic change in curriculum and assessment. In the mid-1980s we were seeking to reconcile the two old traditions of 16+ assessment – Certificate of Secondary Education (CSE) and General Certificate of Education (GCE) – into a single system for all pupils. With very little training – but with a great deal of good will in schools – the transformation was achieved and by common consent it has been a successful development. But barely had the dust settled on the new formulation before we were at it again with the developments that were to lead to the National Curriculum and its associated assessment regime.

Here we were far less successful. A sorry combination of political ideology and educational muddle resulted in the promulgation of one of the most lunatic schemes of assessment ever to hit schools. It created anger, resentment, frustration and ultimately it got what it deserved – the boot (as did the hapless Secretary of State). The shambles of National Curriculum assessment in 1991 and 1992 united teachers, heads, parents and governors in a series of drastic actions that would formerly have been unthinkable in schools. Hundreds of thousands of tests were written, published and distributed to schools – and teachers dumped them in the waste bin. What dreadful combination of mistakes could possibly account for a normally passive and easy-going profession taking such direct and drastic action? Those who do not learn from history are doomed to relive it, and this book is my attempt to understand and explain what happened. I shall describe and analyse the successes of our assessment developments and I shall attempt to account for the chaos of the early years of National Curriculum assessment.

I write as an 'insider' who was closely involved in the events of the time. During the early 1980s I was inside the debates that were central to the evolution of the merged form of 16+ assessment – the General Certificate of Secondary Education (GCSE), launched in 1986 – and equally I was party to the battles (they were seldom cool debates) that characterised the development of National Curriculum assessment in the late 1980s. I was also fortunate enough to be inside the single biggest research venture in the assessment of technology; the Assessment of Performance Unit (APU) project in design and technology of 1985–91 (see Chapter 3).

In Part One of this book I shall focus on the traditions of assessment that supported the early evolution of technology; how our understanding both of the technology curriculum and its assessment was extended by the APU research; and how the National Curriculum in technology and its associated assessment came to be the way it was. In telling this story, I shall attempt to analyse what seem to me to be the successes and the mistakes, and I shall bring these together (in Chapter 6) into a series of lessons that we should learn from the last few years.

International comparisons

But technology is increasingly a worldwide development in the curriculum. During the troubled National Curriculum years of 1990–93 we were constantly being told how much better things were in other parts of the world – in Germany, for example, or in the Far East. I vividly recall Kenneth Baker's glowing accounts of technology in 'magnet schools' in

New York, and more recently we have been regaled with accounts from Taiwan and elsewhere, where practice is supposedly so developed that pupil performance should leave us gasping in admiration and floundering in their wake.

I decided to conduct my own comparative study of practice in a range of nations that have some reputation in the world of technology. My concern was primarily with assessment practices in technology, but of course this can only be described and analysed in the context of the technology curriculum and this in turn can only sensibly be described in relation to a wider awareness of the school systems as a whole. Accordingly, in Part Two of this book, I present four vignettes of curriculum and assessment practice in technology from other parts of the world and I chose to study the USA, Germany, Taiwan and Australia. In each case I outline the education system, the technology curriculum and its associated assessment practices.

In selecting these countries, the USA was an obvious choice; it is the ultimate technological society and there is more than a little truth in the notion that what happens in the USA today will happen in ten years' time in the UK. However, the USA devolves the majority of its education policy-making to the state level, and I chose to focus on New York State since it is at the leading edge of technology curriculum development. The Federal Republic of Germany, too, was not difficult to select, partly because I wanted another European country to contrast with the UK and partly because – like the USA – it has an immense technological reputation. My investigations in Germany are focused on Thuringia – a *Land* or state of the former East Germany but situated at the geographic heart of the modern Federal Republic. In one place I have, therefore, been able to examine an education system in transition from the closed, paternalistic traditions of East Germany to the open, competitive instincts of West Germany. I chose Taiwan from a short list of five 'tiger' economies on the Pacific rim (I might have chosen Malaysia, Korea, Japan or Singapore). Of this short list, Taiwan proved the most enticing because of the contrasts it represents; it is a formidable modern manufacturing nation, and yet it has roots in a deeply traditional Chinese culture. Finally, I selected Australia as a nation that has its roots in UK traditions of education, but which in the last ten years has progressively moved to develop its own distinctive national curriculum – not least in technology. In Australia I have focused on two states (Western Australia and New South Wales) which are at different stages of development with the technology curriculum and which have very contrasted approaches to their national curriculum.

In these four national case studies, I have attempted to follow the same guidelines, addressing the same issues so as to be able to make appropriate comparisons that in their turn can illuminate our practices in the UK. The dramatic contrasts between the four nations occasionally prevented me from maintaining absolute consistency, but for the most part the approach was workable. In the final chapter of 'Reflections', I have brought together the lessons learned over the last ten years in the UK (Chapter 6) with the lessons that might reasonably be learned from practice in the four case-study nations.

Interwoven and interdependent

Had we not developed sound approaches for assessing pupil performance in process-based technology, then the curriculum would not have been able to develop as it did. I am not, therefore, an apologist for assessment and I do not believe that curriculum development and assessment development are separate stories. Understanding assessment and developing good assessment practices are central to understanding and developing good curriculum. In any assessment regime, one is forced to identify and make explicit what will count as excellent, good, satisfactory and unsatisfactory performance. In seeking to resolve these qualitative matters, and to find ways of enabling pupils to demonstrate their quality, we contribute to the progressive clarification of the discipline. Curriculum and assessment are therefore not separate stories but flip-sides of the same story. The title of this book, *Assessing Technology*, is intended to reflect this duality. It is about how we assess pupil performance in technology, but it is also about how we might assess the quality of the technology curriculum.

In 1990, the UK was the first nation on earth to make a technology curriculum compulsory for all pupils between 5 and 16 years of age. It was a pivotal moment in time. Or rather, it was a visionary moment that was ahead of its time. There are lessons to be learned from what we did and how we did it, and I hope that some of these lessons are made explicit in this book in ways that enable us to learn from our mistakes whilst capitalising on the undoubted successes.

Richard Kimbell
Goldsmiths College, University of London

part one

Technology and its assessment in the UK, 1965–1996

one

Assessment lays
the foundations

Technology in the school curriculum has been shaped by the priorities of assessment. The two stories (defining the discipline and assessing pupil capability) are intimately interwoven in a way that is quite unique in the curriculum.

Technology is, of course, a relative newcomer in the curriculum – emerging from a range of craft-based traditions only in the last thirty years. By contrast, the vast majority of the curriculum of England and Wales is deeply rooted in the mists of our educational past, and Goodson (1985) provides a revealing analysis of this long tradition. His 'histories' (for example, of science, mathematics, religious education and the rest) are typically far more than a century in the making and underline the durability of these traditions, as Williams (1965) observes: 'The fact about our present curriculum is that it was essentially created by the 19th century, following some 18th century models and retaining elements of the mediaeval curriculum near its centre.'

But technology as it now exists, as a mandatory part of the National Curriculum, is different. It does not even get a mention in Goodson's (1985) 'histories'. It is a product of thirty years of such intense curriculum development that each step in the evolutionary chain has come hot on the heels of the last, creating transformation upon transformation.

Such a situation is bound to be intensely unstable. And this internal instability has occurred at a point in history when the whole education service is itself undergoing dramatic transformation. *External* instability has therefore been piled upon *internal* instability. In the last fifteen years in particular, even subjects with deep roots and established traditions have struggled to maintain coherent direction. Historians, for example, were at each other's throats over 'factual' and 'empathetic' models of history teaching. But technology had neither the roots nor the traditions of the vast majority of curriculum disciplines. Rather, it was seeking to create itself amidst the ferment of change. We should not be surprised that this bubbling cauldron created a few explosive reactions.

High on the list of transformations in the last few years stand those concerning assessment. Disenchantment with the limited formal strictures of GCE O-level examinations[1] led to the emergence of more flexible school-centred CSE examinations.[2] Dissatisfaction with the resulting two-tiered structure then led to pressure for their amalgamation into a single system of examining for all pupils. In preparation for this development, the newly established Secondary Examinations Council (SEC)[3] launched a major consolidation exercise in which all 'subjects' in the secondary curriculum were required (in 1985) to define themselves in 'National Criteria'. This exercise in definition led to some of the most ferocious debates I have ever experienced. There was blood on the walls in Notting Hill Gate.

Having fought our way through the National Criteria exercise, we then embarked on the enormously complex process of establishing the GCSE examination itself with all the attendant arguments about course content, examination procedures and educational standards. By 1988 the first cohort of pupils was just completing its GCSE courses and taking the first round of examinations set by the newly merged examination groups.[4] It was clearly time for another upheaval, only this time the upheaval was absolute. We embarked on the National Curriculum.

Once again we were stuck in the thicket trying to define technology, not just in terms of existing practice but in terms laid down by the Education Reform Act of 1988; to accommodate the model of assessment dreamed up by the Task Group on Assessment and Testing (Department of Education and Science (DES) 1987a); and being leaned on at regular intervals by functionaries from the DES and (SEAC).[5] The process of definition took place through the 1988 *Interim Report of the Design and Technology Working Group* (DES 1988a) and the subsequent Statutory Order for Technology (DES 1990).

Again the exercise was controversial, with numerous players competing for ownership of this half-formed entity, technology. We might, however, have survived the process intact had it not been for the utterly lunatic model of assessment that the National Curriculum required. Within weeks of the publication of the Order teachers were struggling to assess pupil performance in technology against 150 'can-do' statements of attainment: a process that ran completely counter to the entirety of teachers' experience of assessment in schools.

On top of the teachers' school-based assessments came the official testing in the form of Standard Assessment Tasks (SATs). Initially for pupils at age 14, then also for age 7, these new assessment instruments made yet further demands on teachers, testing their understanding of the new definition of technology. For many primary schools this was their first encounter with technology.

Within months of trying to teach and assess technology as defined in the 1990 version of the National Curriculum, teachers were told they were getting it all wrong. Her Majesty's Inspectorate of Schools (HMI) wrote critical reports and all the special interest groups that felt they had been ignored or marginalised by the 1990 formulation of technology were out sharpening their knives and grinding their axes. It was a period of grossly ill-informed and very public blood-letting.

In the end it was the teachers who put a stop to the assessment madness by their astonishingly solid refusal to have anything to do with the 1992 and 1993 SATs. But by that time, the problems of technology were being blamed not on the assessment system but on the definition of the subject in the Statutory Order. It was time for yet another rewrite. Over the following two years another three versions of technology were written and debated before we finally ended up with a new Statutory Order (Department for Education 1995). The formulation of this Order was significantly affected by the new approach to assessment involving eight broad levels of judgment in place of the 150 statements of attainment.

This potted history of the last fifteen years is far from comprehensive, but I trust it is sufficient to demonstrate the environment within which technology was created as a school subject. At every turn those of us working within the field of technology were forced to define, redefine, and re-redefine what we were doing. And in most cases this pursuit of ever tighter definition was motivated by the needs of assessment: for GCE, for CSE, for National Criteria, for GCSE, for A level, for National Curriculum.

As I said at the start of this chapter, technology in the school curriculum has been shaped by the priorities of assessment. The two stories (defining the discipline and assessing pupil capability) are intimately interwoven in a way that is quite unique in the curriculum. I do not regard this as a bad thing – but it is a fact. There is enough of the philosopher in me to relish endless debate about what we are doing and why. And the fact that the ground rules keep changing can add a good deal of spice to the debate. But whilst I relish a good argument, there is no doubt that the constant uncertainty of the last fifteen years has militated against technology developing firm traditions based on established values.

But interestingly, despite all the upheavals, there are some strands of thought that *have* become deeply rooted in the literature and in the consciousness of technology teachers. Two of these deeply rooted ideas have been particularly influential in shaping our understanding of technology – and both of them came to prominence because of their misfit with traditional examination and assessment regimes.

Misfit number 1: theory or practice?

When I took my O- and A-level examinations in the 1960s, I was required to engage in two kinds of activity. In one I was required to sit with rows of other candidates in the heavy silence of examination halls, busily writing 'answers' to test questions. In the other I was permitted to use a carefully defined set of tools and materials to mark out, cut, join and finish a practical test-piece of craftsmanship. I was one of the countless candidates processed through the tried and tested routine of 'theory' and 'practical' tests. The entirety of my supposed expertise was subsumed and examined under one or other of these two headings. The 'theory' tests were about memory and writing, and the 'practical' tests were about organisation and skill.

I was always fascinated by the fact that there was absolutely no connection between these two kinds of examination. Whilst in everyday life – and even in most of school life – I was expected to operate as an integrated whole, as soon as it came to examinations I could be neatly parcelled up into two entirely separate packages. The world of thoughts and ideas was suddenly quite removed from the world of action. The idea that one might think and have ideas *about that action* was dangerously radical and well beyond the scope of the examinations of the day.

What I did not at the time realise, however, was that I was in at the birth of a quite new development; by 1970, a radically new form of examination had squeezed itself into the picture, and no one was quite sure whether it was to be treated as a 'theory' or as a 'practical'. It involved writing and other kinds of 'desk-work', but it also required practical activity and the manipulation of tools and materials. It was the brainchild of George Hicks,[6] the chief examiner for the London University O level in design and technology. The difficulty of placing this new form of examination within the formal constraints of the GCE structure is evident in the title that was eventually settled for this exam paper. It became the 'pre-practical', and required candidates to work from a tightly constructed design brief and design and make a part-product that was subsequently to be fitted to the product that was the focus of the practical examination. For example, one year candidates had to design and make an angle adjustment system that was subsequently fitted to a hot-wire cutter so that angled pieces of expanded polystyrene could be cut. In another year candidates had to design and make a levelling device that was subsequently to be fitted to a surveyor's theodolite stand.

It is difficult to overestimate the impact of this single initiative in assessment. At a stroke, the pre-practical examination had welded theory to practice – lending legitimacy to the notion that it is right and proper to exercise thought and imagination in the world of products and manufacture. However, one of the lessons that candidates learned through this pre-practical examination, was that in order to gain maximum marks it was necessary to make one's thinking very clear. It is all very well having lots of ideas for a levelling device, but if the examiner failed to see them, the pupil was given no credit for them. So the idea of design drawings – collected into a design portfolio – was a natural extension of the pre-practical. At the school in which I was teaching it enabled us for the first time to mount exhibitions of imaginative design solutions that pupils had developed and gained credit for even within the academic, hide-bound GCE tradition. Naturally the amount of credit that candidates could gain in this way was strictly limited, but it was a very important step in the evolution of technology.

Misfit number 2: process or product?

In retrospect we can see the London pre-practical examination as an early and somewhat primitive step towards establishing one of the core features of technology in schools – the need to understand and be able to assess the *process* of design and development. There were many things that could be tested by written papers and practical tests, but these traditional assessment strategies were unable to get to grips with this underpinning process. Assessing the 'real-time' capability of a pupil to work through a design and development process just did not fit with the normal conventions of examinations.

However, the London O-level examinations team was not alone in seeing the centrality of the process to technology, and it was another group entirely that took the lead in reconciling this problematic misfit. Two technology-related research projects were launched in the late 1960s: Project Technology at Loughborough University and the Design and Craft Education Project at Keele University. By the end of the pilot phase (1968–70) of Project Technology the research team was quite unequivocal about the centrality of the process of design and development: 'Technology is a process which can be observed fully only from the inside; it is an activity, not a readily definable area of knowledge' (Schools Council 1970, p. 4). The team's subsequent work confirmed this early diagnosis: 'The essence of school technological projects is the full and practical involvement in all stages of the technological design process' (School Technology Forum 1974, p. 7). The idea began to take root that 'design projects' should be the defining feature of a course in technology and it was the Design and Craft Education Project at Keele University that began to wrestle with the problem of relating an abstracted 'design process' to a model of assessment.

Articulating the process

The Keele research team, under the direction of Prof. John Eggleston, produced the first comprehensive guidance to teachers about running design projects, and once again we see the importance of assessment to their developing work. For their most influential strategy was to create a 16+ CSE examination in association with the North Western Secondary School Examination Board (NWSEB). As Eggleston and his team were subsequently to write:

> It may be argued that external examinations at 16+ exert too powerful an influence as determinants of the curriculum, and that freedom from such examinations would enable greater variety and more exciting work to be undertaken ... [however] ... While industry, parents and students alike value examinations ... they will continue as a major control mechanism of the contents and attainments of secondary education.
>
> (Schools Council 1974, p. 38)

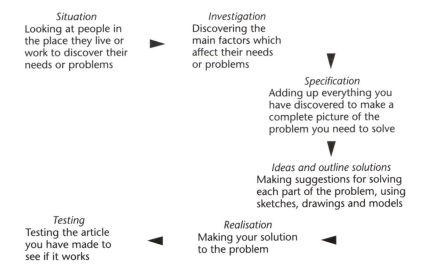

Figure 1.1 The design and development process as specified for the experimental CSE examination by the NWSEB.

Eggleston understood how schools work. He knew that the model of design that his research team was beginning to articulate would get nowhere without the external stamp of approval that in the context of England and Wales could only be provided by an examination. 'A Course of Studies in Design' was the answer they developed and piloted in 1970 in association with the NWSEB, and it contains some absolutely seminal material about the process of designing. Figure 1.1 shows what (at the time) the process was seen to involve. With the 20 : 20 hindsight with which most of us are gifted, there are several features of this articulation with which we might wish to argue. But as a product of its time (1970) it was quite remarkable. In addition to the description of the process, there are three additional things for which this initiative deserves recognition as one of the great landmarks in the development of technology.

First, having established and formalised the process (Figure 1.1), the project team went on to translate it into a model for assessment (Figure 1.2). Each stage of the process became, in turn, the focus of explicit assessment on a sliding scale from 0 (no real attempt) to 5 (comprehensive grasp of the capability). The final mark out of 25 was therefore seen as a measure of whole capability. Again the team's approach might now seem very naive, but it was the first time it had been done.

For the first time it became possible and legitimate to assess the whole process of design and development that pupils pursue over an extended period. At a time when most project work assessment (for example, in metalwork) was solely about the quality of manufacture, this scheme required teachers to make judgments about pupils' grip on the whole process of design and development, including the manufacture.

	0	1	2	3	4	5
Situation and brief						
Investigation						
Solution						
Realisation						
Testing						
Total	(out of 25)					

Figure 1.2 The assessment model derived from the process of design (NWSEB 1970, p. 9).

Second, and despite Eggleston's comments that examinations 'will continue as a major control mechanism of the contents and attainments of secondary education' (Eggleston 1996), the Course of Study in Design deliberately avoided the specification of course content. As the course booklet explains: 'It is not therefore possible to itemise a syllabus for practical work under headings of specific knowledge or motor skills because these may vary according to the individual needs of candidates and the requirements of different design problems' (NWSEB 1970, p. 2). This was brave stuff. One might almost say that the course was so focused on the *process* of designing that it was content-free. In reality, however, the scheme allowed schools to link design project work assessments within this course to the 'theory' papers of pre-existing courses – for example, in domestic science. Nevertheless, the Keele team had seen and expressed the logic of the situation. If the *process* of designing is to be the core concern, then the *content* must be a secondary matter.

Third, the Course of Study in Design grappled with the pedagogic issue of helping teachers to teach it, using a 'project book' which was designed to take pupils through the process step by step. For each of the steps in the process there was a page in the book, and each amounted to a list of questions that pupils ought to be addressing at that point in the process. So, for example, when pupils were 'investigating' for the design of playground equipment, they had to think about

What social factors affect it?	e.g. Does it involve one person or more?
	What are the relationships?
What material factors are involved?	e.g. Must they be light?
	How strong must they be?
	(NWSEB 1970, p. 3)

But when pupils were making their solution, the booklet steered them to different questions.

In which order shall I make the pieces?
Will I need any special materials not in stock?
How long should it take to make each part?

(NWSEB 1970, p. 6)

Taken together, this pilot examination represented a giant leap forward from the world of craft teaching and its single-minded assessment of making skills. Pupils were not only being empowered to make their own decisions about manufacturing issues, but also being encouraged to originate and pursue their own design tasks, often derived from outside the school. The last word on this initiative should go to a teacher who was involved in the pilot years of running the course. Reflecting on the development, the teacher perceptively picked out both the major pedagogic strength and the major difficulty in running the course. And interestingly, they have remained the key classroom issues for technology through the succeeding twenty-five years:

> any course which sets out to make the student think and plan ahead, and then forces him [sic] to set down his thoughts in a series of steps, can do nothing but good . . . [but] . . . students find it difficult to plan ahead . . . because they are not used to making their thinking explicit.
>
> (Schools Council 1975, p. 63)

However, my principal concern here is with the *assessment* contribution of the project, and here there are two things to be said, both concerning the transferability of this model of design practice.

First, the description of what designing is all about has stayed remarkably consistent over the intervening twenty-five years. The number of steps is sometimes elaborated, and the relationships between them is occasionally tinkered with, but the central idea remains the same. Indeed, the four design and technology attainment targets from the 1990 National Curriculum represent an amazingly parallel statement to Eggleston's from 1970. The description of the processes of design and development has become so commonplace, that it has almost become an accepted truth.

However, there has been another developing trend in that period, and it brings me to the second factor affecting the transferability of the model especially in relation to the reliability of assessments made within it. If the teacher is to make a judgment (on a 0–5 scale) about the quality of a pupil's investigation in the project, how does the teacher set the level? What level of quality is to count as level 1 or level 3 or level 5? And how can we know that all teachers will make the same decisions about setting the levels? In the early days, what typically happened was that the performance of the pupil group was distributed across the range of marks so that the best were given 5 and the worst 0. In short, the scale of excellence was defined by the quality of the group of pupils. It was a norm-referenced system. As a result, if teachers from two schools came together to discuss 'standards', they might quite conceivably be using two quite different scales.

This was increasingly seen as unacceptable, and the need for transferability of standards of excellence in relation to the description of designing led to a series of attempts to define what we mean by excellent, good, satisfactory and poor performance. In short, we were embarking on the road to criterion-referenced assessment, laying down in assessment criteria the qualities of excellence that were believed to be important.

This next step – of defining performance criteria – illustrates once again how the evolution of design and technology as a subject for study in schools has been tied to the evolution of examination and assessment requirements. As I shall attempt to show in the next chapter, this process of definition has been fraught with problems.

Notes

1 The GCE (General Certificate of Education) was a 16+ examination designed for high-ability pupils. It supported option choices for A-level (18+) courses and subsequently for university entrance.
2 The CSE (Certificate of Secondary Education) was a form of 16+ examination designed for school leavers of average and below average ability.
3 The SEC was set up as a quango with statutory responsibility for overseeing all matters to do with examination and assessment in secondary schools.
4 The former GCE examination boards (typically centred on universities) were compulsorily merged with the CSE examining boards (typically centred on geographical regions) to form five 'competing' examination groups. (Southern, London and East Anglian, Northern, Wales, Midland).
5 The SEAC (School Examinations and Assessment Council) took over from the SEC when the looming requirements of National Curriculum assessment in *primary* schools rendered the 'SEC' title inappropriate.
6 At the time George Hicks was head of the Design and Technology Department at Goldsmiths College; he later became a schools inspector and eventually Staff Inspector for Design and Technology at the DES.

two

The road to atomisation

In search of criteria

The articulation of the process of design and development enabled early assessment schemes in technology to be used to measure pupil performance against the whole process instead of simply in terms of the quality of manufacture of the end-product of that process. However, the descriptions were rather sketchy, and when teachers were in dispute over whether a given piece of work should be awarded an A or a B, there were no established criteria against which to justify any conclusion.

Increasingly, therefore, in the late 1970s and early 1980s there was a growing awareness that we ought to define these standards in advance – in criteria that could be applied to the work of all pupils in an even-handed way. The opportunity to act on this matter presented itself with the work of the SEC and specifically in the planning for the new generation of GCSE syllabuses for 16+ examinations.

One of the fundamental tenets in the development of the GCSE was that norm referencing of the sort that had formerly existed in the vast majority of GCE and CSE assessment was unreliable and unhelpful because it did not identify in clear and positive terms what pupils were capable of doing. All it did was to distribute pupils across a mark range. In the new regime, GCSE General Criteria were specific in requiring examinations that ensured proper discrimination and provided opportunities for pupils 'to show what they know, understand, and can do' (Secondary Examinations Council 1985, para. 16). Here was a clear imperative to draw up criteria to enable us to remove the concept of 'average' or normed performance. A pupil's capability was no longer to be described by comparison to *other pupils* performance, rather it was to be *defined* through a series of positive 'can-do' descriptors. The assessment process would then require teachers to identify which descriptors applied to each pupil. If a pupil was given 4 out of 5 for 'evaluating' it was not simply because she was nearly (but not

Figure 2.1 The GCSE cycle of designing (Kimbell 1986, p. 10).

quite) at the top of a rank order of other pupils, but rather because she was capable of meeting the defined requirement for a mark of 4:

the performance required to achieve a particular mark is therefore specified in advance in the list of criteria on the form. It is therefore both more precise and more useful in a situation in which it is imposs-ible for one teacher to know exactly what norms will be used by another teacher . . . the norms are encapsulated in the criteria.

(Kimbell 1986, p. 38)

As far as the articulation of the process of designing was concerned, the 1986 GCSE formulation (Figure 2.1) might be seen as a next step forward from the 1970 model, though clearly derived from it. There were two developments from earlier models, one of minor significance and one crit-ical refinement. The minor issue concerned the closing of the loop, and the recognition that the completion of one design cycle typically creates a whole mass of new problems and opportunities that can be the starting point for more designing. The major issue concerned the interaction of the steps within the cycle. This arose from increasing unease at the rigidly lock-step approach to designing that was starting to emerge in practice in

The candidate's evaluation:
0 – has not been attempted;
1 – is irrelevant;
2 – is relevant but superficial;
3 – represents an honest attempt to appraise his or her work but lacks objectivity and is either incomplete or not altogether relevant;
4 – is complete and largely relevant but lacking in objectivity;
5 – is thorough, objective, relevant and concise; it would provide a useful source of reference for later material.

Figure 2.2 GCSE 'criteria' for the quality of a candidate's evaluation (Northern Examination Association 1986).

schools.[1] This is a matter to which I shall return later in this chapter and in the next.

The transition from GCE/CSE 'norms' to GCSE 'criteria' resulted in the development of a series of 'can-do' statements that were intended to characterise performance at a range of levels. For example, in the 1970s CSE examination, the quality of 'evaluation' was a single judgment on a 0–5 scale. For the GCSE equivalent in 1986, each point on this scale was identified through a unique descriptor (Figure 2.2), and the process of assessment for the teacher amounted to identifying which descriptor best fitted the performance of each pupil in relation to their evaluating.

Clearly, these descriptors (assessment criteria) represented an attempt to embody the received wisdom of what excellence entails. But they were in reality based on little more than the best guess of the chief examiner for that course. The criteria were often arbitrary, and were in any case liberally littered with normative words, such as 'thorough', 'objective' and 'relevant'. How thorough is thorough? How relevant is relevant? The statements were sufficiently vague to make the teacher's task of assessment just as difficult as it had always been. The criteria helped to the extent that they identified that evaluation was something to do with appraisal, relevance, thoroughness and objectivity. But it was of little help beyond that point. Suppose, for example, that a pupil's work was thought to be 'objective but superficial', not an uncommon combination. Where was the teacher supposed to place it on the scale?

Despite these difficulties, the GCSE innovation was a huge success, not least because the vast majority of teachers believed in it as a matter of principle. They were fed up with the inequalities of the former GCE/CSE regime. They had too frequently been placed in the invidious position of deciding whether to enter pupils for (typically) a dull, formal, high-status GCE examination course or a more interesting, relevant but low-status CSE examination course. This decision was always tricky, but it was particularly difficult when dealing with the mass of pupils in the middle of the ability range. A single system of examining for all pupils at 16+ was therefore widely held to be a great step forward.

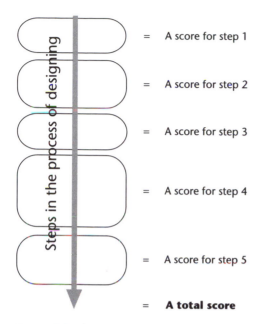

= A score for step 1

= A score for step 2

= A score for step 3

= A score for step 4

= A score for step 5

= **A total score**

Figure 2.3 The assessment procedure developed from 1970 and culminating in GCSE systems in 1986.

... and yet more criteria

A mere four years after these innovative GCSE days, and after two years of National Curriculum development, the Statutory Order for Technology was published in 1990. Technology was now a 'foundation subject' in the National Curriculum. I shall be dealing in detail with this development in Chapters 3 and 4, but here I intend merely to use it to indicate the next step in the relentless march towards criterion-based assessment.

It was a huge next step, even if it was not recognised as such at the time. All the experience of assessment in technology had accustomed teachers to the idea that there is a generic process called designing; this is divided up into sections; each section gets a block of marks; and the assessment 'criteria' enable the teacher to decide how many marks the candidate should be given for each section. These are then added up to give the final total score (Figure 2.3). In this regime, criteria were used by teachers to guide decisions about the balance of excellence: 'Does this piece justify 12 out of 15, or would 10 out of 15 be more like it?'

The new world of National Curriculum assessment was to be totally different in the sense that there were to be no marks to be added up. The Statutory Order (DES 1990) sought to lay out – for the first time – a comprehensive description of the progression of capability that is required between ages 5 and 16 both in terms of the *programmes of study* that teachers use to plan their teaching in school and in the *attainments* that pupils

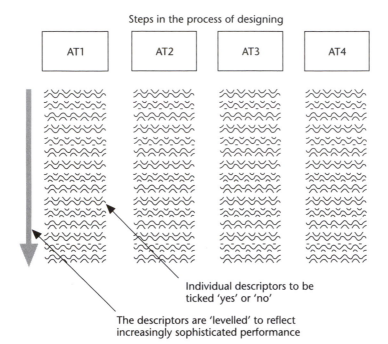

Steps in the process of designing

Individual descriptors to be
ticked 'yes' or 'no'

The descriptors are 'levelled' to reflect
increasingly sophisticated performance

Figure 2.4 The new assessment regime for the National Curriculum.

should seek to demonstrate through those programmes. The four original attainment targets (ATs) again reflected the process of design and development and the statements of attainment (SoA) were intended to provide a comprehensive criterion-referenced assessment scheme within those ATs. It is important to note that there were nearly 150 such SoA, each intended to describe a specific quality at a particular level.

Whilst the description of the process (in the ATs) remained more or less the same, the really big change was that the criterion statements (SoA) were no longer to be used to support a balancing judgment about the allocation of a number of marks. There were no marks any more. The criteria (SoA) were now a set of simple yes/no propositions that the teacher had either to agree with or not in relation to pupils' work (Figure 2.4). Guidance from SEAC (1989, p. 24) summarised how these SoA were to be used:

Teacher assessment is criterion-referenced; a child is assessed in relation to a criterion given by a Statement of Attainment . . . The SoA can provide a reference for the level of achievement met . . . Pupils' successful achievement of SoA provide

- a map of the progress of the whole class;
- help to pinpoint gaps and prompt direct action;
- give an instant picture of what has and has not been achieved by individuals and groups;
- help to identify the need for remedial action . . .

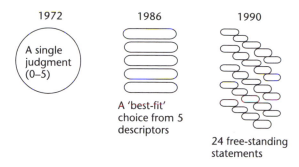

Figure 2.5 The progressive atomisation of assessment over twenty years.

Over the next few years, and after uncountable hours of labour, teachers were to see these SoA as providing anything but 'an instant picture' of anything.

Looking again at the assessment of 'evaluation' in the designing process it is possible to illustrate the progressive atomisation of assessment over the twenty-year period up to the launch of the National Curriculum. In Eggleston's pilot CSE course (in 1972) it had been a single judgment of capability on a 0–5 scale. This became (in 1986) a choice of one 'best-fit' descriptor from five possibles, and then (in 1990) a series of 24 independent SoA (Figure 2.5).

It can be argued, of course, that these are not directly comparable, since the first two examples were for 16+ examinations whilst the National Curriculum covers all ages from 5 to 16. However, the 24 SoA for 'evaluation' were distributed as shown in Figure 2.6, making at least the top 14 (levels 5–10) directly comparable to the former 16+ examinations.

These three examples – CSE, GCSE and National Curriculum – are by no means the only ones (or even the most extreme ones) that I could have

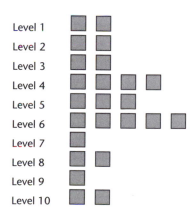

Figure 2.6 The distribution of criteria for assessing 'evaluation' in the Statutory Order for Technology (DES 1990).

chosen to illustrate the trend towards criterion-based, atomised assessment. Significantly more extreme versions exist. For example, the 'Graded Assessment' schemes[2] of the 1980s typically mapped out hundreds of 'achievements' (and associated assessment boxes) to be ticked when single skills have been demonstrated by pupils.

The even more recent development of General National Vocational Qualification (GNVQ) courses[3] within Key Stage 4 in schools confirms this relentless trend, for – if anything – it is even more atomised than National Curriculum assessment was initially intended to be. Since GNVQ courses are currently of increasing significance in schools, it is worth a brief diversion to examine their assessment regime.

GNVQ courses

The policy with GNVQ courses is that rather than specifying in a syllabus what will be taught, they specify the competences that pupils must have acquired as a result of following the course. The *output* is specified rather than the *input*.

The pilot courses in GNVQ Manufacturing[4] have undoubtedly created an interesting and different relationship between teachers and their courses. No formal evaluation reports are yet available, but the impression has been created that teachers in the trial schools have worked very hard in collaboration with industry representatives and have generated interesting and challenging assignments for their students. Since there is no syllabus to fall back on, the planning of courses has had to be exhaustive.

My concern here, however, is with the assessment regime; and specifically with the trend towards atomisation that I have identified above. Assessment for GNVQ is based on its 'unit' structure and – as an example – GNVQ Manufacturing (at foundation level) is made up of three compulsory units and three 'key skills':

- Unit A Manufacturing products
- Unit B Exploring manufacturing operations
- Unit C Making a product

- Key skill 1 Communication
- Key skill 2 Application of number
- Key skill 3 Information technology

Each of these units of study is subdivided into elements – for example:

Unit C Making a product
C1 Suggest design solutions from the given brief
C2 Plan for production
C3 Prepare materials, components, equipment and tools
C4 Make a product to specification

Each element is then further subdivided within its specification in the following terms:

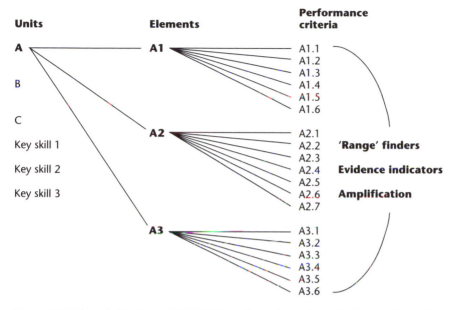

Figure 2.7 The subdivision of GNVQ Manufacturing units: a single unit (here A) has 19 performance criteria, and there are six units.

Performance criteria	'a student must be able to . . .'
Range	suggesting some 'context' parameters to help define the performance criteria
Evidence indicators	to identify the kinds of evidence that might be produced
Amplification	to illuminate further the key terms and depth of study required.

Thus a student's capability in GNVQ Manufacturing is subdivided into something like 100 performance criteria (Figure 2.7) – which then become the basic units of assessment. It should be noted that to pass, students must 'show evidence in their portfolio which satisfies all the element re-quirements' (NCVQ 1994), which means that the teacher has to record 'yes' or 'no' against each of the criteria. In relation to each criterion, either the student has achieved it or she has not, and this is recorded for all of the performance criteria in all of the units.[5] One GNVQ teacher de-scribed this system in the following terms: 'we can tick them for having bread – and butter – and cheese – separately; but we can't score them for the quality of sandwich they produce'.

I trust that the reader can readily see that this GNVQ assessment regime fits neatly into a long line of progressively more atomised assessment systems. One can see why these regimes have evolved. It is important not just to be able to say something is good or poor. We need also to be able to unpick why it is good or poor – identifying strengths and weaknesses. And it seems logical then that if these criteria are made the basic units of assessment in the first place (as in National Curriculum SoAs or GNVQ performance criteria) then naturally the assessment becomes more diagnostic and therefore more helpful to pupils in showing them how they might improve their performance. An analogy that is frequently cited in support of criterion-referenced assessment schemes makes this point quite neatly; students need to know where the goal-posts are if they are to score goals. It is a fair point, and its persuasiveness has led us progressively down a path of being more and more detailed in spelling out what we want pupils to do and what will count as 'good' or 'poor' work.

But the benefits of this policy have to be seen – and evaluated – against the very major drawbacks that arise as a result of pursuing the policy. These drawbacks are numerous and serious. And their impact exists at many levels – from day-to-day matters of manageability in the classroom, to underlying principles of the meaning and purpose of technology in schools.

Atomised assessment: six problems

Assessment in schools is a 'high-stakes' activity: important in determining pupils' futures; immensely time-consuming for teachers; and very expensive for schools. As we continue to develop our assessment practices, we should take a closer look at the dangers – for pupils, for teachers and for the system as a whole – that arise through the pursuit of ever more atomised assessment. I would draw attention in particular to the following six difficulties.

Do it my way

A criterion-referenced assessment scheme defines in advance the qualities that are to be identified and credited. This might sound an obviously desirable state of affairs, but it has the serious drawback of creating a highly exclusive arrangement that is only able to credit those things that are expected to arise. The assumption underpinning this position is that we know the 'right' and 'proper' way to design and manufacture things; and this 'right' way is the only way that will be acceptable. Given the very recent emergence of designing activities in the curriculum, it would be astonishing if we were able to say with confidence that this (and only this) procedure is the 'right' one. All the evidence is to the contrary, as academics and practitioners alike are constantly – and quite properly – disputing how the process of designing should best be described and taught.

All the descriptions of designing and making that contribute to assessment schemes are procedural: they describe a process, not a product. And at heart, the process is creative and generative. The further we move towards a position that defines a 'proper' way to proceed through this process, the more we risk valuing the plodding and orthodox over the inspired and unexpected.

Underlying the problem of defining the 'right' procedure lies the assumption that it has to be right for everybody. Atkinson (1995) has done some revealing work in this area, contrasting the approaches typically adopted by girls and boys in their GCSE course-work. She documents the reasons for the higher scoring of the girls, illustrating their greater facility at fitting their work into the logical, rational, step-by-step process that GCSE (and GNVQ) syllabuses demand. This leads teachers to encourage their pupils to go back over their design folders at the end of the project, 'to re-work or "pretty-up" existing work and fill in gaps in their design process . . . in an attempt to present the required evidence for assessment' (Atkinson 1995, p. 45).

There are no marks for innovation and creativity – especially when you do not demonstrate (step by step) where the ideas came from. In a world bounded by pre-defined criteria of excellence, everyone will do it my way (that is, the examiner's way). And ultimately this converts an exciting and creative process into what McCormick and Murphy (1994) have characterised as a conformist ritual. I shall return to this point in Chapter 6.

Processes become products

One of the first consequences of this ritualising of the process is that whatever steps exist in the examiners' 'design *process*', rapidly get transformed into *products* that can be weighed and measured:

> investigation as an *activity* becomes an investigation *folder* and active design *thinking* becomes a folio of *drawings*. The evaluation *report* at the end of the exercise is the only direct evidence of evaluative *activity* and therefore becomes synonymous with it. The process has become a series of products.
>
> (Kimbell 1991, p. 142)

This need to see activities in terms of the manifestations that arise from them is inevitably associated with the business of assessment. But it becomes an ever greater problem the more detailed and specified we make the 'desired outcomes'.

One of the more bizarre illustrations of this tendency arises when assessments are made of the process of idea generation. This is the creative heart of the process – where one might expect syllabus writers and examiners to be somewhat diffident about laying down hard and fast rules. But no such luck. The assumption is made that since innovative people have lots of ideas, we can count up the ideas and use this as a measure of innovation. Thus was born the 'three-ideas' paradigm:

> The concern is that students should demonstrate divergent thinking at the start of a project . . . In order to demonstrate divergence they must have three different ideas from which they pick one and develop it. Typically, having got an idea as a starting point, students want to get on and explore it to see to what extent it can meet the demands in

the task. But the three ideas paradigm demands that they immediately forget the first idea and come up with a completely different idea as another starting point, and then, having got a second, they must find a third. Any [similarity] between these ideas renders them 'not different' and accordingly the mark scheme will not credit the student as a fully 'divergent thinker'.

(Kimbell 1991, p. 144)

The nonsense of this paradigm is so obvious that it is nothing short of astonishing that it was ever allowed a place in any assessment regime. But it was, and still is. I would be a wealthy man if I had a pound for every design sheet that I have seen that conforms to this paradigm: the sheet of A4 paper carefully ruled up into a set of boxes for 'idea 1' and 'idea 2' and so on.

Creative and divergent thinking are difficult qualities to judge, but counting boxes is simple. Assessment through ever more detailed and pre-specified elements encourages us to transform a creative process into a set of pre-specified products.

The wood and the trees

Imagine you are doing a jigsaw without the benefit of the picture on the box. If you pick up a single piece of the puzzle it tells you very little about the whole picture and even less about the quality of that picture. The same argument exactly transfers to the world of assessment. Small, individual judgments – like individual bits of the jigsaw – make sense only when they are contextualised by a wider field of vision.

The world of digitised computer images makes this point neatly (Figure 2.8). Each pixel is either yes or no – black or white (just like the SoA). In isolation, this pixel conveys no meaning. The information in it is so decontextualised and at such a minute level of detail that it is even impossible to identify where it comes from on the 'real' image.

Another way of looking at the same issue is to put oneself in the role of a biologist who discovers a new life-form and who needs to identify and catalogue it. One would start by making observations with the naked eye: 'it has three legs and seems to swim quite well'. Then one might wonder how it 'hears' and, if it is not obvious to the naked eye, one might inspect it with a hand-lens to find its ears. Ultimately, one might take a series of blood or tissue samples and make microscopic slides of them to study the fine detail of the new find. The point is that one would not *start* with this fine detail. One would not seek to identify the find by combining the results of dozens of microscopic slides. This detail only makes sense in terms of the broader information that needs to precede it. The identification process is one that starts with big pictures, and moves to progressively finer detail.

Exactly the same can be said of assessment. As I shall show in succeeding chapters, the rules of National Curriculum assessment forced teachers

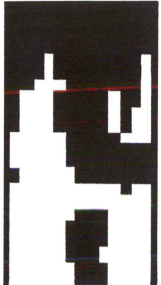

Figure 2.8 A digital image and a section of pixel detail.

to look at bits of detail rather than at the whole. Instead of gradually unpicking the strengths and weaknesses of pupils, teachers were reduced to a primitive and apparently arbitrary process of ticking or not ticking countless boxes. In trying to make sense of all the detail, they too often lost sight of the big picture.

Less means more

It follows (as night follows day) that as units of assessment get smaller, they have also to get more numerous in order to cover the same ground. The price of atomisation is proliferation, and an interesting parallel can be found in the engineering tool-box from years ago.

Go/no-go gauges were precisely ground instruments that gave a clear (yes/no) answer to a simple question: 'Is this bar 20 mm in diameter?' If the gauge fitted snugly on the bar the answer was 'yes'; if it did not then the answer was 'no'. It was a very limited instrument that was only capable of supporting that one single decision. For effective engineering, therefore, you needed a great store full of them, all of slightly different sizes. Go/no-go gauges were therefore not measuring devices at all, but *checking* devices. The 20 mm diameter gauge was not used to measure whether a bar was 10, 15, 20, or 25 mm in diameter, it was used as a precision check exclusively on bars that were known to be (or supposed to be) 20 mm in diameter. Effective use of go/no-go gauges therefore depended on a prior *judgment* about the size of the bar. A skilled fitter could make far more efficient use of these gauges than an unskilled one.[6]

There are two points to this story. First, it provides an illustration of the fact that the smaller the units of assessment become, the more you need of them. But there is also a second point, which relates to the use of small-scale assessments. As with the operator of the go/no-go gauges, the only intelligent way for the teacher to make sense of atomised, categorical assessment of this kind was to make a prior overview judgment in order to select the appropriate criteria of validation. This relates back to the point above about processes becoming products, and is a matter to which I shall return in later chapters.

You say yes, I say no

It is often assumed that small-scale judgments are easier to make than larger-scale, more inclusive ones. But time and again with National Curriculum assessment it became evident that teachers did not find it easy to distinguish between a 'yes' and a 'no'. When deciding whether to credit the SoA or to deny it, the teacher was necessarily involved in a calibration exercise to decide the quality threshold at which a 'no' becomes a 'yes'. In a recent subaqua examination I had to demonstrate that I could tread water for one minute with my arms above my head. The instructor tells me that the results of this test are usually clear, you sink or you do not sink. It is (generally) good digital data. But few school-based assessments are so clear-cut.

One statement from the technology Order (DES 1990) requires that pupils be able to 'use specialist modelling techniques to develop design proposals'. How do we calibrate the achievement threshold for such a statement? At what level of capability does a 'no' becomes a 'yes'? Does it refer to a 5-year-old squeezing out some Plasticine, or to an 8-year-old experimenting with a Lego mechanism, or to a 15-year-old modelling in a computer-aided design system? And what does it mean to 'develop a design proposal'?

In reality of course, designing at all levels of capability involves a degree of modelling. But the simple yes/no assessment system required that all pupils be put into one of two camps – the modellers and the non-modellers. We should not be surprised that teachers made different judgments, and that accordingly the reliability of assessments was low. Some teachers said 'yes' because they interpreted the detail at one level, and some said 'no' because they interpreted it at a different level. And yet both would comfortably have agreed on a larger-scale judgment about the quality of the pupil. The supposed precision of assessment brought about by detailed criteria was often illusory.

No criterion is an island

Finally, we need to recognise that individual judgments necessarily interact in the assessment of capability. It is a bit like judging the quality of an omelette. However good the eggs are – and the herbs, and the butter, and perhaps the cheese – the key question is how well they are blended to work together and enhance each other. To treat the judgments as independent points to be scored is seriously to misjudge the interdependence of the elements that go to make up technological capability.

The original version of the technology Order (DES 1990) contains countless examples of such interdependence:

Pupils should be able to:

- record the progress of their ideas
- describe and edit their design proposals
- detail and refine their proposals
- review the detail of their design
- apply knowledge and skill to select ideas for different parts of the design
- review how to make best use of materials
- identify and incorporate modifications
- evaluate the ways in which materials have been used.

Quite apart from the overlap in these snippets (drawn from levels 3–8), the levels of interdependence are obvious. To take but one example, how would we distinguish between 'detailing and reviewing design proposals' on the one hand and 'reviewing how to make best use of materials' on the other? The multiplicity of detail confuses and ultimately confounds itself.

Do we really need to assess (in isolation) the quality of the butter in order to know when we have eaten an exquisite omelette? Moreover – even supposing that we had a series of assessments for all the separate bits – would we be happy to accept these as an aggregated judgment, or would we rather rely on our tasting of the whole omelette?

To summarise

The search for criteria of assessment in technology was begun through a desire to be clearer about what the activity involved and hence what targets should appropriately be pursued by pupils. Over a period of twenty years the process of designing (which is now generally accepted as the core of the technology curriculum) has been described for assessment purposes in ever more detailed ways, culminating in the 150 National Curriculum SoA. And in recent years, the following six difficulties have sharpened into ever clearer focus:

- the danger of *exclusivity* as the process becomes a set of rituals prescribed by examiners;
- the associated tendency to transform creative *processes* into pre-specified *products*;
- the splintering of real images (real pupils) into digits of *meaningless detail*;

- the *proliferation* in assessment brought about by the splintering process;
- the uncertainty in knowing when a tiny bit of detail is a *no* or a *yes*;
- the confusion created by the inevitable *interaction* of the bits of detail.

Given these problems, which have become increasingly clear over the last few years as schools have been attempting to cope with increasingly atomised, criterion-referenced assessments, one can see why Satterly (1989, p. 42) pointed out that

> criterion referenced testing . . . is appropriate chiefly in the evaluation
> of learning where objectives can be clearly stated, where criterion
> performances can be established and where objectives are organised
> hierarchically. . . . It is for this reason that most of the published
> criterion referenced tests to date are in areas of elementary skill.

Even as Satterly's comment was in the process of being published, the whole of pupils' learning experience in schools was being reconstructed in these terms. Far from being restricted to the domain of elementary skills, we were moving to create a wholly criterion-referenced curriculum and a wholly criterion-referenced assessment regime to go with it. It was the task of the National Curriculum Design and Technology Working Group to establish the hierarchical objectives in technology, and ironically it was they who quite explicitly decided that – in design and technology – it was inappropriate to make assessments in this way. In their Interim Report (DES 1988a, para. 1.30) they explicitly acknowledged the difficulties to which I have referred above when they reported: 'These considerations point to the conclusion that because Design and Technology activity is so integrative, the approach to the assessment of pupil performance in this area should ideally be holistic.'

So here is a real conundrum. Technology has been defined through its interaction with succeeding generations of assessment systems. And these generations have moved remorselessly in the same direction – towards ever more detail in the assessment criteria. And just as we get to the pinnacle of splintered detail – with NC assessment against 150 free-standing SoA – the very same group that derived this detail make a quite contradictory statement about the necessity of holistic assessment.

It was exactly at this pivotal moment that the first major research project in the assessment of pupil performance in design and technology was beginning the process of analysing data. This project – for the Assessment of Performance Unit[7] – was premised on assumptions that ran somewhat counter to those that have been outlined above. We believed, for example, that it was important to recognise that there are different ways of performing well in design and technology and that reliable assessment does not necessarily demand that markers make endless isolated assessments and 'add up the answer'. We were exploring the relationship between holistic excellence and performance in individual elements of the activity – not in order to identify a magical combination that would provide the prescription for all future performance, but to illustrate a variety of approaches and (hopefully) to give insights into ways of supporting and promoting the development of capability. Our work was therefore partly to do with understanding the processes involved when pupils engage in design and technology, and partly to do with the problems of making reliable and helpful assessments of their performance.

As England and Wales were embarking on the most atomised assessment regime ever to be implemented in their schools, our assessment research for the APU was leading us in a quite different direction. It is time to examine this research, both for what it tells us about the design and technology activity and to provide a different perspective on the assessment of performance.

Notes

1 McCormick and Murphy (1994) subsequently described this as the 'ritualising' of the process.
2 The 'Graded Assessments' system – sometimes linked to GCSE certification – allowed pupils to be assessed for a level when they were 'ready' to take it. Pupils could be tested at any time through the year and different pupils in the same class might be sitting different levels of test at the same time.
3 GNVQ courses are operated by three 'awarding bodies', Business and Technician Education Council, City & Guilds, and the Royal Society of Arts (RSA). These bodies are the vocational equivalent to GCSE examining boards, and they are overseen by a supervising body, the National Council for Vocational Qualifications (NCVQ). As the School Curriculum and Assessment Authority (SCAA) supervises the GCSE examining boards, so it is the role of NCVQ to regulate the awarding bodies for GNVQ and ensure that they are operating to a satisfactory level.
4 At the time of writing there are about 24 pilot schools, each operating a single teaching group of about 15 students.
5 This is only the first layer of GNVQ assessment. A second layer involves making judgments of quality – how well the criteria have been achieved. This is seen as a separate activity called 'grading' and has additional criteria for the award of merit and distinction.
6 It is interesting to reflect on the fact that as the engineering work-force became more educated (or at least more literate and numerate) the extremely limited go/no-go gauges disappeared in favour of more flexible measuring devices (vernier gauges and micrometers) that adapt to the size of the bar and yet render just as much precision.
7 The APU project in design and technology ran from 1985 to 1991 at Goldsmiths College. I was one of the directors of the project.

three

Research lends a hand
The Assessment of Performance Unit, 1985–91

In 1985, we launched the APU project at Goldsmiths College in response to the brief prepared by the DES.[1] This brief required that we devise tests to enable us to report on the performance of 15-year-old pupils in design and technology. I do not intend to describe here all the events within that project or the findings that derived from it since that has already been done in our full report (Kimbell *et al.* 1991). My purpose here is to discuss the two central issues illuminated by the APU research. First, I shall show how we derived a description of the process of design and development that pupils pursue. This description has to be sufficiently flexible to allow for a variety of approaches and yet still retain coherence. Second, I shall show how this description bears on the practice of assessment.

Describing the process

As we reported in our first 'framework' publication in 1987:

> The first task for the research team has been to derive a coherent and acceptable description of the activity on design and technology, noting the features of performance which, because they are central to the development of capability through the activity, will be used in monitoring.
> (Kelly *et al.* 1987, p. 7)

There are two key points in this sentence. First, we described design and technology as *an activity*. That is to say, it is not merely a convenient way of packaging an accumulation of knowledge and skills. Whilst knowledge and skills are of course involved in design and technology, the activity is not defined by that knowledge and skill. As early as 1981, this view had been very forcibly put by the Working Group within the DES that had been responsible for generating the brief we were subsequently given:

both the acquisition of an understanding of design and technology *by* a child, and the detection of that understanding *in* a child, are contingent on the child's engagement in purposeful and comprehensive activity. In order to assess performance, therefore, it is necessary to examine activities.

(APU 1981)

Second, the focus of our assessment was on the word *capability*. The original 1981 Working Group had talked about testing for *understanding* of design and technology, but we believed that the commitment to activity-based testing involved far more than the measurement of understanding. It does of course involve understanding, but any 'meaningful and purposeful' activity in design and technology would also demand practical skills (for example, of drawing and modelling), procedural skills (knowing what to do next), judgment (for example, in identifying and balancing priorities) and even emotional toughness (for example, in coping with the risk environment of tasks without 'right' answers). All these can be summed up in our use of the generic term capability. Hicks (1983, p. 1) alludes to this quality in the following terms.

Teaching facts is one thing; teaching pupils in such a way that they can apply facts is another, but providing learning opportunities which encourage pupils to use information naturally when handling uncertainty, in a manner which results in capability, is a challenge of a different kind.

We spent a great deal of time in the next couple of years developing test activities that could provide valid data on the capability of pupils as they pursued 'meaningful and purposeful' design and technology tasks. Perhaps the greatest challenge was the problem of time, since real design and technology projects are typically spread over an extended period of hours, days or even weeks, whilst the majority of our testing had to be short-term 90 minute activities. Mindful of the problems I outlined in Chapter 2, we rejected the idea of describing the activity in terms of the products that result from it, and instead concentrated on the task-focused thinking and decision-making processes that result in these products. We were more interested in *why* and *how* pupils chose to do things than in *what* it was they chose to do:

Procedural capability is at the heart of the matter, for in design and technology it is the driving purpose of the *task* that prevents conceptual understanding being merely intellectual detritus, and communicative facility being merely organ grinding (suitable for house trained monkeys).

(Kimbell 1991, pp. 145–6)

We gradually came to see the essence of design and technology as being the interaction of mind and hand – inside and outside the head – and the

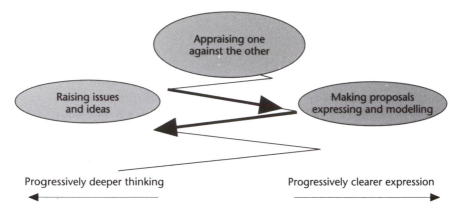

Figure 3.1 A schematic representation of the APU model of activity.

activity as being best described as *iterative* as ideas are bounced back and forth, formulated, tested against the hard reality of the world and then reformulated. We coined the phrase 'thought in action' to summarise the idea and I subsequently described it in the following terms:

> When engaged in a task, ideas . . . are inevitably hazy if they remain forever in the mind and this inhibits their further development. By dragging them out into the light of day as sketches, notes, models or the spoken word, we not only encourage the originator to sharpen up some of the areas of uncertainty, but also lay them open to public scrutiny . . . The act of expression pushes ideas forward . . . [and] the additional clarity that this throws on the idea enables the originator to think more deeply about it, which further extends the possibilities of the idea. Concrete expression (by whatever means) is therefore not merely something that allows us to see the [designer's] ideas, it is something without which the designer is unable to be clear what the ideas are.
>
> (Kimbell 1991, p. 142)

This iterative model of the process is outlined in Figure 3.1 and is fully explained in Section 2 of the final research report (Kimbell *et al.* 1991).

Using this model as a guide, we produced videos to contextualise technological tasks; we developed 'concept-models' of half-developed solutions to focus pupils' activity; we sub-structured the 90 minutes of activity into smaller 5, 10 or 20-minute sub-activities to facilitate the iterative active/reflective process; we designed pupil response booklets that were supportive of pupils working through this process; we developed the concept of the pupil as a member of a design team, responsible for a part of the process; and we derived a series of tasks that were defined at different levels of detail – some allowing broad scope for intervention and others with a much tighter focus.

After numerous trials and a pilot national survey in 1987, we were confident that we had developed a test activity format that allowed pupils to demonstrate real capability on meaningful and purposeful tasks. And the result (in the 1988–9 survey) was a huge collection of 20,000 test responses from pupils that needed to be assessed. We were delighted that our activities had generated an amazing and diverse array of responses – however we did not (at that point) have a fully developed means for assessing them. But we did have a procedure.

Developing an assessment framework

The question that lies at the heart of the assessment debate is: 'What do we mean by good?' As soon as we began to generate responses from pupils we began to confront this problem of sorting the 'good' from the 'poor'. We were looking for a set of yardsticks by which we could reliably measure the performance that pupils had produced. The problem, however, was how these yardsticks were to be calibrated. From where were we to derive the standards?

Our problem was made more complex by the macro-educational setting of the time, since we were acutely aware that the development phase in our work (1986–7) coincided exactly with the first generation of new GCSE examinations. This might be thought an advantage, since we could simply have adopted the measures of excellence provided by the GCSE groups. The problem with doing that, however, was that their procedures were never designed to test the validity of their measures of excellence. Their assessment rubrics (inherited from previous subject-based syllabuses) were developed by examiners, and were typically based on previous under-standings about what constitutes excellence. In this situation, assessment becomes a self-fulfilling prophecy: if excellence is defined as A + B + C and a pupil produces A + B + C, then – by definition – the pupil's work is excellent. The problem with this arises if one challenges the original defini-tion – and this challenge might be of two kinds: excellence is *really* only A + C (that is, B has no part to play) or excellence is *really* A + B + C + D (that is, an important quality has been left out). How are we to decide the truth of these challenges? How can we decide between two people who argue about the basic constituents of our definition of excellence?

The GCSE assessment system could not help here, since all it was designed to do was to measure pupils against a pre-determined scale. The definition of excellence (in the syllabus and other supporting documents) is converted into an assessment filter for excellence, and pupils' work is poured through the filter to arrive at a score (Figure 3.2). This conventional procedure is of no use if one is challenging the truth of the filter itself. It cannot answer the question: 'How do we know that our filter contains all the "right" elements?' What if it is missing some that are really important? Or what if it has some that are simply mistaken?

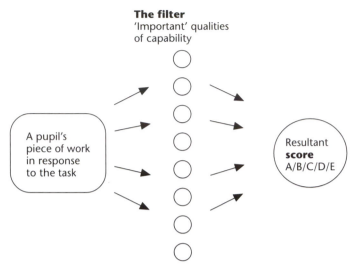

Figure 3.2 A conventional (for example, GCSE) model of assessment.

The measure of excellence that is provided by this approach is only as good as the filter itself – and at that time (1986–7) we had no means of knowing whether or not the conventional GCSE filters were right. We therefore developed a different approach to assessment that would allow us to scrutinise the validity of the filter itself:

> Our experience of assessment in design and technology (in a variety of forms) led us to the conviction that it is often easier to identify a high quality piece of design work than it is to say in detail *why* it is high quality. Precisely because of the integrated nature of the activity and the complex interactions of the various aspects of it, holistic assessments of excellence – which allow us to take these interactions into account – have been far more commonplace in design and technology than in many other, more analytic, areas of the curriculum.
>
> (Kimbell *et al.* 1991)

In association with a selected group of experienced teachers, advisers and examiners, we began the process of assessment by dividing large batches of responses into broad piles 'excellent', 'moderate' and 'poor'.

Our confidence in teachers' ability to make these broad judgments was amply justified. With remarkable consistency, different markers were able to attribute these overall quality judgments. This was, however, only the first step in the process since we recognised that holistic assessment has limitations. It is no good saying 'This is good, but I don't know why', especially if the purpose of the work is to help teachers to develop their understanding of the multitudinous forms in which pupil capability manifests itself. Accordingly, we devised a means of getting inside the holistic mark

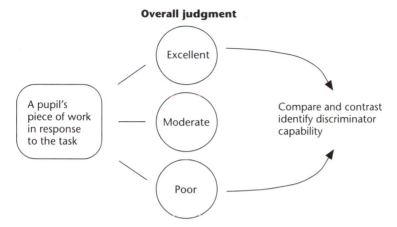

Figure 3.3 A research model of assessment.

to the central traits of good (and poor) performance. But the trick was to do this without defining these traits too rigidly in advance.

The strategy was adapted from a well-established technique in experimental psychology. Having established a pile of work in which all the pieces were unanimously agreed to be excellent examples of design and technology – and another pile equally unanimously agreed to be poor – we had to find out what all the differences were between the two piles.

To do this, we picked out one excellent piece and one poor piece and asked a question of the work, such as: 'Does this piece demonstrate awareness of the end-user and how the product will be used?' If the answer was 'yes' for both the 'good' and the 'poor' piece of work then that question did not discriminate between them and was not therefore a discriminator of quality (Figure 3.3). The questions were only useful if the answer was 'yes' in one case and 'no' in the other.

> We then took two scripts – a high scorer (a) and a low scorer (b) –
> and listed all the things that (a) contained that (b) did not, and all
> the things that (b) had that (a) did not. This was done by looking
> for questions ('does this script do/contain . . . ?') to which one could
> answer *yes* for one script and *no* for the other. *When we found such
> a question we had identified a discriminator of capability.*
>
> (Kimbell *et al.* 1991, p. 31)

With a trained group of markers, this technique was pursued with literally thousands of pieces of work, resulting in a very long list of questions that did in some degree discriminate between good and poor work. It then became necessary to see to what extent they could be grouped and prioritised.

> We coined the expression 'fingerprinting' the scripts because, like a
> fingerprint, each script was unique, but by building up a list of discrim-

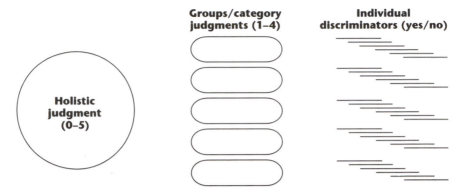

Figure 3.4 The APU assessment framework.

inating yes's and no's it became possible to describe the uniqueness in any particular script. Moreover, as computers are adept at handling such simple (binary) data, it became possible to ask the computer to generalise these descriptors by selecting all high scorers and printing out the discriminating characteristics that they *did* contain and those that they *did not* contain.

(Kimbell *et al.* 1991, p. 32)

Whilst the holistic mark enabled us to *value* a piece of work, the yes/no responses provided a composite *description* of it. Using this approach over a period of 18 months, we developed our assessment model to the point that it contained a single overview (holistic) judgment, six broad categories of descriptors (e.g. communication), 24 four sub-categories, and hundreds of individual discriminators (Figure 3.4). The detail of this schedule and the full rationale can be studied in Section 11 of our final report (Kimbell *et al.* 1991).

Whilst in principle the development of this schedule was as I have outlined here, the reality involved innumerable iterations of examining work holistically – and also applying the developing schedule to examine the detail. There was inevitably, therefore, a degree of backwash between the two, such that the emerging detail began to affect the way one saw the whole. In the end, however, we finalised the schedule in a way that gave us a reliable and usable assessment rubric. It is also worth noting that several of the discriminators that proved to be really significant were not present in any of the GCSE assessment rubrics of the time.

Reliable assessment

I mentioned earlier the fact that during the development phase of this assessment framework, we and our marking team were able to make overview judgments about the quality of pupil responses with remarkable consistency.

It is clearly important that any assessment scheme should be reliable, by which I mean that, when they make assessments, different markers given the same work should produce the same result. The pursuit of *reliability* can therefore be understood as the pursuit of *repeatability*. For reasons that I hope will become obvious, it is worth exploring this issue of reliability more closely in the context of our APU assessments.

It is one thing to have reliable assessments within the confines of a smallish development team with only a few external teachers and advisers. The team that developed the assessment framework amounted to no more than 20 people who came to develop a close working relationship, shared common values, experienced new ideas together and generally grew together. Such a relationship maximises the possibilities that they will make common judgments about pupils' work. However, the major survey in 1988–9 produced 20,000 pieces of work from 700 schools in England, Wales and Northern Ireland, and we needed a very substantial marker team to cope with this amount of work. We ultimately recruited and trained 120 markers for this task. A central concern in this exercise was the absolute need for reliability.

We developed a range of training materials – based on the need for the markers to understand the model of activity described above – and this was accompanied by a wide range of exemplar work from pupils. We subsequently engaged the markers in assessment exercises at both holistic and detailed, analytic levels. The assessment framework required assessments to be made at three levels, the first two of which, the holistic overview judgment and the judgment of categories, were on sliding scales (0–5 and 1–4) and the third categorical (yes/no) data on individual discriminators.

The stark outcome of the marking process was that inter-marker reliability was at its highest with the holistic judgment and at its lowest with the categorical yes/no assessments. At the outset, we found this somewhat surprising – since we had been brought up on the belief that small and closely defined qualities lead to reliable assessment, and conversely that broad interrelated judgments will be subject to all kinds of error. Indeed our DES observers did not at first believe the reliability statistics on the holistic judgment and we had subsequently to demonstrate a second time that we could generate high reliability. For readers with an interest in the hard numbers, the inter-quartile, inter-marker correlation on the holistic marking ranged from 0.55 to 0.9 with a median of 0.74.[2] However, the correlations were less good for the category judgments (with a median of 0.49), and even worse for the detailed judgments. The full details of the statistics are presented in Section 9 of the final report and the appendices thereto (Kimbell *et al.* 1991).

Clearly there were some very interesting things going on here in terms of the ability of our assessors to hold standards in their minds and to interpret pupils' work through these standards. I shall explore some of these in the following section.

Interpretations of the APU assessment experience

There are three issues to be dealt with here: the first concerns the *nature* of holistic and atomistic assessment; the second *relationship* between them; and the third the concept of *sliding scales* of excellence.

Holistic and atomistic assessment

I have already pointed out that we were initially surprised by the reliability statistics that we produced for the holistic assessment, but on reflection – and after further examination of our markers in action – it became apparent to us why the statistics came out as they did.

Teachers of design and technology are constantly dealing in a world of uncertainty. And this uncertainty is made manifest through the dominant teaching and learning strategy that is adopted in design and technology – the project. Within the project, teachers have to operate through the whole process of design and development – from inception (brief) to completion (review of outcomes). There is no right solution to a design task; only better or worse ones. Moreover, teachers are constantly having to help their pupils to keep in mind the full range of variables that a project raises – aesthetic, technical and human. The central ethic of teaching and learning in design and technology is holistic, requiring teachers and pupils constantly to seek to integrate these concerns into a whole solution. Whole tasks, whole projects, whole solutions. I am not saying that this is good or bad. I am merely saying that the vast majority of teaching that I observe in design and technology is of this kind. The new strictures of the National Curriculum – with focused practical tasks and disassembly tasks – are beginning to make inroads into the terrain of 'the project', but still – for now – it seems to me to reign pretty well supreme.

Teachers are also very good at recognising which of their pupils are doing well, and which need more help. And, at the end of the project – or year – assessment will typically revolve around some form of exhibition in which once again the whole process has to be laid bare. Holistic assessment in design and technology is therefore not only commonplace, it is just about all there is. Teachers do not typically test for individual skills or knowledge, nor do they assess individual bits of procedural quality. They are comfortable with talking about 'Jane's great project' or 'Paul's weak project' – making these global judgments not out of sloppiness, but as a balanced reflection on the whole process. They trade the strengths against the weaknesses just as they help the pupils to do when deciding on a course of action in the midst of the uncertainty of the project.

Building on this holistic teaching background, and with the addition of a carefully designed training schedule, we were able to show the reliability of holistic assessment. 'Suffice it to say here that, given suitable training, there is among teachers a sufficiently established public construct of capability to make holistic assessment a valuable and reliable tool' (Kimbell *et al.* 1991, p. 238). I believe that the strength of the holistic assessment that we observed in our 120 markers was due in large measure to the holistic teaching and assessment that is the bread and butter of being a design and technology teacher. We no doubt managed to focus it somewhat through our training regime, but we were working with people whose professional disposition was to see things in the round.

This also goes some way to explaining the problems that these same teachers experienced when trying to make the atomised, small-scale judgments. One of these small descriptors was concerned with designing from the user's point of view – and specifically in terms of safety.

Does the work show an awareness of safety for the user?   Yes/No.

Teacher A looks through the folder and sees no mention of safety. She is aware that the pupil mentioned it fleetingly a week or so back, but is that enough to say that the work 'shows an awareness' of safety? On balance she decides 'No'. Teacher B looks at the same folder and the product and sees 'implicit' awareness. He notes the 'safe' contours of the form and remembers that, in one of the 'user' trials, a parent mentioned that she would be happy for her three-year-old to play with it. On balance he decides 'Yes'. If the teachers were to debate the matter, they might argue for hours about this or that nuance within the project and the pupil's awareness or otherwise of safety issues. But if we were to ask them the question 'Is it a good project?' their uncertainty would typically vanish. 'Oh yes we agree that it's a great project – but we're not sure about that safety question!'

The assumption that it is possible to use small, clear discriminators as a means for assessment in design and technology is a snare and a delusion. It may be possible where very simple and discrete matters are being dealt with, but it certainly cannot be done in a complex teaching and learning environment. This is the same issue that I have already outlined in Chapter 2 in terms of the progressive move towards criterion-referenced assessment in the last few years.

Underpinning this move has been the belief in 'competence' testing – that any expertise can be broken down into a discrete list of competences that can be tested, and, as we shall see in subsequent chapters, this was one of the big ideas driving the development of the National Curriculum. We can describe in attainment targets and in statements of attainment all that might be meant by expertise in design and technology – or English or music.

The assessment data that (in 1989) began to emerge from our APU exercise, ought seriously to have warned against pursuing this approach. We were getting data from 120 able and experienced teachers that proved they were largely incapable of making these small atomised assessments with any acceptable level of reliability. The data also showed that they were quite capable of making reliable judgments at broader, more holistic levels.

The relationship *between holistic and atomistic assessment*

To illustrate the relationship that might best exist between these two approaches to assessment, I shall use an example from a different field.

I have a colleague who works for a major accountancy and business management firm in the City of London. His job is to go into any business that invites him in, to evaluate its performance and suggest improvements in its organisation or working practices. When he first descends on a company, he concentrates all his energy on seeking answers to three central questions:

- What is being sold?   (i.e. what products/ services)
- To whom is it being sold?   (i.e. what is the customer base)
- What do they do to create   (i.e. what processes are involved) their product?

The answers to these three questions sum up (he believes) the rationale for any successful business. However, as my colleague delves deeper and deeper into the workings of the organisation, he engages a business management technique called 'drill-down'. He drills down through these big questions to expose the more detailed questions that lie underneath. For example, on the surface, the answer to the question 'What is being sold?' might be 'wheelbarrows', but properly to understand what it means for the company to be selling wheelbarrows, he needs more detailed information. He might, for example, need to know:

- What does the company buy in (as raw material/resource)?
- What does it sell on (as product/service)?
- What (therefore) does it do to add value?
- How fast is the cycle of input/output?
- How scarce/valuable is the commodity being sold on?
- How stable is the demand (over months/years)?

In exactly the same way he can 'drill down' through the other two big questions to flesh out details of the customer base for the company and to uncover details of its working practices.

Not content with this level of detail, he might then drill down through another layer. He could take any of these second-level questions and drill for a third level. Thus he might take apart the notion of 'how fast is the cycle of input/output?' and ask the following questions:

- What are the constraints on the cycle (for example, delivery batches)?
- Which of these constraints might be controlled by the company (for example, the weather can't)?
- Is it serial (end-on), parallel (side by side) or continuous production?

The point, I hope, is obvious. A few key primary questions lead to rather more secondary questions, which in turn lead to lots of tertiary questions (Figure 3.5).

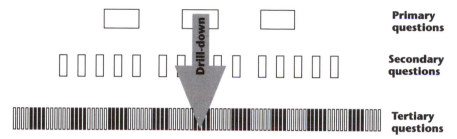

Figure 3.5 The diagnostic process of drill-down.

The point on which I would like to focus attention here is the relationship between these levels of question. The second-level questions only make sense if one is trying to get more information about the first level. And the detailed questions only make sense in terms of the secondary level. To walk into the company and ask about serial or batch production – without initially establishing what is being produced and for whom, would be daft. It would offend common sense, let alone business practice.

The order of events is therefore crucial, and the message is that the big picture must come first. The detail can then be used to flesh it out – to hang substance on the skeleton provided by the answers to the first three key questions.

I believe that exactly the same relationship exists between holistic and atomistic assessment in schools. Small-scale (atomised) assessments can be helpful, but only if the tiny snippets of information that they provide can be fitted into a big picture that has first been provided by bigger-scale judgments. One of the reasons for the success of the APU assessment strategy was the *order* in which we asked our markers to operate. Whilst at different points in the assessment process they were required to operate at three different levels, they always started from the whole judgment and 'drilled down' through it to expose these more detailed layers (Figure 3.6).

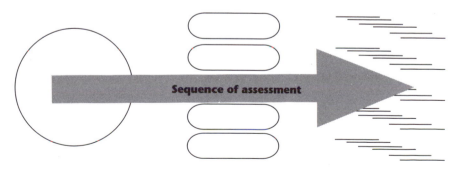

Figure 3.6 The sequence of assessment used by APU assessors.

Viewed in this way, there is a clear rationale for the separate existence of the three layers. Initially we are concerned with whether – in general terms – a piece of work is good, poor or indifferent. We then need to identify some of the principal strengths and weaknesses within it that might help to explain that judgment. And finally, we piece together some of the detail that explains why those strengths and weaknesses exist. Each successive layer illuminates judgments that existed at a higher level.

I shall return to this point in Chapter 5, when we examine the National Curriculum assessment regime. We shall see what happened when this simple, common-sense order of events was ignored.

Sliding scales of excellence

One of the truisms of school life is that teachers will tend to operate towards the middle of whatever assessment scale is operated in the school. If a class full of projects is being marked on a 10 point scale, you can bet that there will be lots of 4s, 5s and 6s; very few 1s and 2s or 8s and 9s; and absolutely no 0s or 10s. There are, of course, very good reasons for this 'bunching' tendency at the middle and for the absence of marks at the extremes. However good a piece of work might be, one can imagine something that is better; and conversely, however poor it is, one can imagine worse.

A number of strategies have been used over the years to help this distribution process. We can develop *criteria* to help to identify quality. We can assemble sets of *exemplar* work to illustrate quality. And we can develop a *moderation* process that helps to share concepts of quality.

As part of the process of developing the APU assessment procedures (as opposed to the framework) we decided that we ought to understand rather better how teachers engage in the act of assessment and hence how criteria, exemplars and moderation support the process. And close observation of our teacher/markers showed that the process was not a simple, single act, but rather that there was a two-stage process. First there is the 'pitch', which might be characterised by the expression 'I think it's about a 6'. The teacher commits herself to a particular judgment of quality. Then there is the 'check' which amounts to the teacher checking the judgment against other reference points (e.g. other pupils' work). This two-stage process (Figure 3.7) is made possible by the fact that the pitch is made on a sliding scale. The initial judgment can be slid up or down a little to calibrate it properly against other points of reference. This allows some flexibility in the assessment process and gives the teacher confidence that she is doing justice to all pupils. The vast majority of teachers' marking work in schools is based on this model of sliding-scale assessment. Figure 3.8 shows this process at work in one school in the context of GCSE project assessment. Initial judgments (the pitch) result in all the work being laid out in order; and subsequently neighbouring cases are examined in detail to check that the initial pitch was fair in each case.

Figure 3.8 (a) Teachers (doing GCSE assessment) lay out folders of work, from best to worst;

(b) they then study the detail in neighbouring cases to check their judgment.

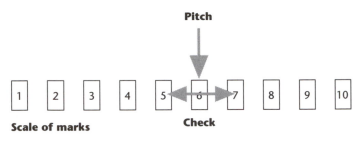

Figure 3.7 The two-stage assessment process.

The problem arises when the sliding scale disappears and is replaced by bipolar options: yes or no. The 'pitch' can still of course be made. But it cannot be adjusted by the 'check', by sliding up and down a scale, since there is no scale to slide up or down. This is the world of certainties, where the pupil is either right or wrong and there will be nothing in between.

There are (at least) two consequences of this. First, it makes the teacher far less confident in making the 'pitch', since so much hangs on it. Teachers know that it has to be right first time. They therefore err towards generosity since to do the reverse might unfairly penalise a pupil. The second, related consequence is that teachers are forced to do something that all their training and experience has conditioned them to dislike. They must separate pupils into sheep and goats: those that can from those that cannot. And they are forced to do this when they know very well that the reality is that no one can and no one cannot. In most educational assessment it is a matter of *how much* or *how well* one can do it rather than whether or not one can. Teachers live in a world of relativities, but yes/no assessment forces them to live in a world of certainties.

APU research and the National Curriculum

As I pointed out at the outset of this chapter, there were two major tasks that guided our APU research. First, we were required to find a way of describing design and technological activity that would be helpful to teachers and that would respect the diversity of pupil performance, and I have touched on the strategies we employed to encourage pupils to demonstrate their capability. Second, we needed to develop strategies that would enable us to make reliable assessments of pupil performance.

The lessons flowing from this research were coming into focus by 1989, and by 1991 we had interpreted their consequence and published our full report. But well before then, some critical decisions had already been made about the formulation of the National Curriculum for technology – and about its assessment. The Task Group on Assessment and Testing (TGAT) had already (by 1987) developed its model of assessment for the National Curriculum, and the Design and Technology Working Group had (by 1988) published the fruits of its labours. This was bad timing from our point of view and prevented us from making effective representations either about the definition of the discipline or about its assessment.

As it turned out, the original (1988) formulation of technology had much to commend it, and we were not displeased with what was published. There were inevitably a number of problems with it and I shall explore some of these in the following chapter. But whilst we were – at the time – philosophical about the description of the activity, we were outraged by the model of assessment that was overlaid across it. Virtually every element of assessment policy for the National Curriculum ran counter to the things we had discovered in our research and illustrated in our report. The nation was about to embark on a gigantic and hugely expensive experiment in assessment based upon utterly flawed principles. We had reported that 'holistic capability is greater than the sum of its parts and cannot be reduced to any intellectual formula; as greatness in footballers or violinists cannot ultimately be reduced to "performance indicators"' (Kimbell *et al.* 1991, p. 147). And in 1990 we embarked upon the most rigidly atomised and formulaic assessment that it is possible to imagine. It was bound to end in tears.

Notes

1 This is now the Department for Education and Employment (DfEE).
2 Rank-order correlation works by having an assessor and a team member rank-order a range (say 50 pieces) of work, without of course seeing each other's ranking. The rankings are then compared. Assuming every single piece is in exactly the same order, the correlation is +1. Assuming the rank orders are exactly the reverse of each other, the correlation is –1. A completely random distribution gives a correlation of 0. In our main APU survey, the median correlation of 0.74 is highly respectable in judgmental assessments of this kind.

four

A pivotal moment in history
Technology as an entitlement in the National Curriculum

I have described in earlier chapters some of the issues and events that, taken together, led us to establish technology as a central component in the education of all children in England and Wales aged 5–16. These issues and events involved the formulation of a new concept of process-centred technological capability – new not just in the sense of being new in England and Wales, but also, in its time, new and original in the world. However, I shall deal with international issues in Part Two of this book, and the purpose of this chapter is to tell the story of how our view of technology was developed and modified through the successive attempts to enshrine it within the statutory framework of the National Curriculum.

The Education Reform Act 1988

The framework within which technology was to be described – indeed within which all subjects were to be described – was established in the Education Reform Act of 1988 (ERA). I do not intend to dwell on the detail of the Act, except in so far as its requirements bear upon the way in which technology was to be defined. The ERA did not in itself specify any of the substance of the curriculum. Rather it specified a framework within which this substance was to be presented.

It specified that there would be three core subjects (English, maths and science) and seven foundation subjects, including technology. It required that they each be presented in terms of attainment targets 'that offer general objectives, setting out areas within which pupils will need to develop their attainments' (DES 1989a, para. 3.11). And it required that each subject should have programmes of study (PoS), that would 'set out the essential matters, skills and processes which need to be covered by pupils at each stage of their education' (DES 1989a, para. 3.12). In a nutshell, the PoS were supposed to spell out what would be taught (and hopefully learned); whilst the ATs would be the 'targets' against which the assessment system

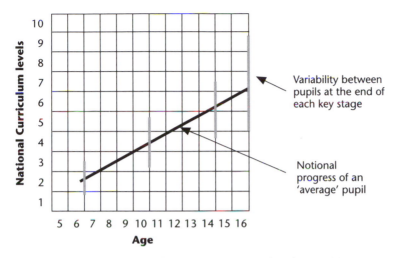

Figure 4.1 The age and levels structure presented in the TGAT report.

would measure pupil progress. And this progress was to be charted across the four 'key stages' of compulsory schooling (ages 5–7, 7–11, 11–14, and 14–16).

The details of the assessment arrangements will be discussed in Chapter 5; suffice it here to say that the work of devising the assessment system was handed to a newly established Task Group on Assessment and Testing. This group created the model within which subsequently a series of subject 'working groups' were to devise and detail the definition of their respective subjects.

The TGAT model can most simply be described as in Figure 4.1, showing the notional progress of pupils up the age scale (5–16) and hopefully up the ten designated levels of performance. Testing at 7, 11, 14 and 16 would identify the level of each pupil, but the norm of performance was 'expected' to sit on this steadily rising line.

My concern here, however, is to examine the work of the subsequently formed Design and Technology Working Group, whose task was to interpret the frameworks presented by the ERA and the TGAT in terms of a description of design and technology. Specifically, the Working Group was asked 'to advise on attainment targets and programmes of study for design and technology' (DES 1988a).

The 1988 Interim Report, the 1989 consultation stages and the 1990 Statutory Order

The significance of the task facing this group should not be underestimated. For the first time ever (in the entire world, to the best of my knowledge), a course of study in technology was to be devised that would cover all the statutory years of schooling (age 5–16) and that would provide a model through which the progress of individual pupils could be monitored.

One of the remarkable achievements of the 1988 Working Group was to place on record the centrality of the act of designing and making, along with the aspiration that the ultimate objective of the whole programme is to establish technological 'capability' for all pupils. By 'capability' I mean that combination of skills, knowledge and motivation that transcends understanding and enables pupils creatively to intervene in the world and 'improve' it. Capability in technology provides pupils with the bridge between what is and what might be, and as a basis for school programmes, it combines intellectual, practical and emotional qualities in a quite unique way.[1]

The concept of 'capability' in technology was fully articulated in the interim report of the Working Group (DES 1988a). In a profound introductory chapter to that report, the following definition of 'design and technological capability' was offered.

> Our view of design and technological capability is that, at the very least, it covers all of the following:
>
> (i)   pupils are able to use existing artefacts and systems effectively
> (ii) pupils are able to make critical appraisals of the personal, social, economic and environmental implications of artefacts and systems
> (iii) pupils are able to improve and extend the uses of existing artefacts and systems
> (iv) pupils are able to design, make and appraise new artefacts and systems
> (v)   pupils are able to diagnose and rectify faults in artefacts and systems.
>
> (DES 1988a, paras 1.42–1.43)

This is a formidable list of requirements. It requires (especially in ii.) a wide-ranging understanding of technology in society, coupled (especially in i. and v.) with the detailed depth of knowledge and skill that is more typical of the restricted scope of hands-on 'doing' courses. At its heart, however, lies the essence of capability (in iii. and iv.) to identify shortcomings in the world and engage in designing and making in order to 'improve' things.[2]

But this view of capability in technology did not just emerge from nowhere in smoke-filled committee rooms. It represents the latest phase of development of a story that is at least 30 years in the making (see, for example, Penfold 1988; Kimbell 1991). And at the heart of this 30 year development lies a fundamental shift of emphasis from the study of *technological outcomes* (making them and understanding their social impact) to the exercise of a *technological process* (of design, development, manufacture and testing) that generates the outcomes.

We should not underestimate the massive significance of this move, particularly in the context of pupils learning in schools. It is a move from receiving 'hand-me-down' outcomes and truths to one in which we generate our own truths. The pupil is transformed from passive recipient into active participant. Not so much studying technology as *being* a technologist.

Defining attainment targets

The development of this proactive, process-centred view of technology may well be mirrored in other areas of the curriculum ('process' science and 'process' maths, for example). But uniquely in technology it is the process that defines the discipline. DES (1988a) proposed six ATs for technology, five of them focussing on this process:

AT1 Explore and investigate contexts for design and technological activities

AT2 Formulate proposals and choose a design for development

AT3 Develop the design and plan for the making of an artefact or system

AT4 Make the artefacts and systems

AT5 Appraise the processes, outcomes and effects of design and technological activities

These were seen to sit within a single 'profile component',[3] 'design and technological capability'. Since the National Curriculum subject was called 'technology', the report proposed that there should be a second profile component for information technology capability, with the sixth AT.

This was in many ways a very bold set of proposals, since it placed the entire focus of assessment (which was of course the purpose of ATs) on to the *process* of design and development. The knowledge and skills that for most subjects dominated the ATs were repositioned for design and technology into the PoS. The philosophy that underlies this decision is clear. Teachers need to teach knowledge and skills, so they need to be specified in the programmes of study, but pupils' capability will be assessed through their ability to *make use of* that knowledge and skill in tackling real designing and making tasks. The ATs therefore can focus on the process and not on the knowledge and skills: 'We have argued that because knowledge is a resource to be *used*, a means to an end, it should not be the prime characteristic of attainment targets for design and technology' (DES 1988a, para. 2.19). Since our aim is the development of technological capability, we do not need to assess knowledge and skills for themselves. Rather we need to assess how well pupils can manage the skills and knowledge they posses in order to tackle technological tasks. It is this *tackling of tasks* that should therefore be the focus for assessment and hence the stuff of ATs. The Working Group even went so far as to say that the approach to assessment should 'ideally' be based 'on the systematic observation of pupils' work throughout a design and technology task from recognition of the need to appraisal of the product' (DES 1988a, para. 1.30).

AT1 **Identifying needs and opportunities**	AT2 **Generating a design proposal**	AT3 **Planning and making**	AT4 **Appraising**
Through exploration and investigation of context (home, school, recreation, community, business and industry) pupils should be able to identify and state clearly needs and opportunities for design and technology activities	Pupils should be able to produce a realistic, appropriate and achievable design by generating, exploring, and developing design and technological ideas and by refining and detailing the design proposal they have chosen	Working to a plan derived from their previously developed design, pupils should be able to identify, manage and use appropriate resources, including both knowledge and processes, in order to make an artefact, system or environment	Pupils should be able to develop, communicate and act constructively upon an appraisal of the processes, outcomes and effects of their own design and technological activity as well as of the outcomes and effects of the design and technological activity of others, including those from other times and cultures

Figure 4.2 Design and technology attainment targets in the NCC consultation document of 1989.

The Working Group was bold in making this separation of teaching and assessment, and was quite right to do it. But this report came as a real shock to many who had naively assumed that ATs would be categories of knowledge and skills to be taught and tested. On first seeing the report, one senior civil servant was heard to observe 'this could be the rock on which the National Curriculum could founder'. We shall examine in the following chapter the extent to which this observation has been justified by events.

Following the consultation exercise, and the further work of the Group, the original five ATs were modified down to four. A good deal of further work was completed by the Group and then the report was handed over to the National Curriculum Council (NCC) which was required to consult and then report to the Secretaries of State (for Education and for Wales), summarising the proposals and detailing any advice or recommendations. Thereafter the Secretaries of State could move to publish a draft Order.

Interestingly, the NCC consultation report (DES 1989b) further strengthened the position on ATs. They emerged for formal consultation in the form shown in Figure 4.2. Each AT was supplemented by a raft of statements of attainment that were the 'criteria' against which performance was to be measured at each of the ten levels of the National Curriculum. I shall explore this matter in detail in Chapter 5.

The NCC consultation exercise led to no great transformations. There was some fiddling at the edges with terminology, and some attempts at a simpler level of language, but the position on ATs remained effectively unchanged. It was subsequently published and enshrined in law as the Statutory Order for Technology (DES 1990). The single significant change between the consultation document and the Order was that each of the SoA was assigned an example (in italics) in an attempt to clarify in classroom terms what it meant. For example:

AT1; level 2; SoA (c)
ask questions which help them to identify needs and opportunities for
design and technology activity

Example
Find out how the school cook chooses the menus for school dinners

With this helpful set of additions, the attainment targets for design and
technology passed quietly into the law of the land. It was a defining
moment in the development of the technology curriculum, but before
examining the events that flowed from the establishment of the Statutory
Order, we need briefly to examine the other half of it – the PoS.

Detailing Programmes of Study

Whilst the ATs enshrined the essence of technological capability as the
target for design and technology in schools, the PoS were intended to
provide the *means* by which teachers might help pupils to reach that
target. They make interesting reading through these early draft stages,
since they went through far greater redrafting changes than did the ATs.
It was as if there was far greater uncertainty about them.

The interim report set out to identify the core of knowledge, skills and
understanding which should constitute the stuff to be taught within the
PoS. The difficulty of identifying this core was summarised by two sharply
contrasted views aired early on in the report.

One position, strongly advocated by some experienced professional
designers is that the body of knowledge in support of design is un-
bounded; designers have the right and duty to draw upon knowledge
from whatever sources seem likely to assist them in their quest for a
solution.

In contrast if we look at the prevailing orthodoxy in much secondary school teaching . . . we find an emphasis on relatively narrow veins
of knowledge concerned with topics such as materials, mechanisms,
structures, energy and electronics.

(DES 1988a, paras 1.23–24)

Given these contrasted positions, the Group sought to build a framework
upon which to structure the knowledge skills and understandings that
pupils need. The Group recognised that the structure 'can be no more than
a scaffolding, to be regularly reconstructed according to the requirements
of particular tasks'; and it finally settled (in the interim report) on the
framework shown in Figure 4.3.

By the time the Working Group had completed its work and handed it
on to the NCC for formal consultation, there were some significant changes
to this formulation. The overarching categories had gone, and there
remained 16 separate categories, as shown in Figure 4.4.

- **Media for design and technology**
  materials and components
  energy
  information
- **Influences on practice**
  business and economics
  tools and equipment
  mathematics
  aesthetics
- **The characteristics of design and technology products**
  systems
  structures
  mechanisms
- **The applications and effects of design and technological activity**
- **Skills for design and technological activities**
  exploring and investigating
  imaging and speculating
  organising and planning
  making
  communicating and presenting
  appraising

Figure 4.3 Design and technology programmes of study in the interim report of 1988.

Materials and components
Energy
Business and economics
Tools and equipment
Aesthetics
Systems
Structures
Mechanisms
Exploring and investigating
Imaging and generating
Modelling and communication
Organising and planning
Making
Appraising
Health and safety
Social and environmental

Figure 4.4 Design and technology programmes of study in the NCC consultation document of 1989.

However, following the consultation, there was a far more radical restructuring, and by the time the Statutory Order was promulgated in 1990, it had reverted from 15 separate categories to four broad groupings:

- Developing and using artefacts systems and environments
- Working with materials
- Developing and communicating ideas
- Satisfying needs and addressing opportunities.

Needless to say, the content of these groupings (being essentially amalgamations of all the former categories) was inevitably less precise, and it
is interesting to note that the formulation of the design and technology PoS
had moved through the following three arrangements: from specifics within
groupings (Interim Report, DES 1988a) to just specifics (NCC Consultation Report, DES 1989b) to just groupings (DES Statutory Order, 1990).
We shall see in what follows that this final – somewhat vague – formulation contributed significantly to the problems that beset the implementation of the Order in the following couple of years.

A moment in history

As the Statutory Order for design and technology was passed into law in
1990, we were witnessing a defining moment in a development that had
been at least 30 years in the making. Despite all the trials and tribulations
that subsequently arose as the full repercussions of National Curriculum
policy hit schools, we should not underestimate the significance of this
moment for technology. Never before had it been an entitlement for all
children to study technology; now it was. Never before had it been the
least bit significant in the primary curriculum; now it was. Never before
had the specialist subjects in the secondary school technology domain
(craft, design and technology; home economics; art and design) been grouped
and expected to provide a single coherent technology experience; now
they were. But crucially, never before had this compulsory (statutory)
experience been described in such incontrovertibly procedural terms; now
it was.

Technology was defined in law (for the first time ever in the world) as
an activity to be pursued, and as an entitlement for all pupils. It was a
great moment.

Emerging difficulties

Teaching one thing, but assessing something different

Given all that I have said above, it should be clear that I think the Design
and Technology Working Group was quite right to settle for capability-
based ATs, supported by knowledge and skill-based PoS. This knowledge
and skill can be taught and learned, but the critical thing to be assessed
is the pupil's capability in putting it to use in a real task.

This raises a really interesting conundrum, since what it means is that the
teacher is expected to teach one thing but assess the pupil for something
else. This problem does not arise where the ATs merely mirror the PoS,
which they generally do for most subjects. But in technology, the PoS
require the teacher to teach the pupil, for example, about 'joining materials in permanent forms'. But then the teacher does not have to assess
whether the pupil can join materials in permanent forms. Rather she has

to assess the pupil's ability to, for example, 'review how to make best use of materials, procedures, tools, and equipment' or to 'use knowledge of materials, components, tools, equipment and processes to change working procedures to overcome obstacles as making proceeds' (DES 1990).

Given the experience of teaching technology through the 30-odd years of its various earlier phases, I do not believe this would have been a serious problem for teachers had it been explained in a straightforward manner. But the issue was never aired; it simply sat in the background as an apparent mismatch between the ATs and the PoS.

Attainment Target problems

The structure of the ATs

A further source of confusion for teachers arose from the inner structure of the ATs themselves. The SoA, through which the ATs were elaborated, illustrate a deeply embedded confusion that further contributed to the turmoil that was later to be evident in schools.

The procedures to be engaged in within a project can be plotted on two quite different axes. First, it is possible to identify the *domains of capability* that pupils might be employing:

- investigating;
- developing ideas;
- planning;
- making;
- appraising etc.

Second, it is possible to identify the broad time phases through which a project proceeds, and these are purely arbitrary ways of dividing up the time that the project takes:

- initiating activity;
- developing activity;
- concluding activity.

We became aware of this issue when we were trying to develop activity tests for the APU project. Our chart of capabilities against time phases (Figure 4.5) illustrates the problem as we saw it. Our four APU test structures were very much based on a time-phase analysis of the activity, and accordingly – in each test – we were looking for *all* domains of capability. The 'early ideas' test prioritised those domains that are typically exercised in the early stages of a project, but it did not ignore the others. And the 'starting points' test did require pupils to generate and develop ideas *and* to evaluate them as part of the process of building a secure starting point. The same was true of the 'developing solutions' test: it also required *all* the domains of capability, but concentrated on the generation and development of the solution.

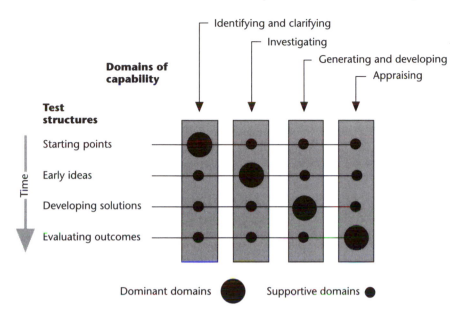

Figure 4.5 The relationship between time phases within a project and the domains of capability employed (Kimbell *et al.* 1991, Section 16).

The problem arises when these two axes are merged into a single axis – which, in my opinion, is what happened with the ATs. It was never clear whether they were to be conceived as distinct domains of capability or as representative of the flow of the activity. This might sound a somewhat arcane difficulty, but its consequences are profound, as we sought to indicate in our response to the emerging framework:

> The point remains however that there is a central difference between *domains* of capability and *phases* of activity and it is less than entirely clear into which category the Attainment Targets are intended to fall. To take a specific example, if AT5 'Evaluating' is a *domain* then all the SoA within it need to be about evaluating. But if it is a phase of the activity (usually the last phase) then it needs to contain all the sorts of things one does towards the end of a project. Thus the SoA might quite reasonably include more practical making/modelling as well as (and in relation to) more investigation of the original need.
>
> The writers of the ATs and SoA have gone out of their way to deny the idea that the ATs should be seen as a time sequence, suggesting – by extension – that they are rather to be viewed as overarching and pure domains of capability. And yet this is not supportable in the detail of the SoA.
>
> (Kimbell *et al.* 1991, Section 16)

Whilst either position (ATs as domains *or* as phases) is entirely defensible, it cannot be both at the same time. Or at least not without some cost. My assumption at the time was that the writers were trying to integrate the domains *within* each AT, in order to avoid the possibility of teachers deconstructing what is essentially a holistic activity. But because each individual AT was (to a limited extent) *internally* integrated, they ended up looking more like a time phase than domains of capability.

In the end, most teachers assumed that the ATs were in fact time phases – starting projects by focusing on AT1, then moving to the concerns of AT2, then AT3, and finishing with AT4. And the cost of this practice was (for example) that evaluating was only ever seen as important at the end of the project, and investigating was only important at the start. By contrast, in the APU tests – that were explicitly designed to represent time phases – *every* test required pupils to clarify, generate and evaluate their developing ideas. The prevailing interpretation of the AT framework did not appear to require this level of integration, and this contributed substantially to the emergence of an unhelpfully rigid, step-by-step view of the ATs.

Furthermore, the interpretation of AT1 as the start of all projects (the first time phase) placed it in a position of huge significance for the teacher. And this had a direct bearing on the confusions that sprang up around AT1, as we shall see below.

The confusion of AT1
The issue of 'what should teachers teach?' became linked with the confusion of ATs as domains or as time phases. And the confusion crystallised around the issue of AT1, 'Identifying needs and opportunities.'

> Through exploration and investigation of a range of contexts (home; school; recreation; community; business and industry) pupils should be able to identify and state clearly needs and opportunities for design and technological activities.
>
> (DES 1990)

There are two aspects of this issue, the first of which is that tasks are seen here to derive from *contexts*. There was nothing desperately new or threatening about this. The idea of setting tasks within a context that helps to make them meaningful has in recent years become a prerequisite of good teaching. In our early work developing assessment instruments for the APU project, we expressed this matter as follows:

> The task must be set in a familiar context that then gives meaning and relevance both to that task and to the appropriate knowledge and skills that people might need to deploy or acquire in tackling it.
>
> (Kelly *et al.* 1987)

The issue was picked up by the Design and Technology Working Group, which lent further weight to the argument:

> pupils will need to bring together and use knowledge, skills, value judgments and personal qualities, the particular components and

combinations being determined by the context and nature of the undertaking . . . as the range of contexts in which design and techno-logical activity is embedded becomes broader, so the demands will expand progressively.

(DES 1988a)

The essence of this move towards contextualising tasks is that 'real' tasks do not and cannot exist in a vacuum, and the *setting* of the task is a major determinant of the *meaning* of that task. If you were invited to 'design a door handle' the task would have very little meaning until you could see the context for which it is intended. It might be for a child's playhouse, or a heavy goods vehicle or an industrial kitchen. In each case the issues that the designer needs to consider are to a large degree defined by the *context*. Equally, the success of the outcome can only be determined by examining its operation in the same context.

None of this would have been threatening to teachers. It is little more than common sense. It was the second half of the attainment target that really put the cat among the pigeons: 'pupils should be able to identify and state clearly needs and opportunities for design and technological activ-ities'. Shock! Horror! Were pupils really being expected to *identify their own starting points* for designing; identify *their own* need that might be met? And, if so, what was the teacher supposed to do other than preside frenetically over the chaos (anarchy?) of a studio/workshop in which every pupil is doing something different? How, in this situation, would teachers ever manage to construct a teaching programme that showed any kind of progression? The wording of AT1 appeared to require teachers to forget their own teaching agendas, introducing new ideas in planned stages. If pupils are busily setting *their own* agendas in response to the imperative in AT1, to what extent can teachers be said to be teaching?

Some very unfortunate activities emerged from the resulting confusion. As HMI reported in 1992: 'In some schools . . . pupils often spent much unproductive time trying to identify needs; the outcomes were rarely sat-isfactory, and pupils sometimes became despondent about their lack of progress' (DES 1992).

In reality, the problem stemmed from a lack of preparation on the part of teachers for what appeared to be a radical development. Few questioned the desirability of basing tasks in real contexts, but typically the only experience secondary teachers had of allowing pupils to identify their own needs for projects was with 16-year-olds in GCSE projects. There was no reason to believe that this approach would work for all ages of pupils. And it did not. The problem here was one of teachers *apparently* being required to abdicate control of task setting. As we shall see, this was not necessary and certainly not desirable.

I have argued elsewhere (Kimbell *et al.* 1991; 1996) that tasks exist on a continuum from broad and contextual to narrow and specific. I have termed this a *hierarchy of tasks* which has – at one extreme – a very open

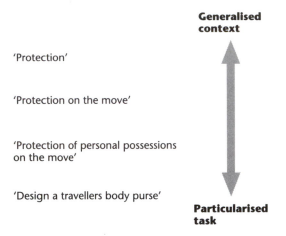

'Protection'

'Protection on the move'

'Protection of personal possessions
on the move'

'Design a travellers body purse'

Figure 4.6 Tasks exist on a continuum from the general to the particular.

and ill-defined context and – at the other – a highly specified task (Figure 4.6). This was a model that we used for deriving test tasks for the APU survey in 1988–9 and about which we were subsequently able to comment in terms of the effects of these different levels of specificity on different sub-groups of pupils (e.g. girls as against boys). It matters little how many steps exist in this hierarchy, but it is important that we see the ever more specific tasks deriving originally from the context and subsequently through each successive layer.

> This progression – from the general to the particular – is nothing more than a recognition that all particular tasks exist somewhere in more generalised contexts. But it does not follow that particular tasks must always be derived through the same progression from the general context. The fact that the hierarchy exists does not mean that it has to be operated in the same way each time when deriving tasks from within it.
>
> (Kimbell *et al.* 1996)

As an example, the teacher might wish pupils to get involved in designing with textiles, and may set the task of designing *a traveller's body purse* to enable the user to carry around money or other valuables whilst on holiday. This specific task exists in its hierarchy in which the overriding context might be 'protection' and which might include the layers shown in Figure 4.6.

There may, of course, be any number of layers in this hierarchy, but the point here is that it is perfectly possible to *start* with the specific task. The significance of the hierarchy is that we would thereafter expect pupils to explore up and down it in order to inform their design of the body purse. They would need, for example, to examine the kinds of personal possessions to be protected, and how this is affected by being on the move, and even ultimately what it might mean to 'protect' them. It might mean to *hide* them or *disguise* them or *fix* them. The task is only the entry point to the hierarchy. We might wish pupils to enter at the specific level or at the general level. But wherever they enter it, they will be exploring contexts to identify the needs and opportunities involved in their task. They would therefore be conforming to the requirements of AT1 as outlined in the 1990 Order.

The confusion that surrounded the wording of AT1 was very unfortunate, and it did lead to some unsatisfactorily unfocused projects, as HMI reported. But again it was completely avoidable. Had the issue of task setting been presented as existing on this continuum of tightness/openness, a great deal of heartache might have been avoided.

Programmes of Study problems

What to teach and *how* to teach

There was an enormous amount of rhetoric flying around at the outset of the great National Curriculum adventure. And much of the rhetoric was explicitly designed to belittle and demean the work of teachers and schools. The politics of derision was at work; schools were failing; teachers were lazy and needed Kenneth Baker's 'contract' to stop them skiving off from school the moment the last bell sounded.[4] The overall tenor of the period was one in which it became acceptable to tell teachers what to do and expect that they would jolly well do it – or else. In the context of the National Curriculum Orders that were being drafted and finalised, this manifested itself as a desire not only to specify what the curriculum would contain (ATs and PoS) but also to meddle in the matter of how this curriculum was to be taught.

In terms of the design and technology Order, the programmes of study not only outlined the knowledge and skills to be taught:

- developing and using artefacts systems and environments;
- working with materials;
- developing and communicating ideas;
- satisfying needs and addressing opportunities.

It also specified that there would be three classes of outcome:

- artefacts;
- systems;
- environments.

And these outcomes would be realised through four classes of materials:

- construction materials;
- food;
- graphic media;
- textiles.

And that the outcomes would be set in five contexts:

- home;
- school;
- recreation;
- community;
- business and industry.

And that all this was to be set into a secondary school curriculum with five former specialist subjects dividing up the work:

- art and design;
- business studies;
- craft, design and technology;
- home economics;
- information technology.

This is multi-level modelling of an awesome kind: four programmes of study; leading to three classes of outcome; in four materials; from within five contexts; 'delivered' by five 'subjects'. It was completely mad.

Whatever the good reasons for having all these features on the teacher's agenda, it is none the less a massive intrusion into the classroom to impose such detail through a Statutory Order. And the same can be said of the other requirements that surrounded the operationalising of the PoS in schools and that formerly had been matters under the control of teachers.

But teachers were left in no doubt about the seriousness of the matter. There must have been hundreds of thousands of copies of the Order circulated to schools – and the first substantive page of text made it clear that this was a command coming with the force of law:

STATUTORY INSTRUMENTS
Education, England and Wales
The Education (National Curriculum) (Attainment Targets
and Programmes of Study in Technology) Order
1990
Made: March 1990
Laid before Parliament: March 1990
Coming into force in accordance with articles 2 and 5.

This level of imposition would only have been possible in the fevered atmosphere of the time – when teachers were going to be told exactly what they would and would not do. Even at the time, there were some who sounded warnings about the level of difficulty that this might represent for teachers and schools:

> however, we do have some serious worries as to whether the proposals will *actually* be practicable in many schools . . . the proposals will pose very considerable challenges to teachers and schools . . . we note the question voiced by some of our respondents as to how

realistic it is to expect the technology PoS for KS3 to be fitted into
a maximum time allocation of four periods in a forty period week.
(Curriculum Council for Wales 1989, p. 17)

Inevitably it could not last. Schools did their best to accommodate the
demands in the Order but were soon found to be struggling. The statutory
curriculum in technology (quite apart from that in the other nine compulsory subjects) represented a massively unwieldy structure.

What to teach and **whom** to teach

The programmes of study were intended to be taught, and in secondary schools it was anticipated that this teaching would typically be done
through existing academic departments. Whilst the terms of reference for
the Working Group had particularly singled out CDT as central to the discipline, the interim report identified five contributory departments (listed
above) concerned with the 'delivery' of the technology curriculum. The
NCC consultation report held to the same line, acknowledging (DES 1989b,
para. 1.8) that 'the skills, knowledge and values necessary for design and
technology activities are to be found at present in' that same list of five
subjects.

The problem of how to manage this exercise was thus thrown back to
schools. In effect, schools had been told: we (the DES) have mandated the
curriculum; you (the schools) have subjects that cover different bits of
what we have mandated; you now have to organise yourselves so that
you can guarantee coverage of the PoS. A plethora of 'delivery models'
then surfaced as schools and LEAs desperately tried to find ways to make
it work, and three broad approaches are discernible.

1 *The status quo – a single-subject approach.* This amounted to little
more than an accounting system, since the traditional subjects carried
on much as before. The difference was that they accounted for their
elements of teaching and learning against the PoS. At the end of a key
stage, it was thereby hoped that all the ground would have been covered
by one or other of the partners.
2 *A federated approach.* This involved a more proactive relationship between the departments. They came together in planning teams to try
systematically to manage the 'delivery' of the curriculum in ways that
would ensure that the whole PoS was dealt with during the key stage.
This federated approach had a number of features that were very constructive. First, it involved the identification of key contributory factors
– what, for example, can home economics or CDT uniquely bring to
this partnership? Second, it required teachers from the subjects to recognise where their work overlapped. Third, it required teachers to take an
overview of whole key stages – planning ahead to make sure that pupils
received an appropriate mix of activities and experiences. But most of
all – to even get started with all this – it required that the teachers from
these subjects sit down and talk with each other about the development

of technological capability. This was in itself an important development. These were important discussions to be having with technology in such a formative state.

3 *An integrated approach*. This amounted to a much more radical development than the other two, since in effect the subjects disappeared to be replaced by a newly constructed 'technology' team. The advantages of this were much the same as those mentioned above in the federated approach, but the difference was that the consequences of decision-making were taken to a much higher level. The approach tended to downplay the significance of the roots from which teachers had grown, and the differences of culture that existed as a result of their different histories. And given that the discussions might ultimately be about reassigning teachers – and even about redundancy – the integrated approach can be seen as representing a strategy with very high stakes.

It might be argued that this reassessment of the contribution of a whole raft of curriculum subjects was an entirely good thing. We need to have things thrown up in the air occasionally so that we are forced to think about what we are doing rather than just accept the current convenient status quo. The problem, however, was that this reassessment came hard on the heels of a series of preceding reassessments. 'Uncertainty' had been the only fixed characteristic of technology for the previous ten years. And essentially the amalgamation of the five subjects was only the most recent of a series of other amalgamations. The 'CDT story' illustrates this point very clearly, since CDT was officially 'launched' as recently as 1985, and in schools that adopted an integrated approach to the National Curriculum PoS, it was absorbed into the technology team a mere five years later.

The CDT story has been fully documented by Penfold (1988), but for the purposes of this brief illustration, the story really comes to a head in the early 1980s with the work of the Secondary Examinations Council.[5] The SEC was established to bring order into the 'anarchy' of the secondary school curriculum, with hundreds of different examination courses all leading to idiosyncratic examinations run by a multitude of examination bodies. The SEC sought to *rationalise* these courses (so that one maths course looked similar to another), and then to *approve* them for the new common system of examining at 16+, the GCSE. Courses not approved by the SEC would not be allowed in schools.

In the early 1980s there was a plethora of subjects in the curriculum that made some contribution to the discipline that we now call technology. These ranged from 'engineering workshop theory and practice' – through 'woodwork' to 'technical graphics'. The SEC brought together the principal exponents of these multitudinous strands and required that they write down what was the central defining nature of the subject. The aim was to produce some National Criteria through which we would define each area of the curriculum. And the SEC did not want 25 different sets of criteria, but just one set that would define what it is that goes on in this domain of the curriculum. There were some painful meetings between the resident experts, leading (in 1981) to a document in which three sets of criteria were proposed, one each for:

technology   (incorporating all the applied science courses)
craft and design   (incorporating all the designing/making courses)
technical graphics   (incorporating all the graphic/communication
                     courses)

The SEC rejected this formulation, and sent the experts back to do further work to come up with a single set of National Criteria. There was a good deal of blood on the walls at the subsequent meetings. Very deeply held views, passionately advocated, led to a level of conflict that made these meetings quite gripping. But gradually a resolution emerged: craft, design and technology. It was moderated through a series of sub-titles, and the 1985 National Criteria emerged as; CDT: design and realisation; CDT: technology; and CDT: design and communication. The critical point, however, was that there was a common core of stuff that was the basis of the discipline: 'to foster an awareness, understanding and expertise in those areas of creative thinking which can be expressed and developed through investigation and research, planning, designing, making and evaluating, working with materials and tools' (SEC 1985, para. 3.1).

I was asked at this point (by the specialist SEC committee) to write a guide for teachers (the orange book) to explain the issues surrounding the implementation of GCSE, including the distinction between the subject of CDT and the three GCSE course strands which might be certified through it.

> the breadth of material that CDT encompasses cannot be contained in one course, even though it is one subject. To make sense of the mass of content that it might contain, the material has been biased for GCSE purposes into three courses. We use the term 'biased' (as opposed to divided) deliberately to indicate that the courses are different in emphasis only. Much of the material will be common to them all and it is for this reason that they are all prefixed CDT. The National Criteria for CDT illustrate the the distinctive contribution of each of the courses *and* the common ground that unites them.
>
> (Kimbell 1986, p. 17)

The point of telling this story is to illustrate that between 1980 and 1985 CDT emerged through a painful birth process that left many of the participants bruised and battered. Much of the content of the contributory subjects had been binned, leaving the common core of designing and making and the three strands of emphasis. It was – in my view – a timely consolidation of what we were seeking to achieve in this area of the curriculum.

But within five years we were at it again. Only now there were four other subjects that had each been through the same rationalisation process. Business studies, home economics, art and design and information technology had suddenly been added to the melting pot, and 'design and technology' was to be distilled from it. It is a rare teacher – and an even rarer school – that relishes this relentless restructuring. It too often creates a perception of winners and losers rather than partners. As with the 'blood on the walls' in the SEC in the early 1980s, there were rather too many gory scenes in design and technology staff meetings in the early 1990s.

There were also, of course, many constructive and purposeful debates that helped many schools to get up and running with the National Curriculum PoS for design and technology. The point of telling this story, however, is to illustrate the enormous historic and cultural pressures under which the Statutory Order for design and technology came into effect.

Summarising the problems

I have tried to outline in this chapter some of the major sources of confusion and difficulty that confronted teachers and schools when they inherited the Statutory Order for Technology in 1990.

There was the confusion created by the fact that the programmes of study required teachers to teach one thing whilst the ATs required them to assess something different. There were confusions inherent in the structure of the ATs (as domains of excellence or as time phases), and there was particular confusion about AT1 'Identifying needs and opportunities'. The programmes of study created a massive management problem through the specification of *contexts*, *outcomes* and *media*, in addition to the PoS categories themselves. And, on top of all that, the whole package was almost entirely new in primary schools whilst, in secondary schools, it was to be put into effect by a new formulation of curriculum subjects, a new federation (or even a new integration) with all the concomitant tensions of management reorganisation that this brings with it.

And it was all to be achieved at no cost. Or, at least, no cost in terms of professional training and development for teachers. The costs were to be incurred in the publication of truly awesome amounts of paperwork to be sent to schools, and in terms of the development of assessment arrangements to which we shall turn in the next chapter. In-service training activities for teachers were left for LEAs and schools to cope with.

Given the scale of the challenge, it is quite remarkable that so much happened in such a short time. The HMI report on the first year of implementation (1990–91) identified the following features of excellence from the schools visited in that first year:

- pupils taught safely by specialist teachers who were confident and familiar with the media, tools and equipment being used, and who knew the standards they should expect.
- the work was well planned, with systematic teaching of skills, knowledge and techniques related to all the ATs and Programmes of Study.

- teachers provided a good range of resources and materials and encouraged pupils to use them to investigate, design, make, test, and evaluate their work.
- specialist teachers used a variety of teaching techniques, and provided pupils with a good balance of activities both as part of an individual lesson and as part of their long term planning.

(DES 1992, p. 19)

But it was not all quite so good as this. Whilst 70 per cent of Key Stage 2 lessons were rated as satisfactory or better, only 60 per cent of Key Stage 3 lessons were satisfactory or better. 'These are disappointing figures and highlight the difficulty experienced by teachers in implementing National Curriculum D&T' (DES 1992, p. 18). But after such a massive upheaval – and given the difficulties and confusions involved – it was not at all surprising. It is interesting to trace how these difficulties and confusions were dealt with in the subsequent redesign of the curriculum, culminating in the new design and technology Order in 1995. But before we do that we should remember, and even restate, the point to which I drew attention earlier in this chapter.

Despite all the trials and tribulations that subsequently arose as the full repercussions of National Curriculum policy hit schools, we should not underestimate the significance of this moment for technology. Never before had it been an entitlement for all children to study technology; now it was. Never before had it been the least bit significant in the primary curriculum; now it was. Never before had the specialist subjects in the secondary school technology domain (craft, design and technology; home economics, art and design) been grouped and expected to provide a single coherent technology experience; now they were. But crucially, never before had this compulsory (statutory) experience been described in such incontrovertibly procedural terms; now it was.

Technology was defined in law (for the first time ever in the world) as an activity to be pursued, and as an entitlement for all pupils. It was a great moment.

Despite all the aggravation, the 1990 Order for technology represents a central landmark in the developing story of technology in schools. And had we not had the courage to press ahead with what was recognised at the time as a difficult and even risky venture, our curriculum would be the poorer for it.

Before moving on from the 1990 Order and its associated difficulties, there is one final matter with which we need to deal. It represented – in my opinion – by far the biggest problem in implementing the Order. I refer to the assessment arrangements. All other problems associated with the implementation of the National Curriculum pale into insignificance when set against the monster that was created to assess the performance of pupils and, by extension, to assess the performance of teachers and schools.

The assessment requirements of the Education Reform Act were articulated through the work of the TGAT and finally confronted the reality of technology classrooms and studios through the words of the Order – specifically the SoA that comprised the ATs.

The chaos that resulted – and the reasons for that chaos – are the substance of the next chapter.

Notes

1 For a more detailed discussion of this issue, see Kimbell *et al.* (1996, Chapters 2 and 3).

2 Again, see Kimbell *et al.* (1996, Chapter 3) for a detailed discussion of 'capability', including the role of values and hence 'improvement'.

3 The idea of 'profile components' emerged as a reporting device from the TGAT report. They were seen as 'clusters of attainment targets which have some homogeneity in relation to the skills, knowledge and understanding which the subject promotes' (DES 1988b, para. 35). TGAT took the view that each subject should have a small number (between four and six) of profile components reflecting the breadth of the subject.

4 The front pages of the press did not report that this contract (emerging as 'directed time' in schools) amounted to significantly less hours than most teachers were doing anyway. There is a wonderful story of a group of faculty heads in Devon writing to the DES to enquire who was going to cover their work during the summer term, since their 1260 contract hours had all been accounted for in the first two terms. The deeply damaging effects of the contract on extra-curricular activity also went unreported, until 1994–5 when ministers suddenly realised the damage that their policy had inflicted on organised team sports in schools.

5 The SEC was established shortly after the Conservative Party (Thatcher) election victory of 1979. Its work in standardising curriculum provision (initially at age 14–16) can be seen as the first link in a chain of actions that led to the National Curriculum in 1990.

five

The shambles unravels
National Curriculum assessment

Many kinds of assessment

A useful starting point for any discussion about assessment is to be as clear as possible about *what* it is that we are seeking to assess; *whose* performance we are concerned with; and *why* we are concerned with it. In the school context over the last ten years these questions might lead to any one of the following answers:

1 'We are assessing pupils – to see how they are progressing in their current work, and in order to design an appropriate next project' (*a teacher response*).
2 'We are assessing pupils – to see what they know, understand and can do at the end of their GCSE course' (*an examiner response*).
3 'We are assessing the success of the teacher/department/school in enabling pupils to achieve good GCSE grades' (*an Ofsted[1] response*).
4 'We are assessing the nation's school leavers – to see if they are doing better than they were five years ago' (*an Ofsted/DfEE response*).
5 'We are assessing the curriculum – to see what changes we might recommend in the revision for the year 2000' (*a DfEE/SCAA[2] response*).

A reasonable person may well decide that *all* these matters are useful to know about. But it is then necessary to decide what would count as acceptable evidence to inform them. Evidence to inform issue 1 might, for example, look like this: 'I spoke to the teacher and she thought that Paul's evaluation is very weak – so she is going to focus on that in the next project.' But this very particular piece of evidence about Paul is irrelevant to issue 3, for which we need to appeal to data about the department, perhaps about levels of training or resources, and perhaps using statistics about the incidence of 'good' teaching or the percentages of A–C grades achieved by pupils. But these measures are in turn quite useless as evidence for issue 4, for which we must appeal to national statistics on a scale that is sufficiently large to overcome the vagaries of particular schools or year groups.

It is simple common sense to assert that the evidence that one needs to scrutinise varies with the question one is seeking to answer, and accordingly each of the five issues listed above needs a different set of data or body of evidence. There is nothing surprising about this, and indeed it is the reason why we have traditionally had quite different forms of assessment in school.

A *classroom record sheet* would traditionally contain all the kinds of information that teachers find helpful when looking at the progress of individual pupils through particular projects or assignments. It provides classroom-based data for the purpose of supporting teaching and learning.

GCSE assessment is a different kind of assessment that provides an overview of what the pupil 'knows, understands and can do' at the end of a two-year GCSE course. It is similar to the classroom record sheet to the extent that it is based on the work of a particular pupil, but it is different in that it is seeking to summarise everything about that pupil's work in technology, rather than report simply on a single project or assignment. And the purpose of this assessment is different. It is not to do with supporting teaching and learning so much as with national certification: with awarding grades that have meaning and currency at other levels of the education service and in other domains altogether (e.g. employment).

APU assessment (see Chapter 3) is different again. The Assessment of Performance Unit (APU) was set up in 1975 as a research branch of the DES, surveying and monitoring levels of achievement in schools. Whilst GCSE data tell us about the pupil, APU assessment was designed to tell us about the state of the subject nationally. APU studies were therefore based on the principle of devising a multitude of different test activities and administering them selectively across the population. The sum total of the APU design and technology tests would have taken any individual 40 hours to complete, but any individual pupil only completed 3 hours' worth. Data on the whole survey was amalgamated from thousands of individual performances, and since we only tested 12 pupils in a school, and only used 700 of the 4500 secondary schools, the testing only made modest demands of schools. Our APU survey – like all other APU surveys – was designed to provide immensely detailed data on national performance in design and technology whilst making very modest demands on any one school or pupil.

APU data can tell us how performance varies with different kinds of task, or in different regions of the country, or in pupils of different gender, or in pupils with different curriculum backgrounds. It provides national monitoring data.

These three examples represent dramatically different kinds of assessment evidence. It is all evidence of pupil capability in design and technology, but it has been gathered for very different purposes and is therefore of very different kinds. It also supports very different kinds of judgment. The differences have long been recognised and the separate systems have therefore coexisted in schools for many years. But this comfortable coexistence was consigned to history by the assessment regime that was ushered in by the Education Reform Act of 1988. At a stroke, the *multiple* purposes to which assessment data had previously been put were to be served by a *single* system – National Curriculum assessment.

When Kenneth Baker established the Task Group on Assessment and Testing in 1987, he wanted it to lay the foundations of a single, all-embracing system of assessment. It was to be diagnostic and formative (for teachers in the classroom), it was to be summative (for certification purposes) and it was to be evaluative (of the education service as a whole).

> Our consultation document recognises a number of purposes which assessment, including testing, may fulfil, and different uses to which information derived from assessment may be put. These include diagnostic and formative purposes...; summative purposes...; and purposes mainly concerned with publicising and evaluating the work of the education service and its various parts...
>
>   I seek advice on a coherent national system of assessment and testing ...that recognises the different purposes... and takes account of how they interrelate with and complement each other...
>
> (DES 1988b, Appendix B)

This would indeed be the holy grail – a single, united system of assessment. A single system that could be used by teachers to guide their pupils; used by employers to make recruitment choices; used by LEAs to guide policy (e.g. on professional development in schools); used by parents to judge the effectiveness of schools; and used by central government to monitor the service as a whole. The single system was to operate at the macro level, i.e. nationally; at the median level of the school; and at the micro level of the pupil.[3]

Golly Gosh – it must be one hell of a system!

The single system of assessment

The central features of the new National Curriculum assessment regime were developed by TGAT. In the summer of 1987, and in advance of the subject working groups deliberating on the content and structure of their respective subjects, TGAT proposed a general model for assessment and testing to which these subject groups would be required to conform. And TGAT itself was given a scant few months to do its work – its report being required by Christmas 1987. The members of TGAT were clearly aware of the difficulty of conflating the multiple purposes of assessment. And as experienced assessors, many of them were also aware of the problem of generating evidence for assessment at a level that is appropriate to the task in hand.

TGAT made the reasonable point that whilst it is possible to aggregate upwards from pupil-level detail, it is quite impossible to disaggregate downwards to the pupil from school-level judgments. The focus of TGAT therefore fell heavily on the formative assessment of individual pupils – with the possibility thereafter of aggregating data upwards for other purposes.

> Some purposes may be served by combining the findings of assessments designed primarily for a different purpose . . . We judge that an assessment system designed for formative purposes can meet the needs of national assessment at ages before 16 . . . It is realistic to envisage, for the purpose of evaluation, ways of aggregating the information on individual pupils into accounts of the success of a school, or LEA . . . the reverse process is an impossibility . . . We recommend that for summative and evaluative purposes results should be aggregated across classes or schools so that no individual performances can be separated out.
>
> (DES 1988b, paras 25–29)

TGAT went on to make a series of recommendations: for ten levels of performance through which pupils were to progress during their 11 years of statutory schooling; for the age points at which, during these 11 years, they should be assessed (7, 11, 14 and 16); and for the reporting arrangements that should apply to the data derived from the assessments. It also began to hint at the practical problems of how the assessments were to be made, and it is here that we begin to discern the birth of the monster that was to become National Curriculum assessment. It had the following structural hierarchy which progressively emerged from the multitude of National Curriculum documents, including the TGAT report.

- *The subject*: 'The National Curriculum is made up of *core* and other *foundation subjects*[4] which are defined by law' (NCC 1992). Taken together the subjects were intended to 'cover the range of knowledge, skills and understanding commonly accepted as necessary for a broad and balanced curriculum' (DES 1989a).
- *Attainment targets*: 'to be specified at up to 10 levels of attainment, covering the ages 5–16, setting objectives for learning' (DES 1989a).
- *Profile components*: 'the profile component . . . will comprise a cluster of attainment targets which have some homogeneity in relation to the skills, knowledge and understanding which the subject promotes' (DES 1988b).
- *Programmes of study*: 'specifying essential teaching within each subject area' (DES 1989a).
- *Statements of attainment*: 'statements of attainment link the attainment targets to the ten levels of achievement specified in the TGAT report' (DES 1988a). There were described also as 'a criterion referenced set of levels' (DES 1988b).

The critical relationships here are between the profile components, the attainment targets, and the statements of attainment, and for technology, the formulation in the 1990 Order was eventually structured as shown in Figure 5.1. There was a clear hierarchical relationship between the three

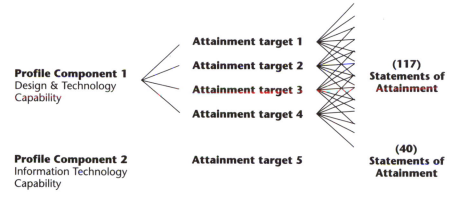

Figure 5.1 The structure of National Curriculum technology (DES 1990).

elements, and TGAT reported, after its consultation exercise and in its supplementary report of March 1988: 'There is general agreement with our concept of the profile component, consisting of a cluster of related attainment targets, as the basic unit of assessment and reporting' (DES 1988b, p. 19).

But the reality behind this cosy complacency was that no one (not even TGAT) had grasped the significance of what had been proposed. It amounted to nothing less than a complete revolution in assessment thinking and the wholesale dumping of years of classroom and examination board experience. In two respects, in particular, it created an assessment monster that proved – after several painful years – to be unforgiving, insatiable and blind.

The first problem: digitisation

There can hardly be a teacher anywhere who has not engaged in assessment using a sliding scale of excellence. The scale may differ: it might be A–E, or 1–10, or 1–100. But the essence of a scale of excellence is that it can report the level at which, or the thoroughness with which, a pupil has responded to a task. It is an analogue system that enables teachers to report on the different levels at which pupils are operating (Figure 5.2).

I have explained in Chapter 2 how sliding-scale systems of assessment were gradually transformed into criterion-related scales that progressively defined what A, B, C, etc. mean in terms of the performance of pupils. The GCSE General Criteria were specific in requiring examinations that ensured

Unacceptable very poor		Sliding scale		Outstanding excellent
Literal or numerical				
E	D	C	B	A
1 2	3 4	5 6	7 8	9 10

Figure 5.2 Analogue systems of assessment.

that if a pupil got 4 out of 5 for 'evaluating' it was not simply because she was nearly (but not quite) at the top of a rank order of other pupils, but rather because she was capable of meeting the defined requirement for a mark of 4:

> the performance required to achieve a particular mark is therefore specified in advance in the list of criteria on the form. It is therefore both more precise and more useful in a situation in which it is impossible for one teacher to know exactly what norms will be used by another teacher . . . the norms are encapsulated in the criteria.
>
> (Kimbell 1986, p. 38)

These criteria can be seen in retrospect as the forerunners of statements of attainment. But with one huge difference. In the early GCSE assessments, the sliding scale continued to exist alongside the criteria. The criteria provided some guidance as to the possible location of a pupil on the scale. Thus, for example, a pupil's evaluative ability in a design project might be measured on a six-point scale, and the 'criteria' in the GCSE assessment scheme provided some simple bench-marks against which to reference the judgment (see Figure 1.2). The criteria were designed to act in concert with the scale.

But the post-TGAT world was to be entirely different. For National Curriculum assessment these criteria become statements of attainment which were to be seen as free-standing bits of capability, with teachers' responses to them limited to 'yes' and 'no'. This was the first startling change. Gradations of quality were dispensed with. The uncertainty and often the hesitancy of analogue assessment on the sliding scale was replaced by the blunt certainties of the digital world. Either she is or she isn't. Either he can or he can't. The vast majority of teachers had never before encountered such a simplistic model of assessment.

Incredibly, this issue never appeared as a matter for debate in any of the National Curriculum documents: not in TGAT; not in the technology Order; not in the NCC's *From Policy to Practice* (DES 1989a); not in its *Starting out with the National Curriculum* (NCC 1992). It was almost as if there was an assumption that the whole of past practice in assessment had been wrong. Sliding scales were history – and we did not even need to question the new certainties of SoA. And yet – as I shall show later in the discussion of Standard Assessment Tasks – this was a major reason for the collapse of the National Curriculum assessment regime.

But we might just have survived this transformation from sliding scales of excellence to free-standing SoA, had it not been compounded by a second – even greater – folly.

The second problem: 'miniaturisation'

The question here concerns the *focus* of assessment. Is the focus on the profile component, or on the attainment target, or on the statement of attainment? There were some fascinating arguments about this, and TGAT opened the batting with a clear preference for the profile component as the focus of assessment and reporting. Given the proliferation of attainment targets in the first round of Statutory Orders (e.g. 14 in mathematics and 17 in science), the focus on profile components appeared a better solution, though the problem here was big enough:

> there is a potentially serious problem because of the size of the burden that could be placed on teachers . . . a single class teacher of 7 or 11 year olds could have to assess pupils in at least 20 and possibly 30 or more profile components.
>
> (DES 1988b, para. 119)

TGAT did not go on to make the obvious point that assessment by attainment target (as defined in the first set of Statutory Orders) would have required teachers to assess about 100 of them for each child. None the less, and incredible as it may seem, this was the approach required by SEAC in 1990 in the first round of development for Standard Assessment Tasks in maths, science, English and technology.

The burdens of making assessment at the AT level were not as severe in technology (with only five ATs) as in many other subjects. But it was a nightmare for primary teachers in particular, who faced the prospect of assessing all ATs in all subjects. As the chairman of TGAT later reflected:

> It seemed absurd to me that SEAC could contemplate reporting separately on such a large number, but it was not until the Examining Groups pointed out that they could not possibly do this at GCSE level with any respectable degree of accuracy that the absurdity was accepted.
>
> (Black 1993, p. 60)

This was the reason for the 1990–91 rewrites of the Statutory Orders. Science came down from 17 ATs to just four, and mathematics from 14 to five. Technology remained unchanged.[5]

The rapid revisions of the Statutory Orders might therefore have been thought to overcome the problem of the burden of assessment for teachers. By 1991 there were only approximately 30 ATs covering the whole of the National Curriculum, and the task was down to something a bit more manageable – even if it was still vastly in excess of anything that had been experienced before. But in fact the problem was greatly magnified – and made utterly unmanageable – by a further step towards detail.

SEAC was making it increasingly clear that ATs were composed of SoA – and teachers would have to show that pupils had achieved the requirements in the SoA. Its attitude is well summed up in a policy document on National Curriculum assessment for Key Stage 1:

> Teachers will be expected to record their assessment of pupils . . . in the core subjects and technology . . . where there is evidence that justifies and supports such an assessment. The available evidence however

must cover attainment of a *complete level* within an attainment target. Where a teacher has evidence that a child has attained beyond level 3, but does not have sufficient evidence to establish whether the attainment is at level 4 or at a higher level, then the teacher is required to record level 3.

(SEAC 1991c, para. 17; emphasis added)

And here is the rub. The teacher has to have evidence of a complete level, that is to say evidence to support the awarding of each individual SoA. This ruling from SEAC was not based on law; it was not part of the Statutory Assessment Order that was in force at the time which barely mentioned SoA. Rather it was an interpretation of the law, and an interpretation from an increasingly macho organisation that was determined to stamp its authority on teachers and schools.[6]

By virtue of this diktat on the achievement of 'complete' levels, teachers were faced with the prospect of collecting evidence of everything that pupils did, so that each individual SoA could be scrutinised and justified – or not. And then the dozens of resulting SoA judgments needed to be transformed via a formula into an AT score.[7] And beyond the AT scores there was a further stage of aggregation into a whole score for the profile component.[8] And it did not even end there, for the Assessment Order (not just SEAC this time) required a further level of aggregation from profile component scores to subject scores, combining design and technology with information technology to derive a 'technology' score.

The bottom line of this whole outrageous rigmarole was that teachers had to manage not so much an assessment activity as an arithmetic activity. And its failing was well illustrated in a case study I was involved in documenting at a forward-looking school in Essex.

The effect in school

This period was marked by a proliferation of different designs for assessment and recording forms, as schools, LEA advisory teams and others sought desperately to find ways to help teachers to record this mass of data. The assessment forms got bigger and bigger; and the boxes on them got smaller and smaller. And this mass of assessment minutiae became more and more meaningless.

The case study in Essex involved a pair of teachers assessing the work of their year 9 pupils. They started with an enormous assessment sheet which contained boxes for all the SoA, and they spent hours ticking the boxes for the 43 pupils. They then started on the arithmetic. They aggregated to AT scores, then to profile component scores and then to subject scores. Then they ranked the pupils by their performance. It was a meticulous and thorough piece of work. But at the end of it they started to question the results: 'Jane can't be better than Joanne', 'Peter must be better than Patrick'. They had a clear sense of who (overall) was better than whom. And this intuitive sense was not confirmed in the assessments. So what should they do?

They could not adjust the profile component scores because they were mathematically derived from the AT scores. They could not adjust the AT scores because they were mathematically derived from the SoA scores. All they could do was go back to the SoA ticks. So they did. And they changed them. Having formerly said 'no' (because Peter was judged *not* to have used appropriate graphic techniques) they now recorded a 'yes' (he *did* use appropriate graphic techniques). By some selective adjustments of this kind – and after lots of supplementary reaggregation – the two teachers got the answers that they felt were appropriate for their pupils. It took an entire afternoon and evening. Eight hours. Sixteen teacher hours. And rather than leaving them professionally extended and satisfied with a good job done, it left them angry, frustrated and convinced they could never go through that ridiculous procedure again.

The two problems I have identified here were the root cause of this fiasco. First, the digitisation of assessment – the removal of sliding scales and their replacement with simplistic yes/no assertions. And this was fatally compounded by the preoccupation with detail (SoA ticking) at the expense of the big picture of overall quality.

A total lack of credibility

Taken together, the twin follies of digitisation and miniaturisation created a situation in which the assessment of pupils' work became far more cumbersome than it ever had been, whilst the results became far less trustworthy. Assessment is – above all else – a matter of teachers exercising professional judgment, and yet teachers were only able to exercise this judgment over matters of fiddling detail, whilst the critical matter of the levels that were recorded for pupils remained in the iron grip of blind arithmetic. Whilst teachers wanted to say something about the excellence (or the limitations) of their pupils, they were allowed only to comment on the 150 or so little sub-sets of it. And even then all they could say was 'yes' or 'no'!

It was a lunatic scheme. And remember, the Design and Technology Working Group (as I described in Chapter 4) had recommended that 'Design and Technology activity is so integrative, the approach to the assessment of pupil performance in this area should ideally be holistic' (DES 1988a). Most professionals in the field at the time endorsed this observation – and yet we ended up with the most atomised and disintegrated model of assessment that it is possible to imagine.

But it was only part of the story. For the other track of National Curriculum assessment was the Standard Assessment Tasks (SATs) that pupils were to complete at the end of each key stage. As one of the development agencies for the technology SATs (1989–91), we at Goldsmiths were thrust into the midst of the politics of National Curriculum assessment, and the story is worth a brief retelling.

SATs and the débâcles of 1992 and 1993

There are several issues that can usefully be highlighted in the work that was done in preparing SATs at the outset of the National Curriculum. I will consider these under the headings of SATs as whole projects, the problem of evidence and making assessments.

SATs as whole projects

We took to heart the statement about holistic assessment from the interim report, not just because it was in the report, but because it also conformed to our experience of assessment in a number of other contexts. And there are two dimensions to this holism: first, there is holism in the pupil activity that is to be assessed; and second, there is holism in the assessment of the pupil's response to the activity.

We took the view that since SATs were supposed to measure the whole capability of youngsters, a whole-task approach was the only reasonable option. We developed SATs that were essentially like carefully constructed course-work projects in which we enabled pupils to demonstrate whether they could (or could not) design and make products using the procedures that were encapsulated in the SoA. Not surprisingly, the other agency developing technology SATs[9] came to the same conclusion. In both agencies SATs were designed to be about 12–15 hours of timetabled (contact) time. As one teacher administering the SATs put it:

> The principle of using a SAT as an extended project that can properly address the integrative nature of the subject, that develops from the d&t curriculum, and that is built on a framework informed by the PoS and ATs, is one which is wholly supported by the staff...
> (Consortium for Assessment and Testing in Schools
> (CATS) 1991, p. 39)

I have often been asked why we did not opt for a different approach – in particular, the approach used in APU tasks (see Chapter 3) that were closer to being 'tests', set in a booklet and completed in 90 minutes. The answer is simple. Each APU test/booklet was designed to tease out a restricted range of abilities. An APU test therefore could never have provided evidence of more than a scattering of SoA. Because of the need (from SEAC) to evidence 'complete levels' (all SoA at a given level) it was simply not an option to use APU style tests. This again illustrates the difficulty of using an assessment instrument for a different purpose than the one for which it was designed. The national data that we derived from the APU survey were an amalgamation of 26 different tests. Taken together, they told us a great deal about what 15-year-old pupils *nationally* could do – but it told us relatively little about what *any individual pupil* could do. It therefore would not work as an assessment approach which needed to measure individual performance.

We were therefore left with the decision to go for whole-project SATs, and innumerable problems arose as to how we were actually to operationalise them. The problems included how to define the tasks in the first place,[10] and how to standardise the conditions under which pupils did their work. These problems were, however, little different from the those that had traditionally been faced by examination boards when setting design and technology examination tasks. The real problem with SATs was about *evidence* for assessment.

The problem of evidence

When a task is being used as an assessment device, not only does the pupil have to design and develop a product in response to the task, but also – at the end of the project – the work must contain all the evidence that is necessary for teachers to award all the SoA at the level at which the teacher judges the pupil to be. That evidence, of course, is partly in the product itself, and partly in the folder of supporting work.

There may well be plenty of assessment evidence in the product and the folder. Evidence, for example, that would allow one to say 'yes' to any of the following SoA:

Does the pupil:

(a) record their ideas as they develop?
(b) specify what they intend to do and what they will need by using simple plans and flow diagrams?
(c) use drawings, diagrams and three dimensional models to assist making?
(d) present an evaluation of their activities, including suggestions for improvements?
(e) devise and carry out ways of testing the extent to which the product satisfies the design specification?

(DES 1990, levels 4–8)

But then again there may not. With (b), for example, what do you do if there is a specification but not one that uses flow diagrams? Or with (c), what do you do if there are plenty of excellent graphics and diagrams but no three-dimensional models? And there were other even more intractable problems. Take, for example, the following list:

Does the pupil:

(v) understand the social and economic implications of some artefacts, systems or environments?
(w) show judgment in seeking advice and information?
(x) review how to make best use of materials, procedures tools and equipment?

> (y) review the ways in which their design has developed during the activity, justifying decisions and appraising result in relation to intentions?
>
> (z) review their own knowledge and draw up a strategy to exploit expert sources?
>
> (DES 1990, levels 4–9)

Most of these SoA – and many more like them – are not readily evident in any but the most meticulously detailed folder. And some defy any kind of evidence – except that direct evidence that results from the teacher seeing the pupil at work. It is evidence about 'recognising', 'showing judgment', 'justifying' and 'reviewing'. This is 'reflective' evidence (where pupils think around and evaluate a set of options and actions) and 'ephemeral' evidence (which is non-permanent). Both are critical to the proper assessment of pupils in technology, but both are very difficult to deal with.

To maximise 'reflective' evidence we developed a system that required pupils to pause for thought at three points in the activity (roughly at the outset, in the middle and at the end). We asked teachers to distribute a 'review' sheet that required pupils to reflect on what they had done, why they had done it and what they were planning to do next.

> Reviews 1, 2 & 3 are like a written viva; used to record thinking, explanation and justification in response to a series of carefully worded prompts under the headings *research*, *having ideas*, *planning*, *making* and *evaluating*. Each review was worded to take account of the general stage at which they occurred . . . near the beginning when the need or opportunity was newly identified; in the middle when ideas were progressing towards the reality of a made artefact; and at the end when the desired outcome has been achieved and evaluated . . .
>
> (CATS 1990, p. 13)

> The pupil's folder and the outcome provide the main evidence of *what* has been done and *how* it was done. The review responses were designed to provide evidence of the '*why it was like that*' kind . . .
>
> (CATS 1991, p. 8)

Not only did this process produce evidence for assessment, but many teachers commented that the reviews provided an important model for good design practice – essentially getting the pupils to be reflective about what they were doing rather than just being carried along by the momentum of the project. As a Coventy LEA report on SAT implementation (cited in CATS 1991, p. 41) put it:

> all teachers considered the notion of reviewing to be paramount in developing d&t capability . . . The inclusion of a formal process of review as an integral part of the SAT was instrumental in providing reliable evidence for some aspects of the ATs and SoA . . . having

completed the activity there is a consensus that this part of the process should be retained.

Making assessments

In the light of our previous research experience for APU, we were convinced that the holism of the projects completed by the pupils should be reflected in the assessment procedure. Apart from any educational argument, there was the reliability imperative from SEAC, and our APU statistics (see Chapter 3) had demonstrated conclusively that, in technology, teachers are at their most reliable when assessing holism and at their worst when assessing the bits.

The first judgment, therefore, was to be an overall measure of quality. Given the ten-point National Curriculum scale, the requirement was to 'pitch' the level as a whole. The second step would then be to check this level by more detailed identification of strengths and weaknesses at the AT level, and finally to validate the judgment by checking off the details of the SoA. It should be noted that one of the distinct advantages of working this way round was that it reduced the SoA to a meaningful and manageable number – those in the level that has been 'pitched' – and (as a cross-check) those one level up and one level down.

Rather than seeing SoA as front-line criteria for assessment, they become back-stop validation devices.[11] Our procedure used them to cross-check a judgment that had already been made, and for which we were seeking confirmation. SAT assessment therefore progressed through these three layers. An initial judgment; an elaboration of that judgment in terms of AT judgments that indicate strengths and weaknesses; and finally a validation of those judgments though a cross-check with the detail of SoA. (Figure 5.3)

At the heart of this process lay the challenge of making the initial pitch, and we knew that we would need to provide some support mechanisms to enable teachers to do this. We therefore developed a series of 'level guides' which were essentially A3 fold-out sheets that summarised all the critical

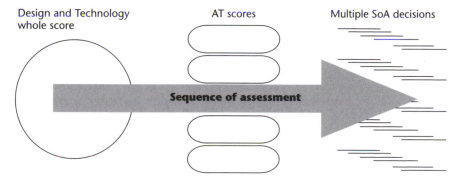

Figure 5.3 The sequence of SAT assessment.

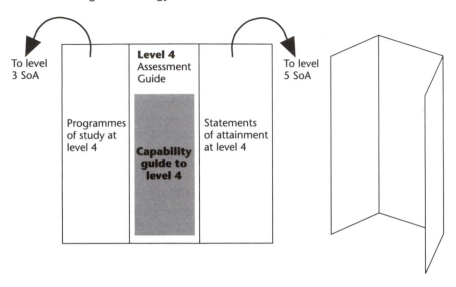

Figure 5.4 The CATS level guides.

information about a level (see Figure 5.4). When folded out, the left column summarised the PoS for the level and the right column contained the
SoA and ATs. The central column was written by us as a capability guide;
summarising the things to look for and the critical components of capability at that level.

A further critical feature, however, was contained on the back of the
folding flaps. By folding forward the left-hand side you turn up the SoA
for the level below, and by folding forward the right hand side you turn
up the SoA for the level above. If you are going to pitch a level, you need
the key information at that level. But having made the pitch, you then need
to cross-check up and down to be sure that you have got it right. The SoA
provided the detail for this validating or cross-checking purpose.

In the CATS technology team we produced level guides for each of
the levels, and they proved valuable for effective assessment. They gave
confidence to the teachers – not only by providing information but also by
providing a mechanism and a protocol for assessment. And this confidence
was subsequently borne out by the reliability statistics which – whilst not
being as good as the APU assessment reliability – were sufficiently secure
to convince us (and thankfully SEAC) of the acceptability of the data:
'The reliability of the tests used in 1991 was probably as high as could
be achieved under the constraints existing' (SEAC 1991b, para. 180).

There was also a clear impression in SEAC that these SATs were good
as a means to exemplify for teachers what the technology curriculum
meant – but less good at pinpointing the SoA detail that could justify solid
AT scores.

The evidence from both development agencies indicates a high level of validity for the questions in terms of their structure as a reflection of technology as defined in the National Curriculum ... the appropriateness of the materials for assessing individual ATs is less clearly demonstrated.

(SEAC 1991a, p. 9)

At the end of the 1991 pilot SAT process, we were reasonably confident that we had developed a SAT structure that reflected a proper, i.e. valid interpretation of what design and technology should look like; was manageable as a classroom activity (it was even supportive of teachers who were struggling to come to terms with the Statutory Order); and it provided acceptably reliable data on pupil performance (though more so at the PC level than the AT level).

SEAC does not approve

But there were two problems. The first was that from SEAC's point of view, these SATs looked rather like a normal piece of curriculum activity. They did not look like a test and they seemed to provide too much opportunity for teachers to influence (and even steer) the course of activity. The second problem goes back to the issue I outlined earlier about SEAC's requirement for evidence of whole levels. The SEAC review of 1991 SATs comments in the following terms:

validation should be based not [on] the extent to which the tests generally match the demands of the curriculum, but also on the extent to which individual questions and mark schemes match the demands of specific performance criteria.

(SEAC 1991b, para. 60)

In short, the demand from SEAC was for 'tests', that had 'questions', which addressed specific 'performance criteria', i.e. the SoA. And this decision made our model of an *assessment project* extremely vulnerable. When we were asked, for example, to identify in advance which SoA would be tested and evidenced by the SAT we could not answer, since the evidence was dependent upon the way the pupil responded to the project. The SAT did not 'target' any SoA in particular.

A related difficulty (for SEAC) was our insistence on the sequence of assessment starting with 'big-picture' judgments of whole capability – and only subsequently moving on to the detail of the SoA. For SEAC, the SoA had become the vital feature of assessment. No argument would persuade the Council from this line and by the time it began to listen (two years later) – it was already too late. The damage had been done and the profession had lost all respect for what SEAC was seeking to impose.

But at the time (1991) our stance on assessment – in terms of both assessing 'real' tasks and the sequence of assessment – was interpreted by SEAC as wooly-minded liberal nonsense. We believed that it was necessarily implied in the Order, and that in any event it was an approach that was supportive of good practice in technology. Indeed SEAC (1991b, para. 185) itself recognised this latter point: 'Technology SATs were not seen as unmanageable in 1991 – even though they were time consuming. Teachers were unsure of themselves in this subject and therefore valued the support the SAT provided.'

In technology, therefore, SEAC's report illustrates the extent to which the SATs could usefully be integral to the curriculum.[12] But within SEAC this tendency to move SATs away from testing and embed them into the curriculum was not seen as a good thing. The pilot SATs of 1991 had penetrated many schools and given advance warning of the workload that was to follow when the SATs were launched nationally the following year. The resulting pressure from schools – in subjects other than technology – was for a lighter form of assessment, and this linked nicely to SEAC's own preference for short, sharp focused tests that did not impose on the curriculum. And consequently the specification for the 1992 round of SATs was threefold: SATs that were shorter; SATs that were sharper, i.e. tightly focused to 'performance criteria' (the SoA); and SATs that would provide a set of SoA scores, not an overall score for technological capability. These demands simply did not fit to our model of SAT assessment, and we were removed from the development process.

It ends in tears: the new generation of SATs for 1992–3

MEGNAP was asked to develop the new generation of SATs that would be far more tightly constrained that those of 1991. And it was presented with an almost impossible task. It tried to retain the concept of whole-project SATs, but at the same time had to make them achieve the unachievable – for example, by targeting particular levels and even particular SoA. The more it succeeded in this 'targeting', the less the whole thing looked like a real technology project.

In the end the SATs were so tightly engineered that experienced technology teachers despaired about the effects of running them. Whilst the 1991 SATs (from ourselves and from MEGNAP) fitted comfortably into the curriculum and were generally perceived as supportive of teachers, the 1992–3 versions projected a very different image. One of the manifestations of the problem was that following the SATs, thousands of pupil outcomes in hundreds of schools looked frighteningly alike. Thousands of drilling clamps (that all worked the same way) and thousands of flashing tent pegs (that all behaved and looked alike). The constraints that were imposed to control the task from the centre reduced very significantly the extent to which pupils could themselves take control of the project. And ironically they therefore reduced the extent to which the activity could be seen as a reliable measure of technological capability.

But these 1992–3 technology SATs became tied up in a bigger battle about SATs in general, and it was a battle that went to the heart of National Curriculum assessment. Teachers did not like what they were being given for assessment purposes and the rumblings of discontent gradually crystallised into a fierce opposition to what SEAC was trying to do. Not only did teachers dislike SATs for pedagogic reasons, but head teachers disliked the effects they had on their schools; and parents disliked the effects they had on their children. A head of steam was building up that manifested itself in an almost complete boycott by the profession of the 1992 SATs.

The hapless Secretary of State for Education, John Patten, was finally forced (in early 1993) to acknowledge that teachers were simply not going to do as they were told in this matter. Even the supportive *Daily Telegraph* (12 May 1993) reported it as follows:

> Bowing to overwhelming pressure, Mr Patten . . . announced yesterday that National Curriculum testing is to be radically reduced from next year . . . action would be taken to reduce the workload of teachers . . . Mr Patten said that the future of the controversial technology tests for 14 year olds would be 'decided later in the light of this summer's tests'. . .
>
> [Mr Patten] continues to insist that this summer's tests will go ahead as planned, despite a threatened national boycott . . . ministers hope that the promised slimming down of the tests and the promise to lighten the classroom workload will gain the backing of moderate teachers and parents and isolate union militants.

It was a vain hope, because the opposition did not reside in a few 'union militants', but was quite universal. By 1993 everyone was militant and accordingly that year's SATs were almost universally consigned to the rubbish bin. And the DES was stunned by the extent of the public rebuke. The week after the 1993 testing fiasco, I happened to be in Sanctuary Buildings, the DES headquarters that Mr Patten must have felt were somewhat misnamed. There was much worried huddling, and frank amazement that the teaching profession could do anything so unanimous and so unequivocal.

The monster of National Curriculum assessment that had been given birth by TGAT and lovingly reared by an aggressive SEAC, was put to the sword by a profession that had finally had enough.

The confusion of purpose

A final area of confusion, to which I would like now to draw attention, arose from the problem I outlined at the start of this chapter: the problem of deciding what purpose is to be served by National Curriculum assessment. As I pointed out, the TGAT report identified the multiple purposes of assessment: formative (for teachers); summative (for certification); and evaluative (for monitoring the education service). Whilst TGAT favoured assessment and reporting at the profile component level, it gradually became policy to focus down to the AT level and eventually to the fine detail of SoAs.

One of the key questions in the development of SATs was the relationship between (and the uses for) two different kinds of assessment data: the scores derived from SATs; and the scores derived from teacher assessment (TA). The problem arose when schools course-work assessments (TA scores) *differed* from the results of the SAT scores, and the problem was neatly described in the 1991 review of SATs by SEAC itself.

> A key decision that remains to be taken about [National Curriculum] assessment in 1992 is the relationship between SATs and TA
>
> - SAT and TA reported separately
> - SAT and TA combined
>   - accepting the TA score
>   - accepting the SAT score
>   - a combination of 50% SAT and 50% TA
>   - a combination of SAT and TA weighted preferentially in favour of one
>   - accepting the schools' decisions after reconciliation for individual cases.
>
> (SEAC 1991b, para. 142)

SEAC was trying to decide whether a decision on SAT/TA resolution would have to be a universal ruling (for all subjects) or whether it might vary between subjects. This might mean, for example, that in technology it might be split 50/50 since SATs and TA were at that time based on activities that were more or less equivalent in curriculum terms; whereas in mathematics the SATs were focused on particular ATs and therefore these scores should override the TA score in that AT.

> If the principal purpose of [National Curriculum assessment] is to provide summative and evaluative information then it may be appropriate to use a *common structure* across all subjects. . . . If however the principal purpose of NCA is formative, then it may be more appropriate to take subject-based decisions . . .
>
> The decision about *whether to combine* scores (i.e. for example by taking the mean of SAT/TA) also depends upon the principal function desired for NCA. If the main purpose is to provide evaluative information at a class or school level then the 'uncombined' test scores alone may be appropriate. On the other hand for formative use at the individual pupil level then some form of combination is probably appropriate.
>
> The precise *method of combination* should also be determined by the purposes of NCA.
>
> (SEAC 1991b, paras 157–160; emphasis added)

In short, SEAC – after two years of SAT development, countless millions of pounds of expenditure and equally countless millions of hours of teacher labour – had not decided what the principal purpose was for National Curriculum assessment. This becomes even more explicit as the review report proceeds:

> It is evident that the SATs of 1991 attempted to satisfy a number of functions. . . . In accordance with the specification to which the development agencies were working, the TGAT model of [National Curriculum assessment] was adopted . . . tasks were produced which attempted to be both formative and summative in function . . . within this framework different priorities were identified. In some subjects (e.g. technology and Welsh as a second language) the SATs were seen to have an important function in exemplifying the curriculum, in other more established curriculum areas (e.g. science and English) this function was perceived to be a lower priority.
>
> (SEAC 1991b, Appendix 1)

The TGAT model of assessment was – like Janus – found to be facing in too many directions at once. It could have worked well in the classroom, providing important information about pupils for teachers, but it did not because it had too much associated baggage as a result of trying also to be a means for measuring the performance of those teachers and their schools. As Gipps (1993, p. 55) somewhat acidly observes:

> The authors of TGAT maintain that their plan has been misinterpreted . . . but there are major technical problems inherent in the blueprint. . . . The notion that one programme of assessment could fulfil four functions (formative, diagnostic, summative and evaluative) has been shown to be false. . . . What is surprising is that the TGAT report was accepted in the first place given the political agenda.

After the débâcle: retrenchment

For the 1991 SATs, the confusion of purpose within SEAC that had been created by the multiple dimensions of assessment in TGAT, had made it possible for us to develop SAT materials that were supportive of the technology curriculum. But from 1992 onwards it became clear where the real purposes lay. The evaluative function – monitoring the performance of schools so as to create league tables and hence a 'market' in schools – came clearly to the surface.

Curriculum-based SATs were rejected and replaced by short, sharp pencil and paper tests that were sat in timed examination settings. Even the technology SATs were emasculated and distorted activities. The 1991 review of SATs had somewhat ominously proposed that 'for the assessment in 1992 and beyond . . . these functions and priorities [i.e. whether SATs should be formative or summative or evaluative] need to be made explicit and understood by all those involved in the process' (SEAC 1991b, Appendix 1). It was made very clear that the priority was *evaluative*. It was made explicit to the developers, and as soon as the materials hit the schools it was equally obvious to teachers, and thereafter followed the boycotts of 1992 and 1993. Some form of government retrenchment (in addition, of course, to the removal of the Secretary of State) was inevitable.

Many teachers did not survive the ministrations of Kenneth Baker, Kenneth Clarke and John Patten as Secretaries of State for Education, responsible, at different times, for the development of National Curriculum assessment. Neither did TGAT survive them. And neither did SATs in technology survive them. The technology curriculum only barely survived them.

Before leaving this chapter, however, it is worth recording the thoughts of one of the principal officers in SEAC. He had been responsible in the Evaluation and Monitoring Unit of SEAC for monitoring the development of National Curriculum assessment, and I asked him (in 1993) to give a public lecture at Goldsmiths College reflecting on the previous three years of frenetic activity. He concluded his lecture as follows: 'it is my hope that a healthy and open debate about the curriculum and its assessment will continue and that we will see a continuing move towards intelligent pragmatism and away from ideological dogma' (Taylor 1993). And so say all of us (that survived).

Notes

1 Ofsted is the Office for Standards in Education.

2 SCAA, the School Curriculum and Assessment Authority was created by the merger of the former SEAC and NCC.

3 Such was the confidence that this system would serve all these purposes, that the APU was closed down. With the new integrated system in place, it was believed that APU surveys would no longer be necessary.

4 Interestingly, technology soon came to exist somewhere between these two states as an 'extended core' subject.

5 However, technology has subsequently been split and 'downsized', as a result of the Dearing revisions of 1995, to two ATs for design and technology and one for information technology.

6 There was a very significant change of attitude in SEAC in 1991, when Lord Griffiths took over as Chairman and Chief Executive. Philip Halsey – the former Chairman and Chief Executive – had deep roots in the education service, as had Duncan Graham at NCC, and these roots had enabled SEAC to retain educational priorities. Lord Griffiths arrived hot from the 10 Downing Street policy unit determined to shake things up and assert the measurement and accountability functions of SEAC.

7 Three different aggregation rules were experimented with, deriving an AT score from various combinations of SoA 'hits'. The first rule required a 'complete' hit; all SoA to be recorded. This was the 'n rule'. There was also an 'n–1 rule', in which pupils could miss one SoA within an AT and level and still get the

level. And finally there was an '$n/2$ rule' in which teachers had to provide evidence for more than half of the SoA within an AT at a level. Needless to say, the three rules produced quite different results.

8 All kinds of options were explored: the 'median' rule; the 'arithmetic mean' rule; the 'geometric mean' rule; and the 'trailing edge' rule. All had strengths and weaknesses.

9 The 'Midland Examining Group National Assessment Project (MEGNAP) consortium was based at Middlesex Polytechnic under the direction of John Cave, Richard Tuffnell and Alf Massey.

10 This was particularly tricky, since the demands of AT1 (at some higher levels) required pupils to derive *their own* tasks.

11 Exactly like the go/no go gauges I discussed in Chapter 2.

12 This was the case with technology SATs developed by both agencies. MEGNAP solved some of the problems in different ways, but the overarching notion of SATs as controlled projects was the same.

six

Lessons we should have learned

The failure and progressive collapse of National Curriculum assessment in 1992 and 1993 can – as I trust I have shown – be accounted for in terms of events, policy decisions and reactions to them. But it is important that we learn from the experience of the last few years, and to that end I would offer the following lessons that we should take to heart.

The limits of law in the classroom

The assessment regime that was dreamed up for the National Curriculum sought ostensibly to provide information about pupils and schools. The National Curriculum was set up by the Secretary of State to define in law the behaviours, attitudes, knowledge and skills that pupils 'ought' to possess. SEAC (a quango accountable to the Secretary of State) then sought to put all children through a series of tests, at regular intervals, to measure their achievement. This can be seen as a constructive move towards making schools accountable for their work, but it can equally be seen as a attempt by central government to take responsibility and control of the curriculum away from teachers and schools and into the office of the Secretary of State.

In the last 15 years, through a series of reforming Acts of Parliament, successive Secretaries of State have taken on to themselves a quite staggering range of powers. But if one is seeking to take power over the curriculum – in a circumstance in which it has formerly been exercised by others – one needs to do more than simply take power to the centre. One also needs to undermine and remove the powers that have traditionally been exercised by teachers and others in the education service.

Over a period of years, the concept of the professional teacher – with responsibility for curriculum building and for defining and maintaining standards of schooling – was challenged and replaced by the concept of the teacher as contractor – working identified hours to others' specification and monitored by external agencies. Internal professional standards were progressively replaced by external contractual standards:

- the teaching contract from the Department for Education which emerged as 'directed time' in schools;
- specified programmes of study from one government quango;
- tightly specified national testing from another government quango;
- league tables constructed by SCAA to the government's specification;
- and school inspections administered by Ofsted also to the government's specification.

As Lockley (1995, p. 17) commented:

> Nightmarishly, the dreaded paperwork seemed to have taken control and I hated the sense of being driven, of having to fit things in ... It was as if the Government was taking revenge on teachers ... One night after hours spent ticking thousands of little boxes I thought if I threw it all in the bin – or made it up – no one would know – because no one ever wanted to see it ... We spent years doing what we thought was important – yet it was as nothing to the people in power, who just changed it.

To whom should teachers turn for support in trying to cope with the flood of centralised directives? They would traditionally have sought support from their LEA teams of advisers and advisory teachers. But this support network was itself subject to just the same erosion from a related strand of government policy. LEAs often had strong traditions in education and strong, articulate individuals running them. To take power over schools it was necessary to eliminate these alternative centres of influence, and the LEAs were squeezed mercilessly. On the one hand, they were prohibited from holding significant sums of money at their own centres so as to fund LEA support services: they were required by law to pass on ever more of their central funding directly to schools. And on the other hand, the schools themselves were encouraged with generous handouts to opt out completely from LEA management. It is a matter of fact that the majority of the advisory positions that (in the 1970s and 1980s) had supported teachers in the development of the technology curriculum, have now either disappeared completely or been converted into 'inspection' roles. The inspection, of course, is run by Ofsted (another quango accountable to the Secretary of State):

> Lines of democratic accountability have been broken as schools ... have been removed from their former control by local government and placed under the management of new trusts and agencies. ... The state system [of education] is fractured by yet another wave of market-based reforms and attacks on the power of local government.
>
> (Hutton 1995, p. 214)

The autonomous professionalism of teachers – to make decisions about the curriculum and make judgments about the excellence of their pupils – was effectively destroyed. A commonplace reaction in schools to this relentless chain of events was teachers washing their hands of the whole business. Sometimes in anger, but more often in despair, I heard teachers say: 'I just wish they would decide what it is they want me to do – and then I'll get on and do it'. By 'they', of course, these teachers meant the Secretary of State and those accountable to him. None of the teachers with whom I worked when I entered the profession in the early 1970s would ever have dreamed of making such a comment. The curriculum was not something designed and imposed by 'others'. Rather it was something that one constantly developed as part of one's professional responsibility.

To those of us who have been working within education during the last few years, the ethic driving this centralisation of power appeared to lie in the desire to transform a profession based on the concept of service into a 'contracted-out' trade, based on the competitive principles of the market-place. The assault on teachers' professionalism was multi-dimensional, and each brick that was pulled out of the wall contributed to the progressive collapse of the concept of the professional teacher. Ironically, as I shall show later in this chapter, teachers' professionalism and experience were desperately needed to make National Curriculum assessment the least bit meaningful or even workable. Successive Secretaries of State appeared to miss this central truth, and when teachers finally withdrew completely from the process it collapsed.

The teacher boycotts of 1992 and 1993 – and the crisis that they caused in government – came as a very rude shock to those who for years had come to regard teachers merely as operatives to be manipulated at will. Finally things had gone too far, and teachers found a focus for their discontent that gave them – for the first time in years – the explicit support of parents and governors. The monumental fiasco of National Curriculum SATs in 1992 and 1993 was a watershed that finally marked the limits of the power of law-makers in the classroom. Send for Ron Dearing!

The National Curriculum rethink that was forced upon the DfE and SCAA[1] by the tumultuous events of 1992 and 1993 was enacted through the review undertaken by Sir Ron Dearing. The process was begun in April 1993; an interim report was produced in July 1993 (Dearing 1993b) and the final report, A Review of the National Curriculum, was published in December 1993 (Dearing 1993a). There are many facets of his recommendations, but they centred upon one principal objective: to slacken and render more flexible the statutory (i.e. compulsory and legal) framework within which the National Curriculum was operating. Specifically, this reduction of the legal framework was to apply both to the definition of the curriculum – through smaller, more generalised and more flexible programmes of study – and also to the assessment regime – reducing markedly the burden of assessment and recording.

The changes had the effect[2] of portioning out responsibility for the National Curriculum: separating issues to do with classroom practice (the domain of teachers) from those that were to do with achievement standards and over which it is perfectly appropriate for the paymaster to exercise some control. If government is paying for schools, it can properly have a view about the outcomes of schooling. He who pays the piper. . . . However, it appears gradually to have been accepted that once having decided on the desired outcomes, it should be for professional teachers to decide how to achieve them.

Reconstructing the technology curriculum

In the technology curriculum, Dearing took the view that much of the detail of classroom practice in the original Order (e.g. about contexts and media) should be non-statutory guidance with no place at all in the legislative framework. This legislative framework should be reserved for defining the outcomes of the curriculum, not for trying to define teaching and learning approaches. A compelling metaphor was commonly used in SCAA at this time, concerning learning to drive. We use the 'Highway Code' as our principal learning tool about the rules of the road, but it is not a legal document. It is effectively non-statutory guidance. The Road Traffic Act is the legal instrument that constrains the way we behave on the road, but no one with any sense would use it as a teaching and learning tool. The argument went that the Statutory Orders should only deal with the outcomes that are to be measured once teachers have done their work through the vehicle of the curriculum.

This single decision about the appropriate limits of the law slashed out a large proportion of the original technology Order, and rendered obsolete the subsequent draft revision of 1992 that had – in my opinion – been a major step backwards. The final 1995 reformulation is something of a compromise: simpler and less prescriptive than the original, but at the same time losing some of its breadth of vision.

Writing in May 1994 at the time of the SCAA consultation on the revision, I described it as a 'Not so much a workshop manual – more a professional guide', and went on to make the following observation:

> It was with some relief that I read through this new D&T Order (May 1994). Its principal strength is that it appears to mark a return to professionalism – to the view that teachers understand about teaching and learning and can be trusted to behave sensibly and appropriately in the interests of their pupils. This is in marked contrast to former versions[3] which took delight in specifying the curriculum – and how to teach it – in minute detail.
>
> (Kimbell 1994b)

Reconstructing assessment

One of the first dramatic changes to the assessment regime was heralded in a letter dated 4 November 1993 to all chief education officers (CEOs) and to all schools. It was sent jointly by the new head of SCAA (Ron Dearing),[4] the Office of the Chief Inspector of Schools for Wales (Roy James) and the head of Ofsted (Stewart Sutherland). The letter followed the shambles of that summer's tests that had seen teachers inflict so much damage to the central tenets of National Curriculum assessment as it had emerged under the guidance of (in particular) Secretaries of State Clarke and Patten. The political fallout for Patten had not yet crystallised into dismissal – but it was only briefly delayed to save further political embarrassment.

The letter enshrines a complete reversal of the former SEAC policy of how statements of attainment were to be viewed; on the need for evidence to justify assessments; and on the role of teachers' professional judgments.

The essential points we would like to convey are as follows.

- In those subjects which have statutory teacher assessment in 1994, the aim should be to arrive at an all round judgment of the level a pupil has achieved in each attainment target.
- There is no need to assess against every statement of attainment individually or to record those assessments on a tick-list: teachers need only consider whether the knowledge, understanding and skills displayed by a pupil correspond on the whole more closely to the statements of attainment at one level than another.
- When it comes to substantiating their judgments, teachers do not need to keep detailed evidence to support the assessment they have made of every child ... they need only collect a school sample of pupils' work that exemplifies attainment at each level. ... How teachers record pupils' progress is, of course, a professional matter for schools to decide.

(Sutherland *et al.* 1993)

The 'of course' must have seemed a bit rich to CEOs and teachers who had just experienced five years in which the very idea of their exercising any kind of professional judgment over such matters had been systematically crushed. That apart, however, the letter reflects a good deal of common sense.

As with the specification of *curriculum*, so too with the model of *assessment*: the limits of the role of law-makers in the classroom had been reached and, in the turmoil of 1992 and 1993, had been exceeded. The Dearing-inspired reconstruction marks a recognition of the essential professional role of the teacher in both domains. The professional role of teachers in developing the curriculum and in assessing pupil performance is a key matter to which I shall return below. For now, however, it is enough to recognise that we have seen the limits of the role of law-makers in the classroom. It was a painful learning process, but an important lesson that we should never forget.

The separation of assessment functions

The letter from Sutherland, Dearing and James indicates a move to separate the evaluative function of assessment from the other two functions (formative and summative). Pupils are still to be assessed individually, but teachers need only make a broad judgment about which level of statements (in overall terms) best describes each pupil's attainment. Thereafter, the collection of evidence is based *not* on pupils but on schools. The school has to compile a portfolio of evidence of what its attainment at each level is like generally across the school. This can then be used, in evaluative terms, as the school's benchmark of excellence.

I have outlined in Chapter 5 how TGAT conflated the multiple functions of assessment into a single system. I have also explained why – in my opinion – it did not work, and the Dearing review began to unpick these three strands of assessment. Particularly in the context of the evaluative function, Dearing's report recognised that if the only purpose of assessment is to monitor the performance of the education system as a whole (i.e. generating system-evaluation data) this could be achieved through carefully devised sampling of *part* of the school population on an annual basis, as APU surveys had done prior to the National Curriculum.

This separation of functions was made manifest in a number of other ways. In addition to system-evaluation data being collected at the level of the school, rather than at the level of the child, the certification role of assessment was further separated from National Curriculum assessment. The confusion here had originally been created by the ten-level National Curriculum scale in which the upper levels overlapped with GCSE assessment. The decision was taken to separate them, with GCSE assessment taking the summative certification role whilst National Curriculum assessment was cut back and applied only to the first three key stages, i.e. 5–14 years. The National Curriculum (5–14) scale thereafter became an eight-point scale.

In late 1993, Rob Taylor, a senior SCAA officer, reported: 'There does appear to be a broad consensus within the educational world that it is more appropriate and useful to separate the various purposes of assessment and testing and then design procedures which are fit for specific purposes' (Taylor 1993). In rapid reaction to the testing fiasco of 1993, the megalithic monster of National Curriculum assessment was being dismantled and it was increasingly recognised that the different *purposes* for assessment in schools resulted in the need for different *kinds of data*. The TGAT notion that one can simply aggregate from one kind of data to the next was recognised as flawed. It is a lesson we should remember.

The limitations of atomised assessment

I have drawn attention (in Chapter 2) to the limitations of atomised assessment when one is trying to assess pupil capability in technology. The six problems that I identified there became apparent to us in the late 1980s in our APU work, and were confirmed in the early 1990s in our work on SATs for SEAC.

Taken together, these problems forced us to the inevitable conclusion that a disintegrated approach to assessment would be not only less valid but also less reliable than an approach that enabled teachers to start with whole judgments and progressively dissect them to diagnose pupils' strengths and weaknesses. All our research evidence suggested that sound assessment resulted from a sequence of activity that started with 'big pictures' of capability and moved through progressive stages into the detail (see Figure 3.6). In the 1991 APU final report we put it as follows:

> It is our view that SoA judgments would be more reliable if placed within a broader frame of reference through the AT and the PC. . . . We are drawn therefore to a procedure that starts with big pictures (PC) moves to more restricted ones (ATs) and ends with the detail. . . . If the SoA judgments do not confirm the overall judgment, then there is clearly something wrong. Either the overview judgment is wrong or the interpretation of the detail of SoA is wrong. In either event the process of reconciliation is likely to be more just and accurate if it is operated from both ends – iteratively, rather than simply by assuming that the SoA is naturally right and the PC naturally wrong . . . [since] . . . our data suggests that the reverse is more likely to be the case.
>
> (Kimbell *et al.* 1991, p. 238)

In the event, National Curriculum assessment was pushed ahead on the assumption that the SoA were all individually and reliably assessable and that good assessments would result from the aggregation of detail. SEAC was quite wrong in this, and the 1993 letter from Sutherland, Dearing and James, already cited, admits as much. Their letter marks a major watershed, and quite specifically requires teachers to start with big pictures – and then not even to bother with all the detail. This was indeed a major about-face. And it is one that has since been underlined in the reconstruction of the level descriptors and in the advice on how teachers should use them. The multiple, free-standing SoA were merged into 'baskets of descriptors' that (taken together) characterise an overall level of performance. Instead of the 150 or so SoA in the 1990 Order, there are just eight of these baskets of descriptors for each of the two ATs in the 1995 Order. And the advice to teachers is simply to identify which basket 'best fits' the pupil's current level of performance. To support this judgment, the 'Exemplification of Standards' documents from SCAA use a single statement that characterises the 'soul' of each level.[5]

At each level, there are key characteristics which help to differentiate the demand of that level from the level below . . . in what follows the

key characteristics of each level are identified . . . [and] are then illustrated in each specific aspect of the PoS.

(SCAA 1996, p. 5)

The message about the limitations of atomised assessment has clearly
been received and accepted at SCAA. We should never forget this hard-
learned lesson, and in retrospect we can only speculate on how things
might have turned out differently had this message been received at the
time it was originally sent in 1990. We should, however, register a note
of caution in relation to the emerging structure of GNVQ assessment (see
Chapter 2). At the time of writing, SCAA is in discussion with the National
Council for Vocational Qualifications (NCVQ) about the future assessment regime for GNVQ courses. It would be reassuring to hear that the
lessons about atomised assessment, learned so painfully within SEAC, have
also been fully internalised at NCVQ.

The false dichotomy of norms and criteria

The conventional wisdom in the history of our examinations systems is that
GCE, CSE and many other examination systems were norm-referenced.
Moreover, norm referencing is thought to be *bad* because it does not
identify what pupils can do, since all it does is to measure pupils against
their peers. By contrast (since we saw the light), GCSE and latterly National
Curriculum and GNVQ examinations are criterion-referenced. Criterion
referencing is *good* because it identifies what pupils should be able to do
and it measures pupils against these identified qualities (not against each
other).

In 1985, at the introduction of GCSE assessment schemes, there appeared to me to be sufficient truth in this to make it believable; criteria
were deified and norms were demonised. And as a consequence we tried
to define criteria of excellence (in words) in sufficient detail to make them
clear and non-problematic, and we proved that it cannot be done. On the
other side of the coin, we sought to persuade ourselves that we were not
assessing pupils against each other, but of course we were. What we have
demonstrated in ten years of troubled assessment is that to separate norms
and criteria (as if they belong to discrete systems) was completely flawed,
for in reality they are two complementary parts of a system that need to
work together to create good assessment.

The issue can be demonstrated in the following story which comes from
a very reliable source and recalls the process undertaken in the (1988)
Design and Technology Working Group. In its early deliberations it was
agreed that a good starting point for defining the National Curriculum
assessment criteria (the SoA) would be to refine a clear statement for level
10 – the ultimate descriptor of what we might expect the most able technologist to achieve. The argument ran that if we had such a clear concluding point it might then be possible to work up towards it incrementally;

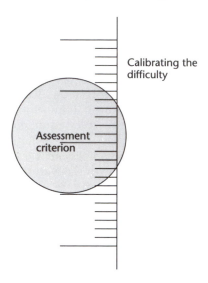

Figure 6.1 The criterion 'target' needs to be 'calibrated' for difficulty.

moving step by careful step towards this Holy Grail. So it was drafted and debated, redrafted and debated, edited and debated, and finally it was honed with infinite precision. The group was happy with it as a statement describing the excellence that should be characterised as level 10. And then they showed it to teachers. And the *primary* teachers said: 'Yes that's what my children do'!

The words did not define a standard because teachers interpreted them to mean things in relation to the students they teach. The very same statement might be interpreted as level 2 or level 10 or even as postgraduate.

This story tells us a great deal about criteria, and the metaphor of the battlefield might be helpful. A criterion acts as a target bearing, but it does not say anything about range. Without the information about range I will never hit the target. Do I drop the shot at 400 m or 800 m of 2 km or 20 km? The criterion bearing might be 340 degrees in each case, but it does not help me to hit the target.

Kimbell's first law of assessment says that *assessment criteria exist on a sliding scale of excellence*. I can make any criterion mean something simple – or something difficult.[6] I can interpret it to fit any level of complexity that I choose. It is slippery and imprecise. And it follows, therefore, that criteria of this kind (on their own) are useless for assessment purposes. To be useful, they need to be supplemented by *other* information that can tell us the range to be shooting at. The question, however, is where we get this additional information with which to *calibrate* the criterion (Figure 6.1). What information do we have – beyond the criteria themselves – to fix their difficulty?

The information that all teachers have exists in the performance of their pupils. If the criterion says 'Is able to use modelling skills' and the age group for which it is supposed to apply is year 7, then teachers can use their experience of year 7 performance to define the meaning. The best pupils in a group can be kept in mind and those of a lower standard can also be kept in mind. These standards then create a frame of reference (group norms, if you like) within which the teacher can understand the criterion. This frame of reference also allows the teacher to understand and interpret any exemplification material that is provided to help illuminate levels of performance.

The mistake is to assume that 'standards' exist in the criteria themselves. They do not. Assessment criteria are slippery and adjustable, and in the 1990 SoA, teachers were given 150 of them; all uncalibrated and presented as if they were a gift from the gods. The ultimate truth. But the standards did not exist in the SoA criteria. They needed to be created. And by far the most effective way to create them would have been to use the experience of teachers. Instead, the assumption was that the SoA were the standard.[7] The arrogant procedures of implementation of National Curriculum assessment frustrated and deskilled teachers. And yet for the process to work it required the empowering of teachers, because without the calibration that only they could provide it was nothing. So it fell apart. Or rather it was torn apart by a profession in revolt.

Let me make myself plain. I am *not* saying that in developing National Curriculum standards one of the options that we had was that teachers should be allowed to create these standards for themselves. It is *not* a matter of choosing that particular option against another one – such as the imposition (by SEAC/SCAA) of a national standard. What I am saying is that it will happen, come what may. Teachers *will* construct a standard from their own experience of their own pupils, because they have no alternative. The points of judgment on the sliding-scale criteria need to be fixed – and the only way (initially) for teachers to get a concrete fix on those points is from their experience of pupils' work.

For the purposes of national assessment, however, the trick is then to develop a strategy that enables teachers to negotiate and move beyond their own standards into a national standard. Before dealing with that problem, however, it is important to register the lesson about the slippery imprecision of assessment criteria and of the need for additional data to fix 'standards'.

The challenge of a national standard

One of the purposes of a national curriculum is that we should have national standards, not local idiosyncratic ones. My point is that initially these fixes on the sliding scale needed to be based on individual teacher norms: the standards that individual teachers think appropriate in the light of their experience of their pupils. The challenge thereafter is gradually to transform these idiosyncratic individualised standards into something more generalisable. And this is a formidable task. We should have built

and resourced a strategy that required individual judgments to be compared and contrasted within schools so as to arrive at school norms of
performance. And then we should have required schools to compare and
contrast their standards with those of other local schools so as gradually
to arrive at local norms. And finally, we should have required local areas
to collaborate in regional groups to generate regional and ultimately national
norms of performance. In the process of reconciling disagreements amongst
teachers at any of these levels (the school, the local area or nationally)
exemplification material can be really helpful – feeding into the debate that
is founded upon teachers' own views of standards in their schools.

As part of the SAT exercise, we had developed a system of *agreement
trials* between teachers making assessments of their pupils' performance
within a school. These trials not only enabled teachers to generalise their
own interpretation of the criteria (e.g. seeing how the same criteria appear
when applied to work in rigid materials and in food) but also helped to
disseminate a sense of quality. Thereafter, the LEAs with which we were
working supported us in running similar activities across schools. It was
time-consuming and hence expensive. But it was also a powerful means of
generating national standards. Arguably it is the only means.

I am reminded of the far-off days of CSE mode 3 moderation meetings
– when we took samples of our work to neighbouring schools to agree
marks. At the time we might have scoffed at all the horse trading that went
on, but we learned from that process. We came away from those meetings
saying 'I now know what my kids have to do to get As and Bs'. And
because of this we developed a clear grip on the standards being used, and
we progressively drove them upwards.

Other than those involved in the SAT trials, the vast majority of teachers
I observed in 1990–93 did not understand that they had a critical role to
play in *defining* national standards.[8] We had moved so far down the road
of criterion-referenced assessment – and power taken to the centre – that
teachers did not believe that they had a formative role in them. They
thought (as did the Secretary of State) that the standards were already
defined in the words of the SoA. They were not. The SoA provided the
target bearings, but they did not and could not define the range. They
therefore did not amount to anything that could be called a 'standard'.

In 1990 – in the early days of SAT trials – this penny was only just
beginning to drop for me. I was just waking up to the central truth about
the importance of performance norms. We had developed SATs and tested
1500 pupils in an 'SAT trial'. We were closeted in a high-power meeting
in Notting Hill Gate, London, scrutinising the data from that trial. We
heard from the science team and the maths team – and then it came to me.
A minister (albeit a junior one) scowled at me and asked what the mean
score was for performance in design and technology in the trial. I reported
– with some confidence – that it was 3.3, i.e. somewhere between level 3
and level 4. What I *should* have said – if I had been quick enough, and
if I had known then what I know now – was: 'Minister, what would you

like it to be? You tell me the score you want and I'll calibrate the criteria accordingly.'

The received wisdom from SCAA, inherited from GCSE days and bolstered by the arrogance of National Curriculum policy, was that we had determined and defined 'what pupils should know, understand and do'. This arrogant certainty recognised no role for teachers to act as agents in defining the national standard. Instead of empowering teachers to do the job, they were utterly intimidated and had no idea that *they* held the key to defining the standard. If only we had presented it to teachers in that way, the sad story of National Curriculum assessment might have been very different.

So here is Kimbell's second law of assessment: *criterion scales need to be calibrated to the performance norms of the pupils involved.* The challenge – for national assessment purposes – was to move from teacher-centred idiosyncratic norms towards nationally agreed norms that are understood and valued by all teachers. The point, however, is that applying criteria is a professional, judgmental matter that required the expertise and experience of all our teachers. It also, of course, required investment in collaborative moderation activities both within and across schools in order to share, generalise, and ultimately universalise the meanings of the criteria: the standards to apply. This is the fifth lesson that we would do well to remember.

Progression and the value of sliding scales

In earlier chapters I have made clear my objections to the absolutist (yes/no) principles of assessment that were embedded in National Curriculum assessment. It was extremely unhelpful to be forced into the position of having to say 'yes' or 'no' about pupils. Because for most of the time, the majority of them are in categories that are better described as 'maybe' or 'sometimes' or 'partly'.

Teachers have used sliding scales of judgment since teaching began. Scales of A–E and 1–10. Sliding scales allow us to talk about better and worse; to discuss improvement with our pupils; to develop a sense of quality. This whole tradition of assessment was cast aside at a stroke by the implementation of the National Curriculum. There was not even a serious debate about the perceived advantages of yes/no tick-list assessment as against sliding-scale assessment. The digital was somehow regarded as superior to the analogue, despite the fact that sliding-scale analogue systems were what teachers had always used. In retrospect, it is quite astonishing that this digitisation of assessment was allowed to get to the lunacy at which it had arrived in the early 1990s without being challenged to justify itself.

And another product of this digitisation was that the authors of the scheme felt obliged to keep inventing lots of different digits to strive for. In the end, National Curriculum assessment was premised on the idea that in order to progress you had to pick up some extra digits – which meant doing something different and extra. This is seriously mistaken, for often all you need to do is the same thing to a higher level of quality.

Quite apart from the traditional 'analogue' understanding of teachers there is also hard research evidence to support the idea that improvement amounts to doing the same thing but in progressively richer ways. During the APU exercise, we analysed the performance of 15-year-old pupils in minute detail. To take but one example, we looked at the range of design issues that they dealt with in their designing. We distinguished between user issues (such as comfort and cost); product (manufacture) issues (such as number of parts and standardisation); and wider societal issues (such as sustainability and environmental impact). But this was with 15-year-olds. What about 7- and 11-year-olds? What kind of progression might one expect in relation to these three categories of design issues? Might we assume (for example) that user issues are all important to 6-year-olds, and that manufacturing issues are of little concern? Readers may remember the arguments around the draft 1992 revisions of the technology Order that suggested that tackling *aesthetic* issues was at one level, whilst tackling *functional*/technical issues was at a another level and tackling *user* issues is at yet another level.

Such sequential notions of progression are seriously mistaken. When Kay Stables was developing the KS1 technology SATs, she showed that 6-year-olds habitually raise user issues, technical issues and wider societal issues in their work:

> [concerning the user]
> Simon decided to make a model roundabout with horses for very young children . . . he expressed uncertainty about the safety of the roundabout for young children . . .
>
> [concerning manufacture]
> Thomas chose to design and make a fabric purse . . . His original plan and the finished purse demonstrate his ability to choose materials and tools suitable for the task. He uses his knowledge of the working characteristics of materials in deciding how best to join materials together . . .
>
> [concerning wider contextual issues]
> Sam decided to design a bedside lamp for himself . . . he started by look-ing at lamps including those from other times . . . evaluating a variety of lamps and their purposes including a candle holder, a paraffin lamp, and an angle-poise light . . . Sam made an observation drawing of a 1920's desk lamp . . .
>
> (Stables 1992, pp. 9, 13, 15)

Capable 6-year-olds deal with these issues at a 6-year-old level, and cap-able 15-year-olds are similarly able to operate with these same issues but at a higher level. This might sound very unsatisfactory to those who seek to characterise progression in terms of more capable pupils doing different things. But the evidence suggests that they do not. Capability is, in principle, the same at any age. It involves understanding the task and responding to it by making proposals; it involves understanding materials, tools and processes; it involves making products and evaluating them critically against the needs of the user and the manufacturer. It involves all of these things for 6-year-olds and 12-year-olds and 16-year-olds. As I pointed out at the time:

> Progression is about unpeeling progressive layers of meaning and consequence; like peeling an onion. Whilst a 6-year-old can see that a product needs to be safe, a 12-year-old might additionally be able to identify a range of risks (fire/cuts/swallowing etc.) and make proposals to counteract them. A 16-year-old might then be expected to unpick the safety legislation that surrounds a product and interpret it through their designing.
>
> (Kimbell 1994b)

This is the assessment equivalent of what Bruner (1964) was saying about teaching and learning: 'Any idea or problem or body of knowledge can be presented in a form simple enough so that any particular learner can understand it in a recognisable form.'

Teaching and learning (on one side of the equation) and assessment (on the other side) have both traditionally depended on understanding and using sliding scales. I am tired of pointing out the inappropriateness of digital, yes/no models of assessment that require an absolutist (black and white) view of the world. Assessment judgments are more manageable, more reliable and more appropriate when set within the frame of reference of analogue sliding scales of excellence.

But it would be a mistake to conclude from this that criteria are not valuable. Of course they are. It is merely to assert that criteria alone are not enough – as sliding scales alone were not enough. The issue is how we can unite them to gain the benefits of both.

Uniting scales with criteria

I have outlined earlier how criteria of excellence play a valuable role in identifying target bearings for assessment, and it is therefore important to see how criteria (on the one hand) and sliding scales of excellence (on the other) might work together to capitalise on the strengths of both systems.

I described in Chapter 2 how sliding scales linked with indicative criteria emerged in the GCSE assessment regime of the mid-1980s, but it is worth mentioning a far more comprehensive system of assessment that pre-dated GCSE by more than a decade. I refer to the Oxford Delegacy A level examination in design. For many years I was a senior examiner for this course, and during that time Malcolm Deere (as chief examiner) was responsible for developing an assessment regime that – in my opinion – has never been bettered.[9]

It identified criteria for assessment; it placed them on a sliding scale; it provided short descriptors along the scale to illustrate what quality might look like at different levels; it left lines blank for teachers to add their own criteria and their own illustrators; it allowed teachers to debate with the examiner and adjust the relative importance of each criterion to each pupil's work; and it required teachers to identify the evidence they were drawing upon to justify their judgments. Teachers were able to develop and maintain a 'picture' of the strengths and weaknesses of each of their pupils in relation to criteria over which they felt they had some influence – and which they accordingly took very seriously. And the absolute requirement to pinpoint the source of evidence that was being used to justify any decision by the teacher, made the whole process immensely rigorous (Figure 6.2).

This rigour was underpinned by the visiting examiner – who interviewed all candidates, with their exhibition of course-work, and subsequently confirmed or modified the judgments of the teacher. As an external examiner, I had a relationship over many years (1975–88) with a significant number of teachers running this course and there is no doubt that, quite apart from enriching all our understandings about design, the teachers' grasp of assessment was enormously enriched by engaging in the debates that arose when this assessment tool was used to examine their pupils' work.

When using assessment schemes of this enlightened kind – that give teachers serious responsibility in not only making judgments but also (within limits) determining the basis upon which such judgments might appropriately be made for individual pupils – the teacher is professionally extended and enriched. Whilst the external examiner ensures the quality control, the real benefit in the whole system is that the assessment exercise becomes a profound piece of professional development for teachers.

Teachers as professional curriculum developers

And this is the central point to which all arguments about curriculum and assessment must ultimately return. I have already outlined the limits of the role of law-makers in the classroom, and I have explained in subsequent sections the critical role that teachers might (should) have played in calibrating, sharing and hence validating the standards that were achievable and appropriate within National Curriculum assessment. But that opportunity was lost – or rather it was squandered. Teachers were to be given all the answers and their autonomy and scope for professional judgment was reduced to the point of irrelevance.

One measure of this centralised arrogance is provided by the weight of paper that landed with regular, earth-shattering thumps on the doormats of schools. On a memorable day in 1990, I answered the phone at college and found myself talking to a government dispatch office. The official informed me that a delivery of National Curriculum documents was on its way and would I please make arrangements to receive it (I wondered if he

Figure 6.2 — The Oxford A-level assessment form

	HEADING	RATING (tick one box below)					Teacher involvement — Which heading needed most help?	Teacher involvement — Which heading needed least help?	JUSTIFICATION — Where appropriate refer to the report, the 'product' log book, notes or sketches, tutor's impressions, any other factors.	Weighting of assessment headings — Very important	Important	Not so important
A	How well was project chosen (considering resources and need)?	Saw real need which could be achieved	Sound target based on slight deficiency in recognising resources	Reasonable need based on adequate recognition of resources	Failed to discern need properly, or resources dimly recognised	Unsound choice, no recognition of resources						
B	Comprehension of project as a whole	No significant omissions	Project considered in very wide context	Adequate scope of relevant factors	Few additional factors outside immediate target	Very limited view indeed						
C	Planning and organisation of work	Tight control on current target	Intelligent changes of target as circumstances changed	Reasonable ability to manage time and effort	Recognised some need for planning	Worked in a very haphazard fashion						
D (i)	Thoroughness in gaining information — By test and experiment	Widest possible range of tests and experiments conducted	Several types of relevant test or experiment carried out	At least one appropriate test or experiment carried out	Only trivial tests carried out	No real tests or experiments						
D (ii)	Thoroughness in gaining information — By search of literature and other sources	Widest possible range of sources explored	Several types of resource researched	Reasonable coverage of data achieved	Only limited information discussed	No real sources consulted						
E	Decision making and consideration of alternatives	Range of possibilities explored; available evidence carefully weighed	Several possibilities considered, with considerable logical deduction	At least one alternative given in reasonable amount of thought	Other possibilities at least recognised	Decisions taken on a random basis only						
F	Quality of manufacture & assembly – having regard to demands of project	Own limitations and demands of design well recognised	Good overall but with slight deficiencies	Adequate degree of skill achieved	Shows some evidence of skill in limited area	Cannot recognise own limits or demands of project						
G (i)	Completeness and presentation of Report — As a record of the project as a whole	Complete and detailed records well organised and competently made	All aspects covered although in variable depth, but with reasonable care	Rather patchy – not striking in any respect	Little more than a diary with significant areas omitted	Shoddy, ill-organised shallow description						
G (ii)	Completeness and presentation of Report — As an explanation of the whole project	Covers underlying thinking completely	Very revealing about underlying thinking	Good in some areas	Gives a very limited picture of the context of project	Gives little or no justification						
H	Quality of evaluation	Able to give good and dispassionate criticism; finished product thoroughly tested	Very fair review with few 'blind spots'; finished product adequately reviewed	Reasonable or adequate view – sees some reason for re-design	Only limited ability to review progress and actions; no post testing	Unable to criticise own actions or design						
I	Self-reliance and initiative	Can be left to work alone most of the time	Needed minimal supervision	Required no more supervision than might be expected	Needed a disproportionate fraction of the teacher's time	Unable to work without continuous help						
J												
K												
L	Interview – Leave for Visiting Examiner											

Figure 6.2 The Oxford A-level assessment form – uniting criteria with sliding scales of excellence and creating a 'picture' of capability.

wanted a red carpet). I suggested that, as with any delivery, it should go to the reception area of the central stores. 'Oh', said the official sharply, 'I was just checking that you have got a fork lift truck'. And he was not joking.

The ethic that underpinned all this paper was that teachers would simply be told what to do. 'The centre' would specify the tools of assessment and the criteria of assessment, and hence the standards of assessment. But my argument has been that standards do not exist in all this paper. They exist in the experience of teachers. And it follows therefore that to raise these standards, we need to extend and enrich our teachers. As (in the 1970s) when we were striving to establish CSE standards, and (in the 1970s and 1980s) in the debates over Oxford A-level examination exhibitions, so again we need to have in place the procedures that allow teachers to debate and share their values and understandings. But now there are some formidable obstacles that did not exist in those far-off days. I was recently in a school which had achieved quite excellent GCSE and A-level results in technology. I asked the department head about the extent to which he was being used in the LEA to help other schools to improve. His reply was double barrelled and devastating. 'First,' he said, I haven't seen anyone from the LEA for years – I don't think they're there anymore. And second, why would I want to help other schools to compete with us?

I wondered how the Secretary of State would have reacted to this. Would she have been pleased to note the extent to which the teacher had internalised the ethics of the market-place? Or would she have been horrified at the barriers to developing and disseminating standards that the policy has created? Since standards reside in teachers, not in documents, my argument is that the need has been for more professional development *in* schools (to help teachers to develop and validate school standards) and more collaboration *between* schools (to moderate and help teachers generate national standards). But the policy of the last ten years has consistently been to shred the LEAs which were the principal source of support in most schools, and to create a competitive environment between schools that is more conducive to secrecy than to open collaboration. Whilst the rhetoric of the last few years has been all about raising standards, the policy has consistently acted to make this harder and harder to achieve.

If there is one thing that we should have learned about standards, it is that they depend more on the understanding of teachers than they do on any form of words in syllabuses, or programmes of study, or level descriptors. You cannot know 'quality' by reading about it. A 'standard' is what *emerges* when a teacher adopts a criterion of assessment and interprets it in relation to the work that s/he is engaged in with students. It is both backward-looking (drawing on previous experience) and forward-looking (shaping the expectations that we have of our current students).

If we are seriously concerned with raising standards in technology, then it is the *understanding* of teachers, the *experience* of teachers and the *practice* of teachers that we should be supporting. The processes that gave birth to technology in the 1960s and that saw it progressively flourish in the 1970s and 1980s were all centred on teachers acting as autonomous professionals in their classrooms and studios and workshops. A teacher in a school would develop an interesting slant on some technology activity. LEA advisory staff picked it up and disseminated it locally, either by using the teacher on courses or by encouraging other teachers to visit the school in question; local centres of excellence were thereby created in many of the strands of activity that comprise technology. HMI picked up on the development and built it into regional HMI conferences and courses or (the ultimate accolade), invited the teacher to run a workshop in the famous Loughborough summer schools of the 1980s.[10] Using this model of progressive dissemination, initiatives that originated in the classroom ended up affecting and informing national practice. Teachers were empowered and technology became ever more effective and more recognised. This is by no means to underplay the importance of national research and curriculum development projects, but technology is a classic example of a subject whose origins lie in initiatives developed in schools. These initiatives needed a sympathetic environment in which to flourish – sympathetic at the local LEA level and at the national level.

It is inconceivable that the meteoric rise of technology that we have observed in the last 30 years could ever have happened by central diktat from DES or DfE or DfEE or SEC or NCC or SEAC or SCAA or Ofsted. Such bodies can never *create* anything – all they can do is impose structures for monitoring and managing what others have created.

The final – and most critical – lesson that we should have learned in this time is that standards of excellence are driven upwards by teachers who understand and innovate; who challenge themselves and their pupils by constantly developing and extending their curriculum. The minute that teachers see themselves as merely applying someone else's curriculum – for reasons they do not understand – is the point at which standards start to decline. The need for a national curriculum – the principle of which which I fully support – is merely for a framework within which innovation can be constantly moving us forward.

The future well-being of technology as a discipline in schools depends upon teachers regaining the initiative of curriculum development that was lost in the early 1990s. Of course, the autonomy to innovate means that schools will not all be doing the same things, and some of the innovations will not work well and may result in disappointment for pupils and teachers alike. But others will work well; and some will be spectacularly successful and will change our whole understanding about technology in schools.

This is the nature of curriculum development, and the final lesson that I truly hope we have learned is that the quality of our technology curriculum and the quality of pupils' work within it are dependent upon our developing and supporting teachers as autonomous creative professionals.

Notes

1 By this time the Department of Education and Science (DES) had been renamed Department for Education (DfE) and SEAC and NCC had been merged into SCAA, the School Curriculum and Assessment Authority.

2 Either purposefully or simply as an unintended consequence, depending on your attachment to conspiracy theories.

3 ... with the honourable and notable exception of the original interim report of 1988.

4 Lord Griffiths, formerly (1991–3) head of SEAC and arguably one of the sources of its aggressive policy on National Curriculum assessment, did not survive the merger with NCC. His reign was one of almost total disaster for SEAC, covering the period of the two SAT boycotts of 1992 and 1993.

5 SCAA officers now discuss the 'soul' of each level (particularly in information technology) in exactly the same way that we developed the holistic 'level guides' for the National Curriculum SATs exercise in 1990 (see Chapter 5).

6 This law applies only in the case of *qualitative* criteria and is rather less true with quantitative criteria. To say that a pupil can file a metal block flat to a tolerance of 0.01 mm becomes a matter of measurement, not of judgment. It is therefore independent of the teacher. It should be noted, however, that *all* the National Curriculum SoA were qualitative and required judgment on the part of teachers.

7 This is not just a problem in England and Wales. As I shall discuss in Chapter 8, in the USA currently a group of 'experts' under the management of the International Technology Education Association (ITEA) is drawing up (i.e. writing down) the new curriculum 'standards' for technology. And interestingly, they are looking to our work within the National Curriculum as a guide. To quote from a recent press release, 'the standards will be developed at grades 4, 8 and 12 ... The project will create teacher preparation and enhancement standards, pupil assessment standards, and program standards ... these standards will provide a framework for assuring a quality articulated technology program at the state, region, district and school level.'

8 In the new (post-Dearing) regime this is now far less true and it is really encouraging to hear of schools engaged in school-wide agreement trials and moderation meetings with other local schools.

9 Malcolm Deere was a member of the Design and Technology Working Group that defined the original technology Order for the National Curriculum. Influenced by the experience of the broad-ranging Oxford A-level design course, he consistently argued for a definition of design and technology that was broader than the traditional confines of CDT. But he was unable to influence the model of National Curriculum assessment.

10 These summer schools also illustrate the important role that was played by innovative colleges of teacher education during the formative years of design and technology. A few key colleges acted as catalysts for innovative teachers and as centres for bringing teachers together to share their innovation.

part two

International comparisons

seven

The Federal Republic of Germany

Thuringia

Situated mid-way between Frankfurt and Berlin, Erfurt is the capital of Thuringia, one of the 16 *Länder* (states) that make up Germany (Figure 7.1). It was, until 1989, part of the German Democratic Republic (GDR), but now it sits at the geographic heart of the new Federal Republic of Germany (FRG). Erfurt, despite having an industrial belt around it, has the flavour of a rural county town – not unlike Canterbury or York. It is a very historic city with a university that dates back to 1250 and some quite magnificent civic architecture: the *Dom* (cathedral); and the *Rathaus* (town hall); and a mass of timber-framed houses in winding medieval streets running into market squares and providing fascinating glimpses into a rich past (Figure 7.2).

The economy of Thuringia is based almost equally on industrial activity and agriculture. When the Berlin Wall came down and Germany was reunited, the economic climate in Thuringia was completely transformed by direct competition from the West and much of its original industry suffered severely. There is now significant unemployment (approximately 15 per cent) and more than a little bitterness at what is perceived to be the cultural imperialism of former West Germany.

A passive, conformist and paternalistic society

The former GDR was a highly paternalistic society in which personal decision-making was dependent – at every turn – on the concept of 'getting permission' from the state. As but a single example, you applied for permission to have a car at age 17, and might be allowed one ten years later. By contrast, in the new FRG if you want a car you buy one (assuming you have the money). The major accommodation areas are comprised of large expanses of soulless high-rise tower blocks built in the 1960s, 1970s and

Figure 7.1 Thuringia, one of the 16 *Länder* in Germany.

1980s. They were conceived as a great advance on the former crowding in the city centres, where a family might have had to walk 200 m to a toilet facility. And these new high-rise residential areas were serviced by an inexpensive tram system for transport into the city.[1]

Some of the teachers to whom I spoke reflected on the down side of the passing of the paternalistic GDR. Children were regularly vaccinated, received regular dental attention, received ten years of schooling and a compulsory year of kindergarten. Now the kindergarten is optional and it is felt that the standard of entry to formal schooling has declined. And children are only vaccinated or have their teeth examined if their parents arrange it and pay for it. Responsibility for so much of life has moved from the state to the individual.

Begging is quite a new phenomenon, probably replacing lots of pointless (but paid) work that was formerly being done under the auspices of the state. Others flourish in the new Germany. They see opportunities to produce things or to provide services that others are not providing. They can start businesses, make profits and buy into a lifestyle that was inconceivable five years ago. This is by no means all exploitative, but it is all opportunistic. The opportunities were simply not there before, but now

Figure 7.2 The historic centre of Erfurt.

they are. And so is a considerable amount of 'social fund' support from the former West Germany and the EU to oil the wheels.

But this has not heralded a new golden age. There are serious problems – of crime, violence and vandalism – many of which did not exist before. Perhaps I should say were not allowed to exist before. Intelligent people are now asking questions about whether some of the former collectivist values of the GDR might not be sadly missing in the sink-or-swim individualist economics of the new Germany. But those who express this too bitterly are gently reminded by others that they would not have dared to speak of the government in this disrespectful way under the former regime.

Surveillance was simply part of life in the GDR. Senior academics were required to write reports to State Security (the 'Stasi') on the 'reliability' of their colleagues and on their students. I heard countless examples of the 'ignorant and arrogant' Communist Party faithful who would not listen to advice they did not like, and who simply, by virtue of being a member of the Party, found it easier to get privileges: cars and spacious, good quality flats. And the best way to obtain such privileges was to be an informer for the State Security.

The collapse of the GDR

Academic colleagues (university staff and school teachers) reflect upon the transformation in a number of ways. Some are bitter, seeing the situation now as essentially exploitative. They cite examples of medical schools that have been closed, or reduced to 'clinics' which have no academic function. The academic staff are then required either to apply for their former positions in new medical schools, in competition with other academics, or to become redundant. Many of these new appointments have gone to academics from the former West Germany. Some see the collapse of the GDR as the inevitable result of an overly passive society emphasising collectivity over individualism. If you had what you thought was a good idea and wanted to develop it you needed permission, which might or might not be granted. It would only be granted if it was seen to be responsive to the 'collective' good. But even then it might be given to someone else – in another place – to develop. This created a culture that discouraged innovation and development and led to acceptance of the status quo, since there was nothing to be gained by doing otherwise.

Lack of individual opportunity, coupled with oppressive and ever-present surveillance by the state, eventually ossified the society to the point of collapse. When the borders were opened to Czechoslovakia (which hence became a conduit to the West) the educated young were the first to get out; the floodgates opened. They were looking for opportunity. Their parents had more security and investment in the GDR and were less mobile. But the GDR was bleeding to death, and eventually had to collapse.

Contrasting pedagogies (the GDR and the unified FRG)

Although this social and economic malaise beset the GDR, many of its scholars will proudly point to the strength of their intellectual heritage. Specifically in terms of curriculum and pedagogy, it is a widely held view that the GDR had immensely richer traditions and practices than did West Germany.[2] And it is not in the least popular, either with academics or with teachers, that the impoverished pedagogy of the West has been transplanted directly into the former GDR and is now standard throughout the new Germany.

Professor Scharlach, a scholar of pedagogy and currently the director of the Vocational Training Centre for Economy and Administration in Erfurt, describes the new pedagogy as very traditional: based in the 1920s, but with updated content. He was greatly disappointed when there was not a sharing of pedagogy between the two systems when the Wall came down. He argues that East and West could and should have informed each other. And as an example of the contrast he cites the role of teamwork.

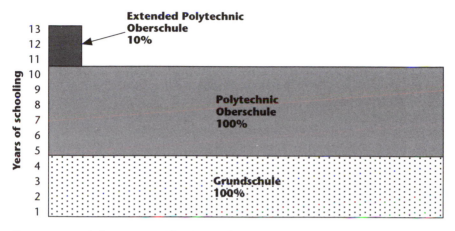

Figure 7.3 Undifferentiated schooling in the GDR.

Education for all in the GDR

The ethic underpinning education in the GDR was the raising of standards for *all* pupils – and group-work was a major instrument of achieving this. The '*Arbeitsgemeinschaft*' was a working group of pupils doing an assignment. Sometimes in groups of five or six and sometimes in pairs, the *Arbeitsgemeinschaft* was of mixed ability, and bright pupils worked with slower pupils and were expected to help them to raise their level of work. *Einer für alle, alle für einen*, in the words of the slogan. Professor Scharlach had researched the effects of this on bright pupils. He showed that the benefit to them resided in the way pupils had to reconstruct and re-express understanding when explaining it to others. This had the effect of strengthening pupils' understanding, and the idea finds expression in the truism that 'you only really know something when you try to teach it'.

But Scharlach also demonstrated the limits of this benefit and explored the damage that can be done within a curriculum that is entirely undifferentiated. However, his work in this area was judged 'unreliable' because (he believes) a more differentiated curriculum would have led to much greater differences in pupil performance; to a more fragmented group of pupils in schools; and hence, eventually, to a more fragmented (self-interested) society. And this would not have been tolerated in the GDR.

The GDR tradition of common education for all inevitably resulted in a single universal system of schooling. Starting at age 6, pupils received four years of primary schooling (*Grundschule*) and then six more years of polytechnic high school (Oberschule). Then, from age 16 onwards only a handful of pupils – perhaps 10% – progressed to the extended high school that gave access to university (Figure 7.3).

The priority for teaching strategies in the GDR was to encourage a general raising of performance. One's contribution to the *Arbeitsgemeinschaft* was

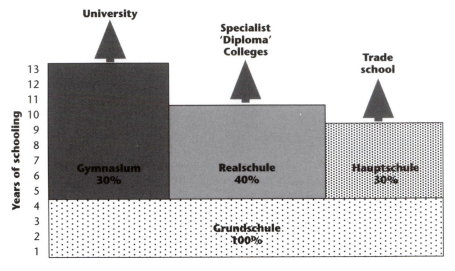

Figure 7.4 Differentiated schooling in Germany.

the priority consideration and inevitably this encouraged a levelling of achievement.[3] Reflecting on this with hindsight, teachers agree that it had very good effects on lower- and mid-ability pupils and – within limits – also on the very able. Pedagogy was strong in helping lower-ability pupils to make progress; demotivating failure was avoided and so too were many of the consequent bad effects that are now (a mere six years after reunification) very evident in some schools. The down side was that very able youngsters were insufficiently stretched, and few succeeded in making it to university. A university education was specifically designed to be highly selective and standards were very high, but the society only needed a very few such educated individuals.

Differentiated education in Germany (the devil take the hindmost!)

Following the reunification of Germany, the central principle of the GDR (raising *all* pupils' performance) was utterly transformed and the pedagogy of the FRG was imported wholesale in the form of a highly differentiated educational regime (Figure 7.4). Formal education in the *Land* of Thuringia still begins at age 6 and, after the first four years of primary school, the system is strictly divided according to a concept of 'general ability'. The 'brightest' 30 per cent of pupils go to the *Gymnasium* (grammar school) and hence to university or to well-placed training and employment. A middle band of approximately 40 per cent attend the *Realschule* and subsequently take up professional careers through diploma colleges for example in teaching or nursing, or pursue technician apprenticeships in industry. The remaining 30 per cent attend the low-ability *Hauptschule* (secondary school). There is some movement of pupils between the *Hauptschule* and the *Realschule* as pupils settle into their schools, but only a very limited amount of transfer into and out of the *Gymnasium*.

It is worth remembering that the transformation from the former (GDR) system to the current system took place overnight, using the very same teachers that had been trained in a former regime and whose personal values were attuned to that regime. Many of these teachers have found it a traumatic experience.

The system is now designed to separate out (and keep separate) the bright from the mid-ability and from the low-ability. The *Abitur* is the certification output of the *Gymnasium*, achieved at age 18 or 19 (i.e. equivalent to A levels). In the *Realschule*, the *Abschluss zeugnis* (final certificate) is a leaving certificate, taken at the end of year 10 (age 16), and it qualifies students for entry to the diploma colleges. The *Hauptschule* ends at the end of year 9 (age 15) and all but a very few students leave with nothing.

The *Hauptschulen* are commonly perceived as centres of failure. There is now a great deal of concern about them since they are very tough places, with difficult, demotivated pupils displaying the inevitably associated behaviour. The pupils are disaffected, typically socially deprived, often children of *Gastarbeiter* (immigrant workers), with little (apparently) to gain from school and no perceived stake in the future of the country. With high unemployment, this group of pupils is right in the firing line, heading for unemployment and (not infrequently) crime.

The heights of the *Gymnasium* and the depths of the *Hauptschule* would never have been tolerated in the GDR, since they would have been seen as socially divisive and culturally destructive. And Erfurt in the new Germany is currently counting the cost and finding it very expensive.

Teachers brought up in a quite different regime are struggling to adapt – and an interesting example of the difference is provided in the notion of 'temporary exclusion' from school. In the GDR truants were collected by the police. As a teacher commented to me: 'Why would you exclude from a school exactly those people who need it so badly?' But now it is acceptable and not uncommon, especially in the *Hauptschule*, as teachers find themselves coping with what they perceive as a lack of 'respect' and 'law and order'.

Curriculum commissions

The school curriculum is written at the level of the Ministry of Education of the *Länder* – in this case Thuringia. At regular intervals, the ministry establishes a curriculum commission (*Lehrplankommission*) to write the curriculum – one for primary and one for secondary schools. The curriculum is composed of subjects; each subject has its curriculum written in the form of aims, content and supplementary notes for guidance, and the level of detail is not unlike that which currently exists in the 'programmes of study' of the 1995 version of the National Curriculum for England and

Wales. Approximately 80 per cent of the members of the commissions are teachers; 20 per cent are advisory consultants from teacher education, from the ministry and from industry. Given that the normal size of the subject commissions is about 10 people, eight of them will be teachers. Within the Commission, the function of the teachers is to reflect on their current work and on the updating they would like to see in the future curriculum. The role of the 'consultants' is primarily to reflect on the strengths and weaknesses of the existing curriculum (in terms of aims, content and/or pedagogy) and thereby to influence the one currently being drafted. In the last five years there have been two such commissions (and thus two drafts of curricula) and a third has just been established to report in 1997. The 'shelf-life' of a curriculum is therefore currently about 2 years. This rapid development is the result of the major upheaval to the education service that was heralded by the change from the GDR to the FRG. It is probably the case, therefore, that curriculum commissions are less frequent in *Länder* that were part of the former West Germany.

The Technology Curriculum

The former GDR approach to technology

In the former GDR all pupils went through a programme of activities in technology. In years 5 and 6 there was a basic programme in technical drawing and materials exploration. But from year 7, the technology programme was related to industry, in the sense not just that it was vocational preparation but also that it was often taught in two-week sections – one week in school and the next in a local industrial plant. This industry-related curriculum was specifically designed to teach technology through the vehicle of the industry that existed locally, and a key player in this teaching was the *Betreuer*, the industry-based mentor or instructor. The curriculum was therefore developed locally, and – in the case of Thuringia – was the responsibility of the Ministry of *Volksbildung* (popular education) in association with the professors at the Pädagogische Hochschule (teacher education college) in Erfurt. They produced a standard text to guide the technology teaching programme right through the years of the *Oberschule* and in association with the local *Betreuer*.

It has to be said that the programme of activities described in the textbook looks arcane in the extreme and reminds me very much of the kinds of things I used to do as a pupil in school (in the early 1960s) in my woodwork and metalwork classes. The focus of the programme was clearly on the building of craft skills – dominantly with hand tools and subsequently with lathes and milling machines. This was extended somewhat by a limited amount of work on 'control systems' such as might exist in washing machines, drill presses and gear boxes. But the dominant pedagogy throughout was one of following rules so as to generate the right answer.

I had discussions with several graduates of this system who spoke with varying degrees of warmth about their experiences in ski factories or furniture factories, which had started as early as year 7 (age 12). The consensus of opinion was that the programme was designed with at least a triple purpose: to induct children into the workings of 'socialist production'; to develop their technological understanding and competence; and subsequently, usually at age 15, to ease pupils into gainful local employment.

In the former GDR this was not just a *part* of the technology curriculum, it was the *whole* of it. Technology was *only* taught in this way, linked directly to local industry. Except in the very early years (5 and 6), technology did not exist as part of a general, liberal education. Rather it was seen as synonymous with (or at least existing in symbiotic interdependence with) industrial education and training. However, it has also to be recognised that this programme existed for all pupils, not just for those who were subsequently to be part of the industrial workforce. It was a requirement in the polytechnic schools, which all pupils attended from year 5 until they left in year 9 or 10. But after the reunification of Germany, not only was the GDR universal polytechnic school system abolished in favour of the FRG tripartite version, but so also was the whole system of technical, industrial and vocational education. It was thought by the federal government to be too ideologically socialist and bordering on the abuse of child labour. And it was replaced overnight by a quite different system.

The dichotomy of technology education in the Federal Republic

There are now two quite different kinds of technology curriculum in Germany. And ne'er the twain do meet. They are taught by different teachers to different pupils in different schools. The two forms might best be characterised as technology of the hand (in the *Hauptschule*) and technology of the head (in the *Realschule* and the *Gymnasium*). In the *Hauptschule* – for pupils who are expected to leave at age 15 for an apprenticeship (if they are lucky) in business or industry – technology exists in the form of a subject called *Wirtschaft und Technik* (economy and technics). It involves a mixture of theory and practice, but the dominant manifestation is of practical activity in a workshop or studio.

For all pupils in the rest of the educational system, this form of technology does not exist. There is a basic course (in year 7) in 'informatics', which includes the basics of information technology (desk-top publishing, spreadsheets, databases, etc.) but, beyond that, technology exists only as an occasional incursion into the science curriculum. In this form it is more like 'applied science' than technology. Pupils in these higher-level schools do not design or make things or study and exploit technological principles. They study science fully, but they only – occasionally – *read about* its exploitation through technology.

The most telling observation in this complete separation of forms of technology curriculum is that the 'economy and technics' curriculum of the *Hauptschule* is substituted in the *Realschule* and the *Gymnasium* by a curriculum in 'economy and law' in which pupils study economic models and constitutional models. But there are no workshops or design studios in which to design and build real models. There are only laboratories. For science. The nearest pupils get to technology is in a room full of computers; but they do not use them for CAD or for control purposes. They program in Pascal, or calculate in Derive, or write reports in Microsoft Word, or scan a multitude of databases.

It is an astonishing and sad story of those who have and those who have not. Those that are judged to have real intellect do not have technology; and those that are judged not to have real intellect do have technology. To understand this dislocation in the curriculum, one needs to recognise that technology programmes in the FRG have never been seen as anything other than a vocational preparation. Linked to a highly differentiated schooling system which separates the sheep from the goats, the technology offering is then provided only for the low-ability who are destined to become the industrial workforce. The rest of the population do not need it since they will never be likely to go into industrial employment. Technology in German schools is purely a vocational preparation activity.

In the *Realschule* and the *Gymnasium*, technology could only exist if a case for it could be built in terms of a general education entitlement. But this has never been seriously contemplated in Germany, as Theuerkauf (1995, p. 19) explains:

> The parallelism that exists between technical vocational training and technology education as part of general education, directs attention to the question of the right of the latter to exist, and thus in how far technology education within the canon of the *Gymnasium* subjects is a general-knowledge subject. Of all the Federal German *Länder*, only North Rhine-Westphalia has settled this basic question in favour of technology education.

In only one of the 16 *Länder* does technology education exist in a form that might be recognised in the UK, and even in North Rhine-Westphalia (NRW) it is only an optional activity that has penetrated about 30% of schools.

Technology in the Hauptschule

So it is only in the *Hauptschule* that a technology education programme currently exists in Thuringia, and in truth the programme is better described as technical education. The programme operates at two levels.

In years 5 and 6 there is a programme entitled simply *Werken* (work). This introduces pupils to working with materials, and the predominant approach is to provide a standard model or product, and to allow pupils

Figure 7.5 Slab-pot making in year 7.

to modify it somewhat before they make it under carefully controlled supervision. The work is dominantly based on handcraft traditions of the nineteenth and early twentieth century – using wood, metal and paper (printing). There is a limited amount of drawing, centred on the kinds of technical drawing that allow pupils to represent the steps of production of their product. There is no design activity, and the end-products from the pupils all look alike, with minor modifications.

In years 7–9 (ages 12–15) this is followed by the *Wirtschaft und Technik* (economy and technics), programme, which divides into three different experiences in the three years. Year 7 has many of the same features as the *Werken* curriculum, with pupils modifying and making products that are designed to teach *making* skills under the strict control of the teacher. Figure 7.5 shows one such class working with clay. The pupils are following the step-by-step instructions of the teacher in order to produce a slab-pot. They all have the same equipment – rolling pin, strip guides (that control the width and the thickness of the rolled clay) and rolling board. Once the slab sections are produced the pupils have some scope for altering the way they go together to make the pot. The exercise is like a very focused practical task.

In year 8 the programme is extended to include a small amount of electrical and mechanical systems work. Whilst craft-based making activities continue for some of the year, the programme additionally includes the study of motors and machinery in terms of functioning systems. The work does not necessitate independent designing or other decision-making activity, and centres rather on practical work based on the disassembly and assembly of pre-existing units. Pupils do, however, learn to use fault-finding diagnostic approaches to systems. The 'economy' part of the subject title comes more into play at this level, as pupils are expected to deal with elements of product economics. Classes are less exclusively workshop-centred, never the less the predominant pedagogy remains very concrete and highly directive. There is a high premium on finding the 'right answer'.

In year 9 the focus shifts again and becomes significantly more challenging, for in addition to further craft-based making activities and further instruction in electrical and mechanical systems, pupils work on what are called 'complex systems'. Such complex systems might be found, for example, in an industrial plant or in a hospital or supermarket where technical systems interact with financial and human constraints. Pupils are helped to build models to illustrate these systems and their interaction. This system modelling becomes (as will be seen in the section on examinations) a significant feature of the final examination. It is challenging and much the most interesting feature I observed in Thuringia.

The basic plan of the *Wirtschaft und Technik* programme for all the Erfurt schools can be represented schematically as follows (Kommunales Technikzentrum 1996):

Year 7   Wood
         Ceramics
         Metal/plastics
Year 8   Sewing
         Kitchen
         Motors
Year 9   System model
         Electro-technics
         Greenhouse ecology
         Computer work

In describing these programmes – particularly in year 9 – it is difficult to provide the reader with a sense of the depth of the work, and it is important to remember that the academic level of these courses is designed to suit the needs of 12–15-year-old pupils in the lowest 30 per cent of 'general ability'. In the section on assessment (below) I include some examples of the level of questions pupils might be tackling in year 9. Given the nature of the client group, these programmes are not deeply intellectually demanding, but parts of them do provide an interesting view of technology for these pupils and (especially in year 9) something that is very unusual in the UK experience. Our National Curriculum has a single-minded preoccupation with *products* (designing, making and evaluating them) and it was refreshing to see German youngsters given the opportunity for extended analytical and modelling studies of whole socio-technical systems. This 'complex systems' strand of work in the *Hauptschule* could usefully be imported to the UK.

However, apart from that unit in year 9, the dominant impression of the *Wirtschaft und Technik* programme is that it is designed to impart a restricted technical body of knowledge and skills. Moreover, the predominant pedagogy is one that requires pupils to follow instructions to the 'right' answer. There is very little use of higher-order thinking skills. As an illustration of this, the assessment of project work (as we shall see below) makes no requirement for pupils to build a portfolio to lay out and justify the thinking that underlies their products. Autonomous decision-making does not feature large in the process, which rather prioritises the proper manufacture of the product to a given tolerance. And since pupils are not generally doing autonomous projects, they do not learn the skills of project management or of person, time and team management. The learning is – and is intended to be – strictly technical.

One can see why this programme does not exist in the *Gymnasium*. Its purpose is not as part of a general, liberal education. Only with a great leap of imagination is the learning transferable beyond the limited confines of producing a technically equipped workforce. And – as I shall show below – this rationale is increasingly being undermined by events taking place in industry itself.

Technology in the Gymnasium

As I have suggested above, technology in the *Gymnasium* is a very different study. The conventional *Gymnasium* curriculum comprises the following academic disciplines which I have listed in the order that they appear in the official curriculum guide for Thuringia: German; foreign language (often English); mathematics; physics; chemistry; biology; geography; economy and law; social studies; music; ethics; sport; informatics (Thüringer Kultusministerium 1996). This curriculum would be normal for all but one *Land*, and technology manifests itself either as occasional elements of applied science within a strictly disciplinary science curriculum or as 'informatics'. In this latter form the official curriculum from the Thüringer Kultusministerium specifies the following elements for study in year 11 and 12:

Year 11   Law and computer crime
          Handling computers
          Applications and systems 1

Year 12   Applications and systems 2
          Problem-solving using Pascal
          Project work

This curriculum exists not only in the *Gymnasium* but also in the *Realschule*. In consequence, a very significant majority of German pupils experience nothing like design and technology as it currently exists in the UK.

However, the *Land* of North Rhine-Westphalia is the exception to this rule and in years 11–13 of its *Gymnasium*, technology has existed as a separate programme since the early 1980s. The programme is based on a two-dimensional matrix that relates *object-centred* constraints such as materials, energy and information to *human-centred* ambitions such as using, evaluating, producing, serving and recycling. This leads to curriculum units described in the following terms in the three final years of the *Gymnasium*:

Introduction to technology
Transformation of materials in technical systems
Transformation of energy in technical systems
Transformation of information in technical systems
Combination transformations in technical systems
Interaction of technical systems with their environment

Each of these is a one semester (20-week) course of three class periods per week. Directives give more concrete shape to this general structure, and *the system of energy supply* runs like a thread through all the six courses. Thus in one course the focus is on the refinery as a system of processing crude oil into fuel oil and its by-products; in another the power station serves as a means for studying energy conversion; and in yet another it deals with the flow of information for automation within the power station. The final course brings all these together and studies the interrelationships between them and their impact on the local, regional, national and international setting (for details, see Kultusminister NRW 1981).

The programme in NRW has been slowly evolving over 15 years, but it has not spread to take in neighbouring *Länder* or even to become an entitlement throughout the whole of NRW. Those of us who have experienced the development of technology in the UK would recognise some of the features associated with the evolution process in NRW: strong advocates in some teachers, strong resistance from other teachers and enthusiasm from pupils and employers.

Since its introduction as a subject at about 30 per cent of the *Gymnasien* in North Rhine-Westphalia, despite strong resistance, technology teaching has held its own on the basis of this concept and has proved to be an attractive subject for pupils that deserves to be treated on an equal footing with other subjects . . . it is welcomed and encouraged by university teachers and by industry . . .

(Theuerkauf 1995, p. 30)

The fact remains, however, that advanced technological studies of this kind exist in only 30 per cent of the *Gymnasien* in only one of 16 *Länder* of the Federal Republic of Germany.

Vocationalism in Germany

Technology in German schools has been shaped by vocational traditions. That is why it is not seen as important in the *Gymnasium*, and equally it is why the *Hauptschule* curriculum is constructed as it is. Accordingly, it is worth reflecting for a moment on how the apprenticeship arrangements, that follow from the *Hauptschule*, currently operate. Since 1955, when the German government linked up with industry and created the 'Contract of Success' that launched the famed 'dual system' of training, it has been assumed that pupils from the *Hauptschule* would move into an apprenticeship that would be jointly funded by industry and by education. The system has been internationally admired – but now (at least in the context of Thuringia) it appears jaded and largely unable to deal with the commercial realities of a post-industrial society. Siemens, Volkswagen and a multitude of other major manufacturers no longer build their manufacturing plants in Germany; they go instead to Brazil or Malaysia or Indonesia where costs (not least labour costs) are far lower. And those industrial plants that do still exist in Germany have a greatly reduced need for workers operating at the level of technical education provided in the *Hauptschule*. Drill press operators and lathe turners are just not needed on the scale that they once were.

So here is a real paradox. On one hand, the whole rationale for technical activity in the *Hauptschule* is vocational – seen to be a preparation for the workforce. And yet, on the other hand, the type of work that is included and the intellectual level of that work are increasingly irrelevant to industry. Industrial companies do not need this primitive technology, so increasingly they are distancing themselves from it. There is now a serious shortage of apprenticeship/training places for pupils leaving the *Hauptschule*, since industry no longer sees itself as gaining any advantage by offering them.[4] It is therefore increasingly difficult for these pupils to find an apprenticeship, and there is a high level of youth unemployment among them. The somewhat cynical observation by those with whom I discussed this matter was that where these pupils did succeed in finding apprenticeships they will no longer be funded by industry, but by a training grant from the local government which in turn receives its training funds from the EU. The new golden calves in Germany are the small and medium-sized enterprises (SMEs) offering training (of any kind) in return for grant funding from the EU via the municipal authority. Professor Dr Dietrich Blandow, director of one of these SMEs, was at pains to point out to me that the training they dispense bears absolutely no relationship whatever to the technology curriculum in the *Hauptschule*.

So we appear to have here a classic example of system lag. The product of the *Hauptschule* system no longer meets the industrial/vocational needs it was originally designed to serve. But this has not yet fed back into the system in such a way as to transform what is going on in the *Hauptschule* curriculum. Currently the feedback in youth unemployability (which might be socially catastrophic if left unchecked) is being muted by subsequent training measures. But there must come a time when the whole rationale for industrial vocational technology programmes of the kind currently offered in the *Hauptschule* will be substantially reviewed. This issue has been recognised in North Rhine-Westphalia in relation to the *Gymnasium* curriculum.

> Technology education at schools providing a general education cannot restrict itself to a technical orientation, it always has also to include the human factor. Technical action is one of the factors giving shape to the social environment . . . and hence has to provide a link with ethics when part of school education.
>
> (Theuerkauf 1995, p. 30)

It is interesting and perhaps inevitable that in Germany this liberal, educational model of the technology curriculum should be emerging at the high-status *Gymnasium*, rather than at the low-status *Hauptschule*.

Assessment and 'standards'

One of the most startling observations about the assessment of pupils and students in Germany, is the simplicity and cross-sector coherence of the approach. It is based upon a simple principle and it is universal – in the primary school, the *Hauptschule*, the *Realschule*, the *Gymnasium*, in the teacher education college and in universities.

The Note scale

Assessment is based on a sliding scale of excellence from *Note* 1 (outstanding) down to *Note* 6 (very poor), and generally anything below *Note* 4 is considered a fail. This six-point system is sometimes supplemented by increments of half points and – particularly in final examinations – is rendered into numbers for aggregation and manipulation purposes before subsequently being translated back into the six-point scale. A pupil graduating from the primary school would need the aggregate level of his/her work to be assessed as at *Note* 1 or *Note* 2 to get into the *Gymnasium*. A student graduating from the *Gymnasium* would need the aggregate level of his/her work to be assessed at *Note* 1 or *Note* 2 in the final examinations in order to win a university place, and the final degree classification at university would again be on the same scale. In exactly the same way, low-ability pupils in the *Hauptschule* – on assignments in industry – will be graded on the six-point scale and the mark entered on their profile. Any curriculum activity in any school will be assessed using this scale and all examinations will be marked in relation to it. It follows from this that the rules defining grades 1, 2, 3, etc. – that is, the criteria of definition – are very flexible. And we should remember that these criteria are applied to the entire range of categories of performance that pupils are expected to demonstrate.

The documents from the Kultusministerium define generic criteria for each of these categories. In technology, for example, these things are defined in the document 'Evaluation scale of curricular units *Wirtschaft*

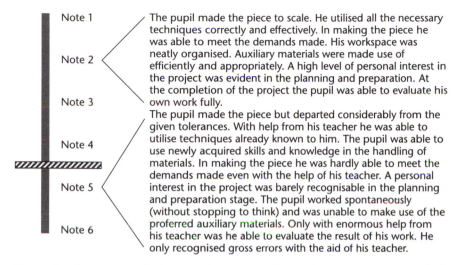

Note 1

Note 2

Note 3

Note 4

Note 5

Note 6

The pupil made the piece to scale. He utilised all the necessary techniques correctly and effectively. In making the piece he was able to meet the demands made. His workspace was neatly organised. Auxiliary materials were made use of efficiently and appropriately. A high level of personal interest in the project was evident in the planning and preparation. At the completion of the project the pupil was able to evaluate his own work fully.

The pupil made the piece but departed considerably from the given tolerances. With help from his teacher he was able to utilise techniques already known to him. The pupil was able to use newly acquired skills and knowledge in the handling of materials. In making the piece he was hardly able to meet the demands made even with the help of his teacher. A personal interest in the project was barely recognisable in the planning and preparation stage. The pupil worked spontaneously (without stopping to think) and was unable to make use of the preferred auxiliary materials. Only with enormous help from his teacher was he able to evaluate the result of his work. He only recognised gross errors with the aid of his teacher.

Figure 7.6 Thuringian Ministry of Education grading scale for 'materials handling'.

und Technik', and one of the categories concerns 'materials handling'. The criteria are outlined in paragraphs of text for each level – not unlike the level descriptions in the UK National Curriculum attainment targets. The criteria for *Note* 2 and *Note* 5 are shown in Figure 7.6. However, the interesting feature of this system is that these generic criteria remain the same throughout the school. In years 6, 7, 8, 9 and 10, the very same overall criteria are used to define excellence. How can this be? Surely this is not fair? Can it be right to grade 10-year-olds on the same scale as 15-year-olds?

However, these questions reflect a misunderstanding of the contributory role of normative data that relate these criteria to the reality of pupils' assessment. There is one additional sentence at the end of the criteria document which reads as follows: 'The level of performance, commitment, and effort was appropriate to the potential of a pupil of his age.' The criteria are intended to mean different things at different ages. As I pointed out in Chapter 6, criteria alone cannot define levels of excellence – they create a target bearing that we can shoot at. For accurate assessment however, teachers need additional data to 'fix' the level of difficulty (the range) of the criterion – and one sensible way of doing that is by using group norms of performance (Figure 7.7). And that is precisely what happens in German schools. The generic criteria (as above) for awarding these grades will be the same in each year. What will change are the specifics of the materials in the lesson (which will be more advanced for older pupils) and the associated expectations of the teacher (which will be higher with older pupils). So along with the *general criteria* for any subject, pupil performance in any piece of work is *normed* against the teacher's reasonable expectations of what counts as good or poor performance.

Figure 7.7 Criteria and norms interact when teachers make judgments.

If a teacher is trying to come to a judgment about the quality of a piece of work from a pupil, then the teacher's judgment is informed by the criteria for the different grades (specified in the curriculum from the *Land*), *and* by the norms applied by that teacher for the particular year's work. The content of the lessons changes from year to year, and the pupils mature from year to year, so the teacher has constantly to modify her expectations about the level at which pupils might be expected (in the words of the generic criteria) to 'manage themselves'. The requirement for 'personal management' will be constant through the years, but the expectation of the teacher will be different from year to year and from task to task.

From year 4 upwards, all pupils expect to be judged against this six-point scale. A pupil might get a *Note* 1 in year 5, and another *Note* 1 in year 8, but of course this does not mean she is the same in year 8 as she was in year 5. The content and demands of the work have progressed; and the teacher is interpreting the generic criteria at ever higher levels of expectation. After six years of battling with UK National Curriculum assessment, the German system for assessment reminds me of former times when I (and most other teachers) used a simple ABCDE scale of judgment for almost everything. An A might mean a different thing in each year, but it was informed by subject-based criteria and normed to the group and the activity.

'Moderating' standards, and teachers' judgment

The system described above for making assessments in the school is clearly dependent upon a great deal of professional judgment on the part of the teacher: judgment in interpreting the curriculum into appropriate activities and judgment in interpreting the generic criteria of excellence into appropriate levels of expectation to apply to pupils' work. By what means is it ensured, therefore, that teachers in one school are making the same judgments as teachers in another? How do we know that standards are consistently applied? When I asked this question – which I did on several occasions with different audiences and in different settings – I was met with looks of blank amazement. It was as if the question itself was somehow improper. Of course the standards are consistent! When I pressed the matter and insisted on knowing how they *knew* that the standards were common, I received answers of two kinds: first, I was assured about the professionalism of teachers and their ethical standards; and second, I was assured that teachers were regularly – through the *Fachberater* (advisory teacher) system – kept abreast of standards of work. The *Fachberater* (literally 'subject consultant') is a key part of the business of curriculum development in Thuringia, and they all belong to the Thuringian Institute for Teacher Education, Curriculum Development and Media (THILLM), under the Ministry of Education. Practising teachers can become *Fachberater* by being recognised as excellent practitioners and by attending courses at the teacher education college (see School Inspection below).

However, whatever role the *Fachberater* play in curriculum development, their role as roving moderators of assessment standards is (at best) somewhat hit and miss. Their visits are not timed to relate to any particular assessment schedule; the work they will be looking at may be very different from school to school; any one school may not be visited for some years, since visits are instigated largely at the request of the head teacher; and there is no formal system to ensure that the *Fachberater* themselves are operating with anything approximating to a common standard of excellence. Whilst they might be an excellent means for spreading a general idea of 'good practice' in the discipline, their system of operation simply does not enable them to operate effectively as a check on assessment standards.

At least two things can be concluded from this situation. At one level there is a revealing and reassuring sense of the professional trust that is bestowed on teachers in Germany. But at another level one has to say that (in terms of classroom assessments) it is highly likely that the standards that teachers apply in making their assessments will vary from school to school. It would be relatively easy to establish a moderation process (internal and/ or external) – possibly related to the *Fachberater* system – that would enable some really valuable debates between teachers about standards of work. But at present these debates appear not to be going on. It is generally accepted, by all those to whom I spoke on the matter, that standards reside (quite properly) in the minds of the teachers. It is almost as if I was being told 'that is where they belong; that is where they should stay'.

School-leaving examinations

The two major school examinations in Germany – as in England and Wales – operate at age 16 and 18, in years 10 and 12. The first of these is the general-purpose 16+ *Abschluss zeugnis* (school-leaving examination), and the second is the 18+ *Abitur*, used almost exclusively for university entrance. In both cases they reflect an amalgam of marks from across the curriculum, providing a measure of a pupil's overall performance. A pupil's record of performance on courses for the *Abitur* will show all the marks from the various subjects, but the grade at the end reflects an overview of the whole (1–6). It is very similar to the high school 'graduation' arrangements in the USA (see Chapter 7).

The Abschluss zeugnis

The school-leaving examination is confused by the fact that the three kinds of school all have different leaving ages. The *Hauptschule* ends in year 9 (age 15) and has a version of the *Abschluss zeugnis* which comprises examination papers in German, mathematics, and economy and technics, as well as some optional subjects. The maths and German papers are set centrally by the *Land* of Thuringia, but the economy and technics paper can be set by the school (as can all the optional subjects), though the content must reflect the curriculum framework agreed by the *Land*. In reality the proportion of pupils taking this leaving examination appears to be very variable. In the inner city of Erfurt, of all the pupils that attend the *Hauptschule*, only 20 per cent are expected to take the examination. The other 80 per cent (i.e. about 25 per cent of the whole school population) will leave school as 'unqualified leavers' with no formal qualification at all. In more rural areas, however, the proportion taking the leaving examination may rise to as much as 60 per cent of the pupils in the *Hauptschule*, and therefore the number of unqualified school leavers is a much lower proportion of the whole school population (approximately 15 per cent). The pupils who do really well in the *Hauptschule* leaving examination (i.e. who achieve an aggregate level of *Note* 1 or 2 on the six-point scale) can transfer into the *Realschule* for year 10.

At the end of year 10 the *Realschule* ends, and pupils sit the year 10 *Abschluss zeugnis*. The papers are (compulsorily) in maths, German, English and economy and law (which embraces IT), supported by a range of options. The maths, German, and English papers are set by the *Land* of Thuringia and the economy and law paper (and the other options) are set by the school. All the marking is done at the school level and results in a mark on the ubiquitous six-point scale. Although there is no formal pass/fail level, anyone achieving an aggregate of less than 4 on the scale is unable to use it for entry purposes into the diploma colleges.

It is worth pointing out here that those who transfer from the *Hauptschule* – having done very well (*Note* 1 or 2) in the year 9 examination – are faced by two major transformations. The subject economy and technics (at which they were clearly good in the year 9 examination) does not exist in the *Realschule* and is replaced by economy and law, with a quite different syllabus and a quite different kind of examination. Furthermore, English is compulsory in the *Realschule* – but only an option in the *Hauptschule*. One has to conclude, therefore, that the leaving examinations in year 10 present these pupils with a significantly greater challenge than they do the pupils who have attended the *Realschule* from the start. The cards are stacked against successful transfer.

The vast majority of pupils in the *Realschule* take the year 10 *Abschluss zeugnis* and, with level 4 regarded as a watershed level of acceptable performance, the vast majority of candidates seeking entry to the diploma colleges do so by reference to their performance on this examination. For students wishing to train as teachers, engineers, printers, and for many other professions, *Abschluss zeugnis*-level entry to a diploma course is the conventional route. It is also possible to excel in this examination and transfer to the *Gymnasium* for advanced academic studies for years 11 and 12, and subsequently attempt university entrance.

Technology in the Abschluss zeugnis

The closest thing, therefore, to a technology examination in Thuringia is the year 9 *Wirtschaft und Technik* examination which is set by the school and which does not need to be validated by anyone beyond the school. I have two examples of such examination papers, one from the Erfurt Technikzentrum school and one from Neuhaus-Schierschnitz (a rural area); and they are substantially different. There is, however, some common ground between them, including the fact that questions extend beyond the immediately technological and into matters of the economy and social organisation. To give readers a sense of the level and type of demand, the examination in Neuhaus-Schierschnitz is a paper-and-pencil test in three parts.

Part 1 (66 marks) tests pupils' understanding of the nature of training, the structure of careers, basic economics, and electrics and switches. For example:

- Explain the dual system of training.
- Compare the rights and duties of trainees.
- Explain with examples the five functions of money.
- Explain the term 'pay agreement' and name four kinds of pay agreement.
- Draw a switch system for a long hall; two lamps need to be switched on from either end of the hall.

Part 2 (30 marks) tests basic technical drawing:

- Four sections have been removed from the cube (shown in oblique). Draw the cube from the front, from above, and from right and left. Space is to be properly apportioned.

Part 3 (19 marks) tests pupils understanding of gears. For example, a belt-drive and a bevel/cog gear are shown symbolically:

- Name the gear systems.
- In what directions will they turn?
- Energy transmission is by . . . (e.g. friction/meshing teeth).
- Give an example of where they might be used.

The examination has a total of 115 marks and pupil responses are marked by the teachers (using a mark scheme) and subsequently the resulting score is translated back to the 1–6 scale. I asked a number of teachers about this process, and concluded that the allocation of marks to sub-sections of the paper is based on the teacher's professional judgment of the relative importance of the various sections; and that the marks awarded to a particular script reflect the unmoderated professional judgment of the individual teacher. Since this whole exam paper is school-based, I assume that the differences between the Erfurt and the Neuhaus-Schierschnitz exam are equally reflected across all the *Hauptschulen* in Thuringia. Typically in Erfurt only 20 per cent of the pupils take this leaving examination in technology, whilst in Neuhaus-Schierschnitz it is nearer 60 per cent.

The origins of the rules surrounding this system are not entirely clear, but we should remember that the German and mathematics papers (and mark schemes) for the exam are set by the Ministry of Education for the *Land*. Perhaps the technology (being vocationally focused) is thought to be a local matter, since the leavers will most likely be moving into local employment, whereas German and mathematics are considered generic and transferable?

Successful students who choose *not* to leave school but to move on into year 10 are subsequently faced with the new subject of economy and law, with examination questions of quite different kinds:

- The social market economy is the existing economic system in our country. It developed from other economic systems and has many characteristic features.
  - Explain the advantages and disadvantages of the social market economy.
  - Explain the difference between taxes, subsidies and investment.
- What means does the Federal Bank have at its disposal to keep the currency stable?
- Explain the difference between civil and criminal law.
- From what age is one criminally responsible?[5]

This is for the year 10 *Abschluss zeugnis*, and I would hazard a guess that very few 16-year-olds in the UK would get very far with an examination paper of this kind. However, as I have suggested above, the down side of this *Realschule* curriculum is that it results in the complete elimination of technology from all levels of schooling above the *Hauptschule* which terminates in year 9.

The Abitur

At the end of year 12 (or possibly 13), pupils in the *Gymnasium* take the *Abitur*. This is the formal examination (equivalent to A levels) that prepares students for university entrance. The curriculum is strictly academic and in the whole of the *Land* of Thuringia it is not possible to study technology. I shall therefore not spend too long dealing with it.

Suffice it to say that these are high-stakes examinations, set by the Kultusministerium, with a formal allocation of marks per question, a formal mark scheme to guide the marking, and a grid to translate the marks back to the 1–6 scale. The *Abitur* is awarded on the basis of a range of these final examinations, the results of which are presented on a 'point credit card' (in the USA it would be called an 'academic transcript'). A total of 840 marks is awarded for examinations in 'basic subjects' and 'special subjects' and the transcript documents performance across the whole range of academic study and eventually reduces it to the 1–6 scale. This transcript (and the final aggregate *Note*) becomes an essential document for university entrance purposes. Only in North Rhine-Westphalia does technology appear on this transcript as one of the option studies carrying approximately 60 of the 840 marks.

School inspection and curriculum development

There is little direct state monitoring of standards in schools. Formerly – in the GDR – schools were monitored by inspectors in terms of their curriculum (content and methods) and for their correctness at a political level.

Now school inspection and the business of maintaining and raising standards are confined to the work of THILLM. This Institute collaborates with the *pädagogische Hochschulen* (ITE colleges) in providing in-service training for teachers. Additionally, however, they (together) train the *Fachberater* who do the inspections. All *Fachberater* are primarily teachers selected by THILLM to help other schools to develop their practice. THILLM ensures that all *Fachberater* are themselves properly able to reflect the state of development of practice in their respective subjects. They are given some freedom from their school duties (up to two days per week) to act in this advisory capacity for the Ministry of Education. They are asked, as subject specialists, to go and see what school X is doing and to offer advice to help it to improve.

These inspections are therefore seen primarily as a device for curriculum and teacher development, rather than a device for school monitoring. Schools are not required to publish examination results (though universities are) or indeed any other 'indicators of performance'. Moreover, the *Fachberater* system operates on an optional basis; a head teacher of a school can ask for a visit from a *Fachberater* to support a particular area of the curriculum. A visit is then arranged and support duly provided, and the *Fachberater* then reports back to the head teacher of the school being advised. If the head teacher did not request the visit, it would not happen.

I found no sense of schools being driven by the agendas of outside agencies. Rather the developments that take place operate at the behest of the school and in collaboration between teachers, the *Fachberater*, and the *pädagogische Hochschule* – which is held in high regard.

A new technology curriculum

There are some significant signs that change may be in the offing for the technology curriculum in the *Hauptschule*, and the change is originating in the *pädagogische Hochschule*. The professors responsible for technology education have for some years been seeking to develop a more imaginative

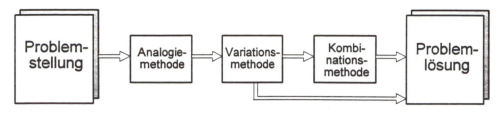

Figure 7.8 (a) Problem – analogy – variation – combination – solution.

programme that (through design-like activities) challenges pupils' thinking and decision-making as well as their technical and practical expertise. In Erfurt, the initiative appears to have started under the direction of Prof. Dr Blandow in the early 1980s with patchy implementation in the *polytechnische Oberschule* in the former GDR. The transformations wrought by the reunification of Germany appear to have upset this development, not least through the dismissal of senior academic personnel in the GDR.[6]

In any event the baton has now been passed to a new generation of academics.[7] Their view of technology teaching is centred on two principles, the first of which would constitute common ground with design and technology teachers in the UK. This is that pupils should tackle 'problems' with creativity and imagination and should seek to design solutions that they subsequently make and test. The second principle is that pupils should be provided with tools to do this designing – and the most important is *analogy reasoning*. They suggest that any problem can be broken down into parts; and that most of these part-problems will have existed before either in nature or in earlier technologies. So if the problem is to do with removing coal from a mine-shaft one of the part-problems concerns lifting (Figure 7.8b). How does nature lift things? How did early man lift things? And can we adapt any of these ideas to our aid? The programme therefore involves pupils identifying analogous situations, adapting and/or combining parts of solutions and thereby developing a new solution to the problem in hand (Figure 7.8c). It amounts to a somewhat more methodical approach to problem-solving than would be commonplace in the UK. Nevertheless, the central thrust of the programme is identical to ours, and for the same reasons. This technology curriculum is seen as an *educational* rather than a *vocational* programme, one designed to help young people to think for themselves in tackling technological tasks.

And it is gradually beginning to penetrate the *Hauptschule* through the *Fachberater* system, since the *pädagogische Hochschule* is responsible for in-service training not only of teachers but also of the *Fachberater* themselves. THILLM requires all such *Fachberater* to undertake such courses, and these new academics are also the curriculum experts advising the Curriculum Commission on the next draft of the *Wirtschaft und Technik* curriculum. The current situation in Germany – at least in Thuringia – reminds me of the position in England and Wales in the 1970s, with a few

Didaktik der Technik
Dr. Bernd Hill

Problemsituation Typ A (Neukonstruktion)

Die Schaffung der Problemsituation erfolgt ohne technische Lösung

Beispiel 1 :   Entwickeln, Bauen und Erproben von
              Fördereinrichtungen

- Problemsachverhalt: Erzschacht im 11. Jahrhundert

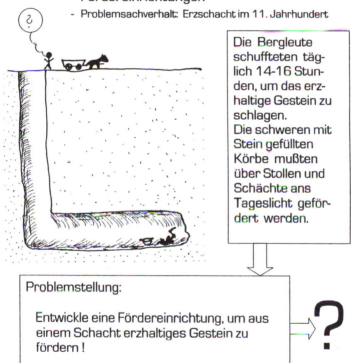

Die Bergleute schuffteten täg-
lich 14-16 Stun-
den, um das erz-
haltige Gestein zu
schlagen.
Die schweren mit
Stein gefüllten
Körbe mußten
über Stollen und
Schächte ans
Tageslicht geför-
dert werden.

Problemstellung:

Entwickle eine Fördereinrichtung, um aus
einem Schacht erzhaltiges Gestein zu
fördern !

?

(b) The problem of removing mining debris.

Didaktik der Technik
Dr. Bernd Hill

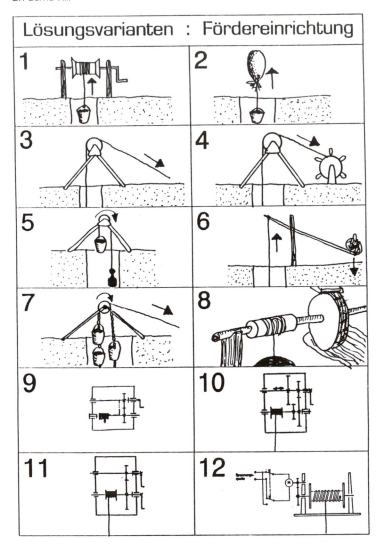

Lösungsvarianten : Fördereinrichtung

(c) Analogous technological possibilities.

centres of excellence developing innovative programmes that are being disseminated to teachers, advisers and teacher educators through the activities of a low-key but sympathetic Ministry of Education.

Notes

1 The tower blocks were designed on the assumption that 15 parking spaces would be adequate for 100 families. There are now estimated to be nearer 200 cars for every 100 families and Erfurt is starting to grapple with serious problems of traffic congestion.
2 Whilst latterly Erich Honecker, the last chairman of the State Council of the GDR, established his wife Margot as Minister of Education and encouraged the development of pedagogy as a science for the advancement of politics, this does at least demonstrate that the study of pedagogy was taken seriously in the GDR, both academically in universities and practically in schools.
3 Interestingly, the exceptions to this general policy were in sports and music, where specialism and excellence were specifically sought for reasons of international prestige.
4 The director of a major vocational training centre in Sommerda in Thuringia, estimates the current shortfall of apprenticeship places in Thuringia to be approximately 20,000.
5 Taken from the Joseph Meyer Regelschule, Neuhaus-Schierschnitz, year 10 leaving examination of 1995.
6 This has been described to me as a kind of educational imperialism by West Germany.
7 Current developments at the Pädagogische Hochschule Erfurt are headed by Prof. Lutherdt and Dr Hill.

eight

New York State, USA

New York is a story in two parts: New York City and 'up-state' New York (Figure 8.1). New York City is a sprawling, international, thrusting, multi-ethnic, vibrant, commercial environment with huge contrasts between rich and poor. The bankers of Wall Street; the fashion centre of 5th Avenue midtown; the urban university in Greenwich Village; the theatreland of Broadway; the shops and businesses of any and every conceivable type – New York City is the commercial capital of the USA. And right along-side (and within) this thrusting commercial environment is the poverty and deprivation of much of the Bronx, Harlem and Brooklyn.

New York State is comparable in size to England. It is a largely rural environment based on communities with more of a shared vision of life than might be expected in New York City. The transition from the one to the other is remarkably sudden. Within a 30-minute train ride of the centre of downtown Manhattan, one can be in rural, small-town America. The state capital, Albany, is about two and a half hours north of New York City (by rail or road). It is a small city – it has only one high school of 2000 pupils – but it is nevertheless the political and administrative centre of the state. That is the rule in the USA: state capitals are never the towns you would expect; they are invariably smallish communities rather than their big commercial centres. The capital of Texas is not Dallas, but Austin; that of California is not Los Angeles, but Sacramento. The idea – I think – is to keep political decision-making close to the heart of mainstream America, rather then have it shaped by the oddities of giant communities.

Education in New York State

New York State has about 200,000 pupils in each year group distributed among some 7000 schools. Approximately half are in New York City and the other half are spread through the rest of the state. The USA has a single – comprehensive – system of schooling. Elementary school (primary

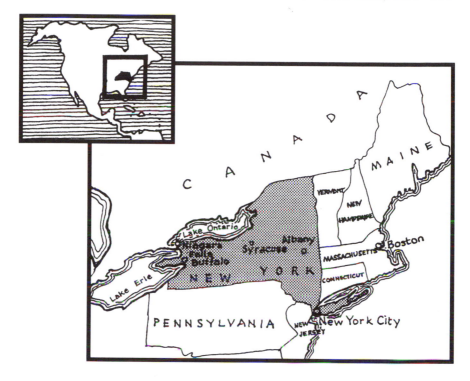

Figure 8.1 New York State.

school) is from grade 1 to grade 6; junior high school is years 7 and 8; senior high school is years 9–12 (Figure 8.2). Legally, the school-leaving age is 16 (end of tenth grade); in reality, however, the majority of pupils do not leave then, but stay on to year 12 and seek to 'graduate' from high school.

Devolved decision-making for schools

There is limited central management of education by politicians in Washington – the centre of federal government. And the current direction of policy is to decrease further the level of federal intervention and get it down to the barest minimum.[1] An example of federal government policy on education would be to legislate the minimum school-leaving age.

There is rather more management at state level: in this case the New York State Department of Education in Albany. In terms of size, this is like policy-making for the UK. The state government – under the direction of the Commissioner for Education and serviced by the State Department of Education – requires schools to follow state policy in a number of areas and especially in relation to parts of the curriculum and its associated testing programme that are mandatory. However, there is a very low level of surveillance, enforcement or support for policy at the state level, as is

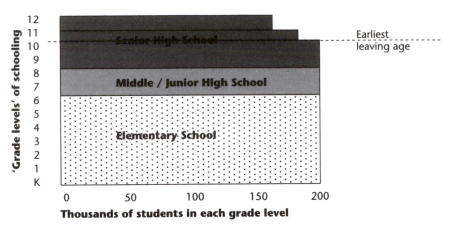

Figure 8.2 The New York State school system.

reflected in the fact that there is only one professional 'State Supervisor' for technology for the whole of New York State. To be effective, this supervisor must therefore work as an interface between state policy and the next level down in the structure of policy and management.

Below the state government there is the school district – which is normally based on the district surrounding and incorporating a town. All the elementary, junior high and senior high schools in the town are controlled to a very significant degree by the policy of the school district, which has its own education committee made up of local people. This ability to 'localise' the curriculum is prized by the community – but can be frustrating to the policy-makers at state level, who might be trying to develop a state-wide curriculum entitlement for all pupils. The school district will appoint and maintain its own support units – for example, through a range of subject specialist supervisors typically based in the high school but responsible for the development of their subject in all the schools in the district. Schools reflect the communities they are in and are politically accountable to them.

Below the school district is the school itself, with its principal and senior management team. At the school level, a further range of policy decisions can affect the direction of the school – for example, in choosing the priorities that shape the development of the curriculum.

This multi-tiered management of education is reflected in (or is perhaps a reflection of) the multi-tiered finances for education. Schools are funded by federal taxes (about 10 per cent); by state taxes (about 50 per cent) and by local district taxes (about 40 per cent) (National Center for Education Statistics 1991).[2]

Not infrequently, these layers of decision-making work in opposition to each other, creating a very confusing patchwork of policy. When there is a Democratic (broadly liberal) federal government, and a Republican (broadly conservative) state government, and a school district with a particular set of priorities, then there is plenty of scope for conflict.[3] In recent years the 'religious right' issue has highlighted this difficulty, with several states in the Midwest 'Bible belt' wishing to focus education towards traditional religious values that would, for example, prohibit the teaching of Darwinian evolution and replace it with an acceptance of fundamentalist Christian creation.

Educational leadership in New York State

In the midst of this devolved structure, the New York State Department of Education strives to focus and direct education policy for its 7000 schools. And interestingly, the Department is headed by a Commissioner of Education who is an educator – not a politician. The Commissioner is appointed by the New York State Board of Regents, which is a body of 16 members who are elected from high-ranking public positions (such as the chancellor of a university, or the head of a major law firm) and who are responsible for policy-setting in the New York State Department of Education.[4] The current Commissioner taught history in New York City; has a master's and a doctoral degree from a teachers' college; and has just come from the post of Commissioner of Education in the neighbouring New England state of Vermont. This does not make him immune to criticism from teachers, academics and administrators, but it does at least ensure that educational decision-making at the state level in New York is founded on something rather more substantial than the homespun dictums we get from successive Secretaries of State in the UK whose experience of education is frequently limited to recollections of their own school days.

The problem of curriculum development

As a result of the highly devolved arrangements for the management of schools, curriculum development is a very patchy phenomenon and there is certainly no national curriculum. A technology curriculum – in a form that would be broadly identifiable with that in the UK – has been developing in the USA for about 20 years, but the development process has had to cope with this highly devolved structure that allows states and school districts essentially to do their own thing, regardless of what anyone else might be doing. Co-ordinated curriculum development is not a feature of education in the USA. Latterly, a degree of coherence is just beginning to emerge through the activities of the International Technology Education Association (ITEA), in response to the 'standards' movement, for ITEA is now overseeing the construction of a set of national standards for technology. The project, entitled 'Technology for all Americans' is pursuing the following ambitious targets

> The standards for technology education will be developed with all Kindergarten through twelfth grade students in mind. They will be

organised around benchmarks at grade four, eight, and twelve. In addition to curriculum content standards, the Project has proposed to create teacher enhancement and teacher preparation standards, student assessment standards and program standards. These standards will provide a framework for assuring a quality, articulated technology education programme at the state, region, district and school level.

(ITEA 1996)

However, even when these 'standards' exist, they will have only an advisory function – with no teeth to ensure that they are implemented. It will be up to the states, the districts and the schools to decide whether they wish to do anything with them.

At present only two states in the USA have any compulsory technology curriculum for pupils: New York is the only state with a mandated junior high school technology programme; and Maryland has a mandated high school course. It is no surprise that both these examples exist on the northeastern seaboard of the USA which is (loosely speaking) the liberal counterpart to the more conservative and fundamentalist South and Midwest.

Schooling and 'graduation'

In New York State, whilst the legal leaving age is 16, the vast majority of pupils carry on to 18 (grade 12), and then seek entry into one of the many kinds of college or university. Leaving school at 16 is widely considered to represent failing at school. The 90 per cent or so pupils who continue in school into grades 11 and 12 are aiming at 'graduation' and this exists at two levels: the Regents-endorsed Diploma and the Local Diploma. Both diplomas are school-leaving awards tied to the whole of a pupil's high school curriculum. They are awarded (or not) on the basis of aggregated test performance across all subjects that pupils take in their final two years. They are therefore very like the *Abitur* in Germany (see Chapter 7), and unlike subject-specific A-level awards.

The two levels of diploma serve (broadly) to divide the graduating population into two ability bands. The Regents Diploma is based on Regents-approved syllabuses and on standardised Regents examinations. And it is achieved by approx 40 per cent of the population.[5] The Regents Diploma operates as the gate-keeper for entry into good-quality higher education. By contrast, the Local Diploma is designed to serve the needs of 'the rest' of the school population: 'The rest take Regents Competency Tests (RCTs) and graduate with local diplomas which rarely are recognised by higher education institutions because they represent non-standardised curriculum designed by schools' (Terdiman 1996, p. 39).

However, this would appear, from my enquiries, to be somewhat less than the whole truth, since it seems that in New York State at present, the Local Diploma (like the Regents Diploma) is taken by about 40 per cent of the population. This raises the interesting question of what happens to the remaining 20 per cent, and the prevailing wisdom is that this is the size of the 'drop-out' group that leave school with no qualifications whatever. The drop-out rate is very much higher in New York City than in the rest of the state, and it is a matter of serious concern to educators.

The 'credit' curriculum

The curriculum in New York schools is built around subjects of study, as it is in the UK. A student will therefore be expected to study English, maths and science and a wide range of other subjects at junior and senior high school. However, the manner of presentation of these studies is quite different. A student timetable will not be an annual construction based on the student's year group. Rather the school will offer a range of course 'units' and each student will select from this range and effectively customise an individual curriculum.

This is made possible by departments in the school planning a range (menu) of one-unit and half-unit courses, published in a prospectus towards the end of each year. It is mandatory for pupils in New York to study science, but this does not mean all pupils do the *same* science. Towards the end of each year, each student will consult with a 'curriculum counsellor' and agree a programme of study for the coming year in all subjects.

In Syosset High School (Long Island) the following science courses are available in years 9–12:

Earth Science	(NYS Regents)	1 credit
Science 9		1 credit
Biology Honours	(NYS Regents)	1 credit
Science Research 1	(NYS Regents)	0.5 credit
Biology	(NYS Regents)	1 credit
Biology Workshop		0.5 credit
Biology English as a Second Language		1 credit
Chemistry Honours	(NYS Regents)	1 credit
Science Research 2	(NYS Regents)	0.5 credit
Chemistry	(NYS Regents)	1 credit
Chemistry General		1 credit
Physical Science		1 credit
Environmental Science		1 credit
Physics Honours	(NYS Regents)	1 credit
Science Research 3	(NYS Regents)	0.5 credit
Physics	(NYS Regents)	1 credit
Medical and Microbiological Laboratory Techniques		1 credit
Advanced Placement Biology		1 credit
Advanced Placement Chemistry		1 credit
Advanced Placement Physics		1 credit
Science Research 4		0.5 credit

None of these courses is compulsory. Students choose the ones they are interested in – and which are appropriate for their abilities and aspirations – in consultation with the counsellor. Because of this level of choice, the courses advertised in the manual are open to market forces. If a programme under-recruits for more than a year or two it will be removed and the department will be expected to offer something more attractive. If a programme consistently over-recruits, it may be offered to more than one group, and hence the department's offering expands.

In order for pupils to make intelligent choices, the school curriculum manual will detail the content and level of each unit course, as illustrated in the following two examples from the Syosset High School curriculum manual for 1996–97:

Biology ESL	1 year: 1 period per day: 1 credit
Prerequisites	Presently in the English as a Second Language program
Required for	Science requirement for graduation
Description	A general Biology programme with emphasis on vocabulary and technical English
Physics	(NYS Regents) 1 year: Alternating single/double periods each day: 1 credit
Prerequisites	Final Grade of C+ or better in Chemistry; plus a pass grade in Maths iii Regents
Recommended for	Average and Above average students who desire an emphasis on a quantitative approach to Physics
Expenses	Regents review book and calculator
Description	Being concerned with the physical principles of force, motion, time, space, matter and energy. Physics is directed toward the student who wishes to broaden the base of his/her knowledge of the physical world. This standard NYS Regents course is designed as part of a complete high school program and serves as an introduction to study of Physics at college. The Regents examination and laboratory work are a required component of the course. SATii Subject Test available.

Since each student's programme of study is individualised, one may choose to do Physics in year 10 whilst another does it in year 12, and in courses without too many prerequisites it is not uncommon for the group to be composed of pupils from years 10–12 studying together. The year group is not a significant organising element in US junior and senior high schools. Courses are based on two semesters each year, from September to January and from February to July. A half-unit course represents approximately a 50 minute lesson each day for one semester. A whole unit therefore lasts for the whole year.

There is an increasing level of specialisation as pupils move up through the school, but this is much less the case than in the UK. In years 9 and 10, for example, pupils would be expected to study eight subjects (including PE); in year 11 this will drop to six subjects; and in year 12 (graduation year) it will drop to five subjects.

Graduation and credit accumulation

Advancement through junior and senior high school in New York is therefore marked by the progressive accumulation of credits. Successful completion of one credit course may provide access to others, and it is through the careful structuring of prerequisite credits that the curriculum is prevented from becoming a 'pick and mix' free-for-all process. The individual counselling of students as they work out their curriculum for the year is a major responsibility.

Credit accumulation reaches its peak at 'graduation', because unless students have acquired sufficient credits they cannot graduate. The minimum graduation requirement for the two diplomas is mandated by the Board of Regents for New York State; to be awarded one of the diplomas, students have to achieve 20.5 credits as follows:

	Local Diploma	*Regents Diploma*
English	4	4
Social Studies	4	4
Maths	2	2
Science	2	2
Second Language	–	3
Health	0.5	0.5
Art and/or Music	1	1
Electives	5	2
Physical Education	2	2
Total	20.5	20.5

Note that technology does not feature in this line-up except possibly as one of the 'elective' subjects. And note also that there is far more scope for electives for the Local Diploma, i.e. for lower-ability students, than for Regents Diploma students.

The Technology Curriculum

The dominant tradition in technology curricula in the USA is of 'industrial arts', known somewhat disparagingly as 'shop' – an abbreviation of 'workshop'. Shop classes are a more industrial version of the woodwork and metalwork of former days in the UK, and it would not be unusual to see boys (almost all the pupils in these classes are boys) handling circular saws

Figure 8.3 A New York State school workshop.

and radial-arm saws as well as vertical and horizontal milling machines
(Figure 8.3). They would also be familiar with a range of electrically and
pneumatically powered hand tools.

This is a tradition that has developed since the 1950s and that has come
to be represented in a series of courses that focus respectively on the
following features:

- craft and machine-tool skills (a US version of woodwork and
  metalwork);
- communication skills (a US version of technical drawing);
- transportation and power mechanics (a US version of motor vehicle
  engineering).

These programmes were at one time very popular with boys, but in the last
ten years have become increasingly disregarded by almost all those who
are seriously concerned with the role of technology in the school curriculum.
The courses make very limited demands on the imagination of pupils –
and even less on their powers of thinking, decision-making and problem-
solving. They require pupils predominantly to *do*, rather than to *think*,
investigate, *plan*, *develop*, *reflect upon* and *evaluate* that doing.

These seriously dated programmes are losing their appeal to youngsters,
who consequently vote with their feet. Small classes are therefore the norm
and this has become such a serious matter in some school districts that
classes (and the associated workshops) have been closed. Nevertheless, the

tradition remains, and it is so deeply rooted that it is still the dominant feature of the technology offering even in the school to which I was taken (Syosset High School) to see examples of excellent practice in technology. The technology offering at this school amounts to 15 one or half-credit courses, 10 of which are of this old-fashioned kind, including the following (as described in the school's curriculum manual for 1996–97):

Production: wood . . . a course to acquaint students with the concepts of woodworking . . .

Materials processing: metals . . . a heavy emphasis is placed on machine operation . . .

Transportation (consumer auto) . . . provides the skills needed to perform owner maintenance . . .

Industrial techniques . . . develops familiarization with appropriate machines, technical drawing and measurement

The technology teachers' association has for years been trying to move the profession away from these deeply traditional programmes. They now entitle themselves 'technology education' teachers rather than industrial arts teachers, and their association is (modestly) called the International Technology Education Association and it has a massively supported annual conference. But still, even in the 'liberal' north-eastern seaboard of the USA and in a school with some excellent and innovative technology, two-thirds of the technology courses are of this very traditional 'shop' variety. How are we to explain the longevity of these curricular dinosaurs?

Undoubtedly one major reason lies in the highly devolved nature of educational decision-making that I outlined earlier. If ITEA were seeking to develop a new and coherent alternative technology curriculum, it would find it very hard to penetrate these devolved decision-making processes. At the state level, Kansas will do what Kansas wants to do, and never mind what New York, California or Texas might be doing. The power of the individual states to steer their own ships will inevitably diffuse any central attempt to develop a new curriculum, however much ITEA might wish otherwise. And further down the devolution chain is the localised school district. Employers and parents in the community – who have influence on the local school board – are typically more conservative about curriculum than educators, and these school boards have to be persuaded of the wisdom of change; and whilst one might be, the next might not. So even *within* a state wishing to develop a new technology curriculum there will be very traditional school districts as well as more innovative ones. Traditional 'shop' programmes therefore survive looking increasingly antiquated and irrelevant, whilst those teachers, teacher educators and administrators with a vision of how things might be improved with a new technology programme find their efforts compromised by multiple levels of autonomous decision-making.

This is a classic example of how choice and diversity – even when driven by market forces – result in a lack of the collective will needed for a coherent change of direction. Even with a sword of Damocles hanging over the 'shop' programmes – in the form of very poor and heavily gender-biased recruitment – there is not sufficient central management of the curriculum to ensure that new technology programmes take over and drive the curriculum forward. The status quo limps on.

However, in New York State there are some members of the Department of Education who have a clear and innovative view about technology in schools and who have been responsible – over the last few years – for some very interesting curriculum developments. And remarkably, they have even succeeded in persuading the Department of Education that the new junior high school course should be made mandatory for all schools in New York State.

'Introduction to Technology': grades 7–8

This introductory programme for pupils aged 11 and 12 has been a collaborative development between the State Department of Education and teachers from various local school districts. It has emerged under the leadership of Mike Hacker (the State Superintendent for Technology Education) and has been developed in recent years to the point where it is now a mandatory requirement of the junior high school curriculum. The 'Introduction to Technology' programme has a strong pedagogic line that is a close reflection of practice in the UK:

> Introduction to Technology is a program which stresses application of theoretical concepts to the solution of practical problems. The course is designed to be taught through activities which should be 75 per cent hands-on 'design and construct' experiences. . . . the programme emphasizes the development of mental process skills such as: creative thinking, decision making, critical thinking, and problem solving.
>
> (New York State Education Dept. 1993, p. 2)

The course is written in modular form with ten modules for study and with associated model learning activities. The modules cover the following broad territory:

Getting to know technology – physical, biological and information technologies; the history and development of technology; and the effects of technology on people's lives.
What resources are needed for technology – people, information, tools and machines, materials, capital, energy (forms and sources), time.
How people use technology to solve problems – design and problem-solving processes, modelling, optimising, graphics and simulations.
Systems and subsystems in technology – systems to satisfy needs, types of systems, analysing and adapting systems, feedback in systems.
How technology affects people and their environment – technology for the human user (needs, ergonomics), technology in the environ-

Figure 8.4 The working environment of the junior high school.

ment (natural, man-made and interacting), desired and undesired effects of technology (solving and creating problems).

Choosing appropriate resources for technological systems – choosing resources (people, information, materials, etc.), combining resources, optimising, choosing software.

How resources are processed by technological systems – converting materials, converting energy, converting information, the computer as a tool.

Controlling technological systems – open/closed loop systems, feedback, sensors, controllers, computer control.

Technology and society – assessing technological systems, impacts on work/careers, scope of impacts (personal, local, national and global)

Using systems to solve problems – systems models for problem solving, systems theory, computers and problem solving.

Each of the modules is conceived as a unit of study lasting for three to five weeks, assuming that pupils have a 45-minute period every day of the week. The programme might therefore be designed to fit in one year of teaching (over 40 weeks in year 7 or 8) or it might be spread more thinly over both years of the junior high school programme.

The programme has been very influential with teachers who are just starting on the challenge of teaching technology. The course specification comes as a 350-page book with a mass of suggested 'Technology Learning Activities' (TLAs) that teachers may use or adapt or ignore. The TLAs

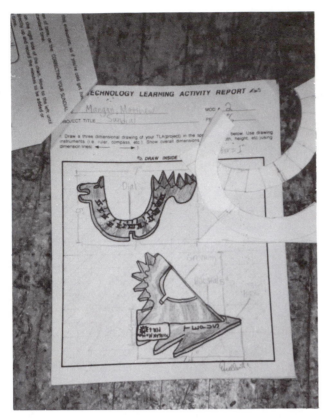

Figure 8.5 A section from a pupil portfolio and model for the sundial.

encompass the major concepts, the equipment that might be needed and an overview of the procedure for the project. It is this procedural overview that carries the pedagogy, suggesting that teachers might try this here or that there to engage the pupils' interest and direct them forward. The TLAs also include a suggested evaluation schedule that teachers can develop into a test if they so choose (I shall discuss assessment and testing issues later).

I observed a 'sundial' project from the first module of this programme that focuses on the history of technology. It was under way in a middle school in Albany and it was a terrific experience. Starting from a pattern established by the teacher, the pupils developed and modelled their own design, tested it in card and then constructed it in plywood. They then got into some splendid work on time and time zones. Since the USA is broken into several time zones the pupils measured their 'own' time in Albany and compared this to their 'time-zone' time, calculating angles of longitude and how these converted back into 'real' time. These 12-year-olds not only learned a good deal about modelling, making and design practice, but also started to talk about time as a socially constructed concept rather than just being 'there' as a natural phenomenon in the world. Moreover, it was patently obvious that they were thoroughly enjoying the work and were seriously challenged by it – both in designing and making the sundial and in calibrating, checking and using it.

It is undoubtedly the case that this junior high school programme has been influential in developing the culture of technology education in recent years, and its influence operates in several ways. It provides a coherent rationale and course plan that innovative teachers can latch on to; it provides the mandatory muscle that encourages all schools to take it seriously; it provides numerous developed project and lesson plans in the TLAs that lay it all out on a plate for those teachers who lack the confidence to take the first step; and accordingly is has succeeded in most schools in changing perceptions about technology. The programme is seen as something quite separate from 'shop' courses: more relevant, more challenging and certainly more popular than the stereotypical craft practices of former times. It represents a major achievement for New York State.

Technology in the high school: grades 9–12

Beyond the junior high school, there is no mandatory curriculum in technology in New York State. There is, however, an elective programme in 'principles of engineering' that has also been developed by the Education Department in New York State and again in close association with innovative individuals from professional engineering societies, universities, schools, teacher education and industry. A distinctive feature of this programme is that it does not confine itself to technology, but takes a much more dramatic stand on the necessary integration of maths, science and technology in engineering studies:

> students usually learn subject matter in the context of the specific disciplines. No wonder the majority of students constantly ask: Why are we learning this? Students in science and maths courses seldom learn how the concepts that they are learning are applied to the design and operation of the technological systems that surround and affect them daily. On the other hand, students in technology courses often do not learn the science and maths concepts that underlie the systems that they are studying. What is needed is learning experiences that are anchored in real world problems and environments ...
>
> (Liao 1983, p. 43)

The programme is intended for pupils between grades 9 and 12 and covers the following fields:

Engineering design – factors affecting it (functionality, quality, safety, ergonomics, appearance, environmental conditions, economics)
– the design process (need, definition of problem, analysis, selection, implementation, evaluation)

Figure 8.6 Group presentation of the telephone system model.

Modelling – descriptive and functional modelling.
Systems – input, process, output, feedback.
Optimisation – modelling the problem, identifying criteria for choice, identifying constraints, arriving at a 'tradeoff'.
Technology-society interaction – technology assessment, making decisions from the assessment.
Engineering ethics – professional, legal and social responsibility, ethical dilemmas, whistle-blowing.

I observed several projects that were part of this programme, including one in which pupils designed a telephone handset for home use by those with specific disabilities; and one in which students were designing a 'smart' road intersection.

In the former case, each group (the pupils on this programme all worked in groups) was given a disability to research and had then to design a handset or equivalent device that would enable the user to cope with it (Figure 8.6). Pupils also had to design a system for 'modelling' the disability so as to arrive at some evaluation of the effectiveness of their solution through a series of tests, as well as trying it out with real users with the disability (Figure 8.7).

The brief for the 'smart' road intersection required the group to produce:

- a 'roadbed' mapping a five-way intersection;
- a series of computer-controlled traffic lights to direct efficient traffic flow;
- a manual override to increase efficiency in unforeseen situations;

Figure 8.7 A visitor evaluates the prototype by 'modelling' the disability.

- a sensing network to determine when traffic flow is unusually high;
- a complete design log and journal with all aspects included.

These five features were then supplemented by a further demand that the intersection should have three other features that the team felt important to make it efficient. The group I watched at work on this problem had got two of their three extras sorted out. One was a cat that popped up in the middle of the intersection bringing traffic unexpectedly to a halt (or crushing the cat). The hand in Figure 8.8 is indicating the cat. The other was a system that sensed the siren of an approaching ambulance, identified which road it was on and automatically switched the lights to allow it through. These are challenging activities that are equivalent to those that we might find in A-level design and technology courses in the UK. And

Figure 8.8 The roadbed under test conditions.

the procedures that the teachers employ are very similar to our own, with much use being made of design and development portfolios and modelling activities of a variety of kinds.

This principles of engineering programme appears really interesting in the extensive documentation of course description and rationale, and where I have seen it in operation it has led to some fascinating and challenging project activities. But sadly, since it is elective and relatively new, the number of students studying it is tiny: some 3% of students across the state.

To summarise, therefore, the pattern of technology courses in New York State is as illustrated in Figure 8.9. There is, however, a gradually developing head of steam behind the evolution of technology courses in New York State, and one illustration of this is provided in the 'Learning Standards' movement that is currently sweeping the USA. This matter might arguably be dealt with in the section on assessment, but I include it here because of its curricular significance.

Curriculum standards

In many states, and also at a national level across states, groups are seeking to define curricular entitlements in many subjects. In technology this emerges in New York State in the *Learning Standards for Mathematics, Science, and Technology* produced by the State Department of Education.

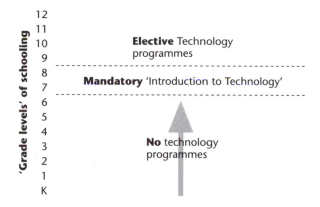

Figure 8.9 Technology curriculum provision in New York State.

This is a new development first published in March 1996 with the backing of the Board of Regents and the Commissioner of Education.

The standards are somewhat like our National Curriculum documents in that they seek to define what the curriculum should address at elementary, intermediate (junior high school) and commencement (senior high) levels of schooling. The standards attempt to differentiate 'content standards' (akin to programmes of study) from 'performance standards' (attainment targets), and the latter half of the document is devoted to samples of pupils' work to illustrate what is intended in the words.

The maths/science/technology (MST) standards in New York State are presented as follows:

Standard 1	Analysis, Enquiry and Design	– the definitions of 'process' in M, S and T
Standard 2	Information systems	– the IT component
Standard 3	Mathematics	– content
Standard 4	Science	– content
Standard 5	Technology	– content
Standard 6	Interconnectedness	– relating M, S and T
Standard 7	Interdisciplinary problem solving	– using strategies, applying knowledge and skills

(New York State Department of Education 1996)

At each of the three levels, technology (standard 5) is defined in terms of

- Engineering design – an iterative process involving modelling and optimisation
- Tools and resources – selected on the basis of safety, cost, availability, appropriateness, impact
- Computer technology – as a tool for design, modelling, communication and control

- Technological systems – to produce outputs such as products, structures, services, energy
- History and evolution of technology – as a driving force in society
- Impacts of technology – positive and negative impacts on individuals, society and the environment
- Management of technology – project management including personnel, time and cost.

(ibid. 1996)

Much of this would be familiar to teachers in England and Wales through the National Curriculum definitions, but there is a somewhat greater emphasis in New York State on the social significance and impact of technology, particularly through the last three elements outlined above. As an indication of the work that is anticipated in these standards, the intermediate level specification for 'Impacts of technology' requires that students:

- describe how outputs of technological systems can be desired, undesired, expected or unexpected
- describe through examples how modern technology reduces manufacturing and construction costs and produces more uniform products

(ibid. 1996)

The standard then goes on the suggest that this is evident, for example, when students:

- use the automobile to explain desired (easier travel), undesired (pollution), expected (new jobs created), unexpected (crowded highways and the growth of suburbs) impacts
- provide an example of an assembly line that produces products with interchangeable parts
- compare the costs of producing a prototype of a product, to the unit product cost of a batch of 100.

(ibid. 1996)

The development of these standards has been a major achievement in New York State, and they represent a very interesting way of defining a technology curriculum. There are many areas of overlap with our own practice – indeed our work in the UK has been very influential in helping colleagues in the USA to define some of the aspects of these standards. And there are also some distinctive features of the New York State standards that do not exist in our own.

But the bottom-line consideration is what impact these curriculum standards have on practice in schools, and the fact is that currently they have very little impact indeed. They do not represent a compulsory curriculum, so they are not in any real sense 'enforceable' standards. What they do is serve as a voluntary benchmark for those who are interested in developing technology curricula in New York State. However, the reality of technology curricula in New York State is that there is virtually nothing happening at elementary level (primary school); there is a lot happening at intermediate level because of the mandatory curriculum, and there is (once again) very little going on in the senior high school since the technology programmes are elective and relatively new.

The standards are therefore principally a rallying point around which to gather interested practitioners, a flag around which to gather and attempt to co-ordinate curriculum development in technology. And the real goal – which the curriculum leaders in technology are desperately seeking to develop – is to have a test that can be used to measure pupils' performance in technology. Such is the all-pervading power of 'tests' in the US curriculum, the view of many is that 'if we had a test for it, it would be taken more seriously' and at the very least it could be used 'to drive compliance' with the mandatory requirements of the middle school technology curriculum. It is time to turn our attention to these issues of assessment and testing in New York.

Testing in the USA

The USA is the land of testing. Standardised testing. Multiple-choice testing. Machine-scored testing. Every day in the USA millions of school children – from kindergarten to grade 12 – take tests. Most are devised by teachers for classroom purposes, but it is the ubiquitous multiple-choice tests – originating outside the classroom – that have garnered the most attention and controversy. The federal government sets tests, the state governments set tests, the school districts require tests, and individual schools frequently opt to use other supplementary tests. And at the culmination of all this testing, high school graduates have to take further multiple-choice tests – the Scholastic Aptitude Tests (SATs) – that are the basic means for qualifying for university entrance.

In a masterly summary of *Testing in American Schools*, the Office of Technology Assessment of the US Congress outlined the current situation as follows:

Commonly referred to as 'standardized tests' these instruments usually serve management functions; they are intended to inform decisions made by people other than the classroom teacher. They are used to monitor the achievement of children in school systems and guide decisions such as students' eligibility for special resources . . . Children's scores on such tests are often aggregated to describe the performance of classrooms, schools, districts, or States . . . they are a fixture of American schools . . . standardized test results have become a major force in shaping public attitudes about the quality of American schools and the capabilities of American students.

(Office of Technology Assessment 1992, p. 3)

There has been a massive expansion of multiple-choice, machine-scored testing in the USA over the last 25 years, and it has become a major industry. Whilst enrolments in school have declined over that period, income from testing (even when adjusted to eliminate inflation) has risen by 160%. Forty-six states had mandatory testing programmes in 1990 compared to only 29 in 1980. And the key to this expansion lay in the development of the 'multiple-choice' testing system and the associated technology that allowed rapid processing of huge quantities of responses.

The origins of the testing system lie in army testing for recruitment in the First World War. A model was developed that was subsequently extended and refined under the 'Iowa Testing Programme' in the 1930s:

> the multiple choice format provided a way to transform the testees' answers from highly variable, often idiosyncratic, and always time-consuming oral and written responses into easily marked choices amongst fixed alternatives, quickly scorable by clerical workers with the aid of superimposed stencils...
>
> (Peterson 1983, p. 6)

The multiple choice item tests were quickly adapted to school use and – in the Iowa Programme – linked to the development of mechanical and electro-mechanical scoring machines that would make possible the streamlined achievement testing of millions of students.

(Office of Technology Assessment 1992, p. 124)

A typical example of such a test question is shown below. It is related to the social studies curriculum, within an option on 'global studies'. The question is from the 1995 examination for the Regents Diploma and reads as follows:

Q22
A major problem that has slowed the economic development of Latin America has been
1   few good harbours
2   the abundance of resources
3   the shortage of unskilled labour
4   the lack of investment capital?

The idea that such a complex question can be reduced to such a simplistic set of propositions about labour, capital, resources and geography would be offensive to most teachers of history or economics in the UK. Even more ludicrous is the proposition that one of these factors is the right and only one, for – by extension – not only must all the others be wrong, but there should be no other possibilities that might have been even more important than any of the above options. In any event the 'right' answer, according to the scoring rubric, is option 4, as one might expect in the major capitalist economy in the world. It seems to me, however, that quite apart from whether or not such tests provide a useful measure of students' understanding of the global studies curriculum, these right and wrong (black and white) certainties that are a requirement of this kind of testing encourage a dangerously simplistic view of the world.

A further interesting perspective is thrown on this form of testing, given the highly litigious nature of US society. People hire lawyers and sue each other for the most amazing reasons and the lawyers have a field day. In this setting, imagine a pupil being denied access to a university place or a special education facility on the grounds of a teacher's judgment. A suitably angry and wealthy parent might contest the judgment and make life extremely difficult for the teacher. But if the teacher is merely passing on highly reliable test scores (even though they are of very limited educational value) then s/he is secure, since there are masses of statistics to fall back on from the test development process. As one of the officials in the NY State Education Department pointed out to me with some pride: 'We've never lost a case yet'. To rely on a process of assessment that required teachers to make judgments would be a very much more risky enterprise in the USA than it is (currently) in the UK. Perhaps its only a matter of time before we follow suit.

Nevertheless, in recent years, increasing concern has been expressed amongst educators about the seemingly endless use of multiple-choice tests in schools.[6] As teachers and curriculum leaders attempt to develop new programmes – not least in technology – they are stymied by tests that reflect neither the content nor the pedagogy that is central to these new programmes. Nevertheless, the fact remains that multiple-choice tests provide both the means and the benchmarks against which the vast majority of US students will have the vast majority of their learning measured.

Assessment and Testing in New York State

Multiple-choice testing is the front-line technique for the vast majority of test purposes in the USA, and in New York State there are broadly four kinds of purpose:[7]

- *Pupil evaluation and competency tests:* designed to monitor individual pupil progress in reading, writing and mathematics. Most operate in the elementary school and are used to identify pupils in need of remedial action – those that fall below the State Reference Point in those tests.
- *Programme evaluation tests:* designed to monitor the performance of schools in science and social studies. Originally (in the early 1980s) these tests were administered only to a sample of pupils and the performance of schools and school districts was aggregated up from the scores of the sample.[8] In recent years, schools have been entering all their pupils for these tests, but since they are designed to monitor schools' performance, pupil scores are not reported individually. Now, however,

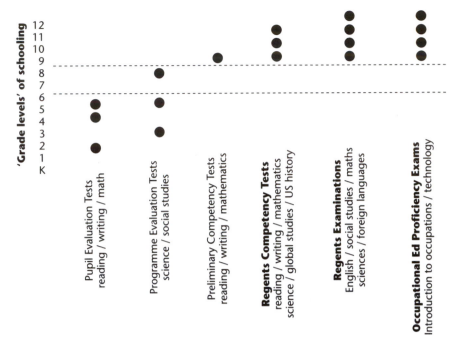

Figure 8.10 The distribution of testing in New York State.

with complete 'in-school' samples, head teachers are using these tests to monitor the performance of departments and even individual teachers.
- Diploma *tests* that are divided into two kinds:
  Regents examinations (for the Regents Diploma) for university entrance, with examinations in English, social studies, maths, sciences and foreign languages in grades 10–12;
  Regents competency tests (for the Local Diploma) for those not going to university, with examinations in reading, writing, maths, science, global studies and US history in grades 9–11.
- *Occupational education proficiency examinations*: in 'Introduction to occupations', and areas of technology (typically 'shop'). These are essentially pre-vocational tests taken as part of a diploma programme, usually for the Local Diploma.

Developing a single diploma system

There is currently much debate in New York State about the two forms of Regents tests, which in some ways reflects the situation in the UK prior to the development of GCSE testing for all 16+ students. Interestingly, New York State is currently embarking on precisely this change – merging the two tests into a single system. The 'lower-level' competency tests are being phased out and (by 2005) all pupils will have to pass the Regents Examinations in English, maths, social studies and science in order to graduate. The whole Local Diploma system is therefore effectively being phased out, and the Regents Diploma will be taken by all pupils.

The development of this new system – or rather the elimination of the former Local Diploma – is being pursued under the banner of raising standards of achievement:

> We're going to stop these low standard [Regents competency] tests ... and virtually all students are going to be on the curriculum to take the Regents exam. ... We have raised the standards and levels of expectation among students and teachers like never before.
> (The Commissioner of Education, in Terdiman 1996, p. 39)

There are a number of issues arising from this merging of systems. Clearly the original Regents exams were designed for their target audience – the top 40–50% of ability. Simply opening these same tests to 90–100% of students might be expected to achieve little beyond a massive increase in the failure rate. There are those in the Education Department who predict precisely that outcome – but there are indications that something more sophisticated is envisaged by those who are planning the merger.

The Commissioner of Education – whose initiative this is – was responsible in his former role as Commissioner of Education in Vermont for the development of one of the most comprehensive schemes of 'authentic assessment' in the USA. Authentic assessment is a US term for *performance* assessment; students are not simply assessed in what they can recall in multiple-choice standardised tests, but rather they are presented with real challenges and their performance on these tasks is assessed. This is clearly a much more sophisticated kind of assessment that requires investment in the development of the tasks and – crucially – investment in teacher development to run the tasks and assess the levels of student performance that result from them. This would appear to be part of the Commissioner's agenda since he has earmarked funds specifically for this purpose.

There are further indications that the Commissioner's long-term agenda is the reform of the Regents examination itself.[9] He is persuaded that there is far too much testing already going on in New York State – by which he means too much multiple-choice testing. He is committed to reducing the level of such testing and he recognises that the new Regents exams – for the whole cohort of students – must look somewhat different than at present:

> In Vermont, Mills achieved national attention for integrating authentic assessment – which encourages critical thinking over rote memorization and analytical projects over multiple choice testing – into the state curriculum. But many educators and the public are suspicious of

the effort, which requires teachers to make judgments and not rely solely on standardised textbooks and testing.

(Terdiman 1996, p. 39)

If the reform of the Regents examination is his real agenda, the next few years will be interesting in New York State. Not surprisingly, the reforms that the Commissioner has in mind are creating something of a stir – and there will be much discussion of the difficulty of maintaining 'standards' in this new regime in which teachers are likely to have to make more significant judgments about their students' performance.

Standards, norms and criteria

With so much emphasis (in the current regime) on tightly constrained multiple-choice testing, it is very difficult to debate and challenge the standards that are currently being applied, since the procedures for applying them seem so objective and clear-cut. Either pupils can answer the tests or they cannot. Either they pass or they fail. And the Department of Education has years of data to demonstrate that these standards have remained remarkably constant through the years.[10]

Using these data, not only are individual pupils measured for graduation purposes but also schools' performance can readily be compared. As an example, Syosset High School (in Nassau County) got 67 per cent of its pupils through the Regents Diploma in 1995, whilst Fishers Island High School (in Suffolk County) only succeeded with 20 per cent. Whilst the socio-economic circumstances of the two schools go a long way to explaining the difference, nevertheless the numbers have some meaning in the sense that they have been derived from a common base line.

But what if Syosset got 58 per cent passes in the previous year? Does that mean it has improved its performance this year, or does it mean that the standards of the Regents Diploma are slipping? The Regents' answer to this challenge is that the pass mark remains where it has been for the last several years: 65 per cent. If a pupil does not get 65 per cent then s/he fails: If s/he does manage to get over 65 per cent then s/he passes. Standards are constant in the Regents Diploma.

That, at least, is the rhetoric. But the reality is somewhat different, as I shall attempt to demonstrate.

One of the features of the multiple-choice test development process is the *pre-test*. Items thought to be appropriate for the test are tried out with a sample of pupils and a consultant group of teachers. This pre-testing is used to establish the 'item difficulty', which is calculated for each test item by reference to the number of pupils who are able to answer it successfully. Only those items that have an 'item difficulty' within the required tolerance are allowed in the final examination. In other words, the standards of the examination are normed in advance to the test population. The pass mark of the Regents examination is set at 65 per cent in order that a given (and constant) percentage of pupils will pass it. It does not mean that the standard of the examination remains constant. If one were to ask whether the students who passed the exam this year know as much about, say, maths as those who passed it in 1970, then this would be a measure of standards. But the Regents examination system cannot answer this question.

The pre-test is used to norm the whole examination to the year group to be tested, but there is no procedure to ensure that 'standards' remain constant. The 65 per cent pass mark is a comfortable but utterly misleading statistic when applied to the debate about 'standards' since its currency relies on the assumption that standards in each year remain more or less the same.

In his attempts to reform the Regents examinations, this assumption of standards is one that the Commissioner will probably need to expose to the light of day, since it is predictable that one of the arguments against changing the testing regime will be that it will result in a loss of these supposedly tried and tested standards.

Graduation: grade point average and profile

The Regents examinations and Regents competency tests are all geared towards students' 'graduation' from high school. The process of calculating and certificating graduation is a complex one with several interwoven elements.

The courses that students take – and the associated course-work – must be passed satisfactorily, and the examinations must also be passed satisfactorily. Graduation is then based on the average performance across the whole curriculum, that is, on the 20.5 course units that make up the graduation requirement. This system is therefore more like the German *Abitur* – which is a cross-curricular certification – than GCSE or A-level certificates which certify individual subjects.

However, the use of these graduation certificates for university entrance purposes has a further twist. A student's whole academic profile is laid out in the certificate and this is summarised in a final mark – a grade point average. But additionally, this mark places each student in a 'class position' – in the top 10 per cent, the second 10 per cent, and so on down to the bottom 10 per cent. This has to be scored on the graduation certificate so that a university can see how a student performed in the context of his/her school. This is then further refined so that the school itself is graded by identifying (for example) the percentage of last year's graduates who are now attending four, three- or two-year colleges. A university might then be faced with a choice between two students: one with a grade point average of 66, who was in the top 10 per cent of his class, and in a school where 10 per cent of last year's graduates are in four-year colleges; and one with a grade point average of 78, who was in the third 10 per cent of her graduating class, and in a school where 80 per cent of last year's graduates are in four-year colleges. Which would you choose?

Technology examinations and assessment

At present there is no formal examination for technology in New York State. The two technology courses outlined above – the mandatory junior high school course and the elective senior high school course – do of course require that teachers return an assessment of the performance of the students on the course. But the assessment is simply a teacher assessment based on assignments devised locally by the teacher.

The nature of these assessments should come as no surprise to teachers in the UK who are familiar with project assessment. A number of categories of work are identified from what might be described as the student's portfolio. These are highlighted and categories of excellence loosely outlined in criteria which are then assessed both by the teacher and the pupil, both of whom are also expected to write some extended comment on their work (Figure 8.11). This assessment regime is stiffened somewhat by guidance in the textbook (the *Introduction to Technology* manual prepared by New York State), which prepares a set of questions covering the conceptual areas for each of the TLAs in the book. Readers will see this identified in the final block of marks.

Many of the same features appear in project assessment forms for the elective high school course in principles of engineering, but there is also a discernible addition. In two schools where I saw this programme running, the assessment prioritised the interpersonal role of students working within a design team. The following criteria, for example, were evident in both schools in addition to the normal ones focusing on the technical development of the product and the supporting portfolio:

- reliability and attendance of team members
- conduct and respect for others
- presentation of work to the class
- all team members played an active part in the presentation
- responses to questions handled professionally.

The idea of the design team is well established in these schools and is clearly an ethic that is explicitly encouraged in the course.

A state test for technology?

The State Supervisor for technology is currently striving to establish a state-mandated technology test as the culmination of the junior high school course 'introduction to technology', since the lack of such state-endorsed testing is seen as a major factor in some schools' choosing to ignore the state mandate for the course. And the means to establish the test *may* have arisen through the Goals 2000 project – a federal initiative that New York State has adopted in relation to the development of assessment practices for the new curriculum standards. The new MST curriculum standard in New York State (outlined earlier) is therefore the focus of considerable

Student	Teacher

Sundial Assessment

All written materials attached in a presentable report
0   loose papers, messy papers, missing papers
10   report poorly organised, messy and missing parts
15   neat report and papers, lacking parts and organization
20   neat papers and report complete and well organized

Design: Geometric construction and theme of sundial
0   compass and protractor not used to develop patterns. No sundial theme
10   compass and protractor used to develop patterns. No sundial theme
15   compass and protractor used accurately to develop patterns. Average theme
20   compass and protractor used accurately to develop patterns. Creative theme

Implementation: Construction of sundial
0   sundial incomplete, poor construction
10   sundial complete, but poor quality of work
15   sundial complete, average skill, few mistakes
20   sundial complete, well done, shows much skill

Evaluation: Testing the sundial
0   sundial inaccurate, more than 1 hour off standard time
10   sundial somewhat inaccurate, within 1 hour of standard time
15   sundial accurate, within 30 mins of standard time
20   sundial very accurate, within 10 mins of standard time

Technology Learning Assignment (TLA) Report
0   no attempt at drawing, questions not answered
10   drawing incomplete, questions incomplete, sloppy
15   drawing and questions complete, a few mistakes
20   drawing complete in color, questions complete, well done, attention to detail

Totals (out of 100)

Student comments ....

Teacher comments ....

Figure 8.11 Project assessment framework for the junior high school course.

development in assessment, and I was able to observe a training day for teacher assessors where the pilot materials were being explored.

The basis for testing is extended tasks which generally take one to two weeks to complete and which involve students explicitly integrating their maths, science and technology in solving problems. The tests are designed to operate at three levels: grade 4–5; grade 8; and grade 11–12, as explained in the MST pilot assessment training pack:

All the tasks emphasise the performance dimensions of
    scientific inquiry
    mathematical analysis
    technological design

use of resources
communication of ideas
teamwork

The tasks have a group component as students work together to brainstorm ideas, perform investigations, and model and synthesize solutions. . . . Tasks also have individual written components in which students describe how they went about their work, why they chose their solution, what they learned, and what they would change if they did the task again.

(New York State Education Department 1996)

The focus of the extended task was on design for devices that maintain the temperature of contained items – keeping them cool or hot – and this took the following form at the three levels

grade 4–5   'ice smart'   design, build and test the effectiveness
                                of small ice boxes
grade 8   'keep it cool'   design and build a container to pre-
                                serve ice for 24 hours
grade 11–12   'cool down'   design and build a container for the
                                transfer of 'organs' for surgery.

(ibid)

The grade 8 test is seen as the priority for technology, since it could coincide with the end of the mandatory junior high school course and thereby act as a success measure for it. A range of materials is provided and the project moves through stages of engagement, exploration, explanation, elaboration and evaluation. It would represent a really good model of integrated curriculum activity and could consequently provide a highly valid mode of assessment. But the experience of Standard Assessment Task development in the UK suggests that it will be much more difficult to secure good reliability in such an open assessment.

Mindful of this problem, the approach to reliability is more through the individual questions that follow the activity, and these questions focus on the following qualities:

• drawing and analysing the central features of the design solution
• identifying strengths and weaknesses in the design
• listing factors that a designer would have to bear in mind (e.g. value for money, durability)
• identifying the design priorities evident in existing equivalent products.

This combination of open but structured project activity followed by specifically targeted questions that relate to it and require students to demonstrate a greater depth of conceptual understanding may provide a model of assessment that takes practice forward in New York State. The pilot materials were well received by the teachers, but I suspect this it is merely the first step on a very long trail.

As I have attempted to show in this chapter, there are two overriding pressures on the education system in New York State: the decentralised, localised nature of much of the decision-making for schools; and the tradition of – and widespread faith in – blind, multiple-choice testing. Initiatives such as I have outlined above provide excellent models of curriculum practice and (if properly implemented) could also provide effective assessments of students' capabilities. But given the traditions and structures in New York State, any such development must fight a real uphill battle to achieve widespread acceptance and implementation.

Notes

1 Readers outside the USA need to keep a sense of scale in this debate. The USA is huge – with almost as great a land area of the whole of Europe. And the population density in the USA is low; some 30 people per square mile, compared to 300 people per square mile in Europe. So it is perhaps justifiably felt that too much decision-making at the centre might be thought of as remote from the reality of people's lives.

2 This funding pattern may in some circumstances be varied – for example, in 'low-wealth' school districts, the state funding may rise to as much as 90%.

3 These conflicts would not be dissimilar to those in the UK between the central DfEE and the LEAs. It is interesting to note, however, that the trend in the USA is towards devolved and decentralised policy-making, whilst in the UK policy-making has been centralised to the point of marginalising the LEAs.

4 The Board of Regents has jurisdiction over the 7000 schools, 248 colleges and universities, 7000 libraries, 750 museums and 25 public broadcasting facilities. In addition to overseeing the Regents examinations – which is the school leaving examination akin to A levels or Highers in the UK – the Board also has authority over the licensing of teachers and 38 other professions.

5 As we shall see later, it is explicitly designed to have (and maintain) this pass rate.

6 The foundations of multiple-choice testing and the associated criticisms of it have been marshalled in a wonderfully ironic work by Samuelson (1987), Was early mental testing (a) racist inspired, (b) objective science, (c) a technology for democracy, (d) the origin of multiple choice exams, (e) none of the above? Mark the RIGHT Answer.

7 The SATs for university entrance are not a state requirement, even though they are almost universally used by universities.

8 This technique would have been similar to APU procedures in the UK.

9 His views on assessment and testing – and many other facets of education policy in New York State – were outlined to me in an interview in March 1996.

10 Regents examinations do not rely totally on multiple-choice testing. Sixty per cent of marks are typically given for multiple-choice components, and a further 40 per cent for essay-style responses in which teachers need to exercise judgment in applying marking criteria. Commonly, the State Education Department

– which runs the Regents examinations – will call in the marked papers from 10 per cent of schools in a designated subject and will scrutinise 10 per cent of those called in. This random check is therefore of 1 per cent of any test cohort and is used to ensure consistency in the allocation of marks – though the process does not lead to any adjustment in the marks. If a discrepancy is found, then the teacher's marks will still stand for that year but the school will be notified of the need for more consistency.

nine

Taiwan: Republic of China

Taiwan: a province of China

Taiwan is an island approximately half the size of England; 400 km north–south and 200 km east–west (Figure 9.1). It lies approximately 150 km off the east coast of China, across the Taiwan Straits. There is a complex relationship between them. China claims Taiwan as one of its provinces, and this is reflected on individuals' business cards and schools' and colleges' letter heads, all of which refer to 'Taiwan R.O.C.'. But increasingly Taiwan sees itself as an independent nation. However, the Chinese government in Beijing is seeking to dissuade Taiwan from any moves towards what it sees as independence, and the tension between the two in March 1996 (with troop movements on the mainland and gunboats in the Straits) was attributable to the Chinese government seeking to influence the outcome of the first ever democratic election of a new president of Taiwan. Despite this activity, the Taiwanese people elected a president who campaigned on a strong platform of independence.

Taiwan has a population of about 21 million, crammed into one-third of the island, the other two-thirds consisting of uninhabitable mountains which run north–south down the central eastern section of the island and rise to almost 3900 m. The eastern side of the island is rocky, with precipitous cliffs falling into the very deep water of the Pacific Ocean. The western side of the island, facing mainland China, is a flat coastal plain where all the population is concentrated. The towns are very crowded and traffic congestion and industrial pollution create serious problems.

Cultural transformation

Taiwan strikes me as a cultural paradox. On one level, it is a thrusting, aggressive, industrial manufacturing economy. On another, it is a deeply religious country, and Buddhism and Taoism – both peaceful, non-assertive

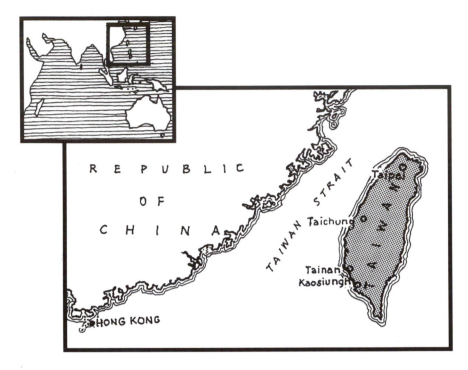

Figure 9.1 Taiwan.

religions – are the established faiths that are actively practised, in innumerable temples, by a significant majority of the population. A further section of the population consists of active Christians – a legacy of successive invasions (and much missionary work) by the Spanish, Dutch and British.

This paradox surfaces all the time, for life in Taiwan is chaotic and ferociously busy, and yet harmony and patience are the touchstones of the major religions: live and let live. Indeed, a major principle of Taoism is the concept of *wuwei*, 'doing nothing', and its central idea is to remain humble, passive, non-assertive and non-aggressive: 'Do nothing, and nothing will not be done' (Laozi, sixth century BC). It is hardly the stuff of commercial and industrial dynamism, and yet the nation is dynamic – in a passive kind of way. I cannot explain this paradox, and neither could anyone I spoke to.

Americanised China

Another interesting paradox is reflected in the fact that whilst Taiwan is historically and culturally a part of China, it is increasingly a bed-fellow of the USA. It has the dollar as currency, yellow taxi cabs (as in New York City), an American education system of elementary and then junior and senior high schools, and a democratic presidential election. When I was put on 'hold' on the telephone on one occasion, the music that kicked in was 'Home, home on the range'! CNN broadcasts US news throughout Taiwan and *USA Today* is the standard newspaper delivered to hotel rooms.

But this does not mean that Taiwan is like America, for in many ways it is the opposite. America worships the individual whereas Taiwan is centred on communal responsibility, conformity and standardisation. The US education system is the most individually devolved system I have ever studied; the Taiwan education system is the most centralised and conformist.

A thirst for education

Taiwan invests heavily in education. It currently spends 15 per cent of all its national tax revenue on it,[1] and additionally (on average) 50 per cent of all local taxes are spent by communities on their schools (the statutory minimum is 35 per cent). All the people to whom I spoke are entirely in support of this. Education is highly valued, and all parents have high educational aspirations for their children.

This thirst for learning is linked by many to the philosophy of Confucius, arguably China's greatest philosopher and the first teacher (500 BC) to open his school to pupils based on their eagerness to learn rather than the nobility of their birth. On three separate occasions I had the same words of Confucius quoted to me: 'If you are my teacher for a day, you are my parent for life.' This respect for education has the effect of making teachers highly valued members of society,[2] and parents instil in their children the need for obedience to their teachers.

There is an almost fanatical pursuit of learning in Taiwan. Pupils study for long hours in school (from 8 a.m. until 4.30 p.m. on weekdays, and on Saturday mornings). Total *teaching* time is typically 39 hours per week, and then there are more hours (often many more hours) of homework. Parents apply pressure to succeed, and pupils compete quite openly with their classmates. It would be very unusual for a pupil to present discipline problems for a teacher, partly because of the learning ethic that pervades the whole society and partly because of the respect that is automatically bestowed on a teacher. One of the consequences of this respect – which becomes obvious when observing a class – is that it is very unusual for pupils to ask questions in the formal teaching setting since this is seen as tantamount to challenging authority. Pupils sit attentively in rows and display a very strong tendency towards patience, tolerance and obedience. The whole atmosphere is highly conformist.[3]

A twin-track system

There are nine years of compulsory schooling incorporating the elementary school (age 6–12) and the junior high school (12–15). Thereafter (broadly speaking) a twin-track system comes into play which directs pupils into

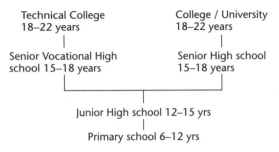

Figure 9.2 The twin-track senior high school system.

the senior high school or the vocational high school (15–18) (Figure 9.2). These are fee-paying schools, since education is not compulsory at this level. The vast majority of pupils continue their studies into senior or vocational high school. Access to these high schools is by successful graduation from the junior high school and by the Joint Entrance Examination (JEE). The details of this examination are discussed later, but for our immediate purposes it is necessary only to be aware of how the results of the JEE are used.

All students in Taiwan take this examination on the same two days in early July, and the results place students in a clear pecking order. Those with the highest marks may go to the senior high schools and those with lower marks may get to a vocational high school. The latter pupils are not attending vocational schools because they are more experienced or gifted in the practical world, but rather because they did not do sufficiently well in the JEE to win a place in the senior high school.

Balancing the two tracks

The vocational high schools have been systematically developed in Taiwan to support the burgeoning manufacturing industries of the last twenty years. As recently as ten years ago, the balance of pupils in high schools would have been 70 per cent in the vocational high school and 30 per cent in the senior high school. Today, the proportions are nearer to 60 per cent and 40 per cent respectively, and the declared policy of the Taiwanese government for the next few years is to get the proportion to 50 per cent in each, raising the general level of education of the population and biasing this away from the vocational schools.

The explanation for this policy lies in the post-industrial aspirations of Taiwan. Much of the manufacturing that made Taiwan wealthy in the 1970s and 1980s has already moved over to mainland China, where labour and other resources are now much cheaper. Responding to this trend, Taiwan is developing new, high-technology industries that need higher levels of understanding and skill than would normally have been present in vocational

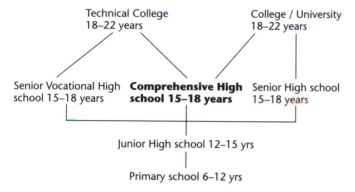

Figure 9.3 The new comprehensive high schools will allow students to follow a balanced course involving both practical and academic subjects.

high schools. The Commissioner of Education for Taiwan is quite clear that the changing economic position of the country requires a changed approach to the priorities of schooling.[4] He points out that a nation must examine its resources and plan accordingly. Taiwan has no natural (mineral) resources, nor any natural hydrocarbon energy supplies. Its only natural resource is its people and he is seeking to maximise the level at which they can work. He is quite convinced – and no one I spoke to disagreed – that vocationally trained production-line workers is not what Taiwan needs any longer. Or at least they are not needed in anything like the numbers that were needed ten years ago.

Related to this issue, it is widely recognised that Taiwan and mainland China need to maintain a strong partnership. As the Chinese economy strengthens, it will be able to benefit from the education and expertise that already exists in Taiwan. And reciprocally, the large-scale, resource-hungry manufacturing that Taiwan finds increasingly difficult to sustain can be located in China. Taiwan would like to see itself as the high-skills, high-technology counterpart to mainland China, which increasingly will cater for the mass manufacturing and heavy industry from which Taiwan originally created its wealth.

A strategy for change

The strategy for this transformation of schooling is (progressively) to change vocational high schools into 'comprehensive' high schools – the first of these have been opened in 1996 and many more are planned (Figure 9.3). The point of these comprehensive schools is that pupils will be able – and encouraged – to select some of their courses from academic areas of study and others from the more practical domains. In the current school system these are completely separated, and this is increasingly seen as a weakness by the education authorities in Taiwan.

Defining the curriculum

The curriculum is highly centralised in Taiwan. The Ministry of Education takes responsibility for ensuring that the curriculum covers the same, approved material throughout all schools of the same type. There are many sets of heavy books that define the 'curriculum and equipment standards' for all subjects in the curriculum and for all levels of schools.

In each subject the 'standard' is drawn up by an expert committee appointed by the ministry. This committee draws heavily from those who are perceived to be the educational leaders in the subject, typically university professors and experienced teachers of the subject. For the standards in vocational high schools there will also be representation from industry. Once the standard has been drafted and approved by the ministry, it is published to all teachers of the subject and will remain the established course for the next ten years, at which time another review will take place.

A 'standard' deals with a single subject, but, since Taiwan uses the American system of presenting a discipline as a menu of free-standing courses, the standard details all the courses that make up the subject. Each course is presented in terms of the following four categories:

- goals;
- teaching time per week;
- syllabus outline (a list of teaching units and a content outline for each unit, each typically for a teaching week);
- guidance notes for teachers.

The standard is a comprehensive document and teachers follow it carefully. In effect it does their course planning for them, even if it does not provide the detail of every lesson. Additional textbooks are of course needed by teachers to develop the detail of lessons, but even these textbooks must first be approved by the ministry and many of them are deliberately commissioned by the ministry. If textbooks do not have the stamp of approval from the ministry Bureau of Textbooks, no school would buy them. The standards therefore ensure that all teachers of the course do (broadly) the same thing, and the supporting textbooks ensure that even the lesson materials look much the same wherever the course is taught. As we shall see below, the use of the standard is enforced by regular visits of ministry-licensed supervisors.

Taken together, the standard and its enforcement regime effectively stifle most curriculum development on the part of teachers in schools. Theoretically it is possible for teachers to develop their own courses so long as they conform to the ministry goals, but in reality the vast majority of teachers and schools do what the standard tells them to do. However, it is recognised that the curriculum needs to evolve, and usually every ten years (on a rolling programme) the standards are revised by another appointed committee of experts.

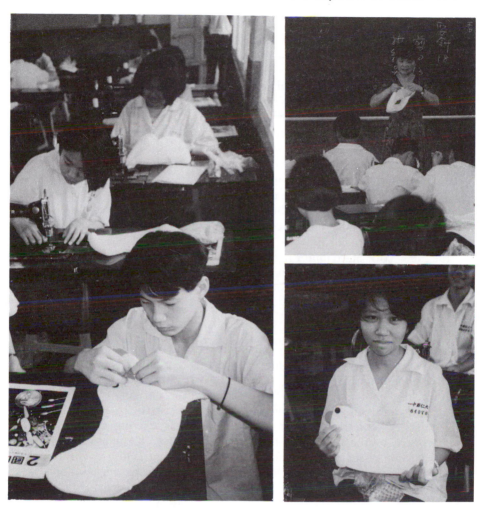

Figure 9.4 Pupils in a junior high school class all making an identical 'chicken' pyjama case with instruction from the teacher.

The technology curriculum

There are two quite different approaches to technology in Taiwan, the educational and the vocational, and I shall outline them in that order.

There is little technology in the curriculum of elementary schools, and what there is arises through supplementary activities in subjects like art and craft. But through junior high school and senior high school, 'industrial arts' is the standard. This is very similar to industrial arts as defined in the USA (see Chapter 8). There is lots of industrialised craft activity in wood and metal and a great deal of engineering drawing and architectural drawing. These programmes in Taiwan are so similar to those in the US system that I have chosen not to detail them here, since the reader can obtain an adequate picture from Chapter 8.

There is, however, a more compelling reason for not wasting valuable space in talking about these outdated programmes in the context of Taiwan, since they are about to disappear in the implementation of the latest ten year rewrite of the standard for industrial arts. More than two years ago, the ministry put together the curriculum committee to reconsider the industrial arts standard, and the committee concluded that the whole thing was outdated. And it has produced a completely new model of technology for Taiwan schools: *living technology*.

It is gratifying to report that this new model of technology education is far closer to that which we would recognise as design and technology in the UK and also like the best technology practice in New York State. Indeed the Ministry of Education has taken – and translated into Chinese – the New York State junior high school programme text, *Introduction to Technology*, that is outlined in Chapter 8.

Living technology

Why the change?

I have already indicated the fundamental redirection of education that is under way in Taiwan. Policy-makers see the economy as needing fewer low-level, industrially skilled workers and a generally higher level of education for the whole population. With 40 per cent of current cohorts able to enter undergraduate degree programmes at university or technical college, the ministry sees this as quite inadequate and is striving to raise it to 50 per cent by the year 2000 and higher thereafter.[5] It therefore projects an expansion of senior high school courses and a contraction in vocational high school courses. The development of comprehensive high schools is another aspect of the same trend – essentially allowing students from what were once vocational schools to take more 'academic' courses.

Within the junior high schools and the expanding sector of senior high schools, attention has now been focused on the nature of the technology curriculum that is appropriate for these students. The traditional Taiwanese link between technology in schools and industrial/vocational employment has been significantly weakened. Students working through junior high school and subsequently graduating from senior high schools might wish to be bankers or lawyers or nurses or commercial traders. What kind of technology curriculum should they experience?

Dr David Lee, Dean of the Faculty of Arts at the National Taiwan Normal University, was appointed to the curriculum committee to reconsider the industrial arts curriculum. He describes the thinking of the committee as seeking to create a technology programme for the the whole of society, regardless of what students choose to do subsequently. The title 'living technology' is meant to reflect the fact that technology is a human creation for human purposes, and the new programme should help all pupils to understand technology better and to develop their creative and critical faculties through engaging with it. The emphasis is on problem-solving; design and development; and on autonomous decision-making for all pupils. It is no longer the traditional industrial arts, and neither is it vocational training and a passport to a job. It is personal enrichment, enhanced understanding and creative engagement. In short, it is education.

What does it look like?
As I have already observed, all teaching in the compulsory years of school-ing is in mixed-ability classes. The very brightest pupils work alongside slow learners – in maths and languages as well as in more practical areas – and workshop activity is project-based much as it would be in the UK. Projects in year 7, for example, typically last about six weeks, for two hours a week. The new programme is intended to be in place for junior high schools (grade 7) in September 1997, and it is intended that it will grow through the system into senior high schools. It is also growing down into elementary schools.

The ministry recognises that this new curriculum will present a major hurdle for teachers. It requires a quite different pedagogy from that with which teachers are currently familiar. Teachers in the UK who have experi-enced the transition from craft teaching to design and technology will be familiar with the problems that are about to hit the technology teachers in Taiwan. The transition from craft teacher (who knows all the skills and answers) to technology teacher (who encourages pupils to think and make decisions for themselves) will be far harder in Taiwan than it was in the UK. In Taiwan pupils do not make decisions – they do as they are told. One can envisage many difficulties as teachers try to manage the transition and pupils seek to learn a completely different way of relating to their teachers.

To support the process of change, the ministry is currently encouraging the development of textbooks and other resources that will in effect present teachers with an 'off-the-shelf' three-year course for junior high school. Dr Lung-Sheng Lee of the National Taiwan Normal University is heading a development team of teachers in preparing such a book, and he sees it as a course with 12 'units' spanning the seventh, eighth and ninth grades (Table 9.1). Each of the units, he believes, must be exemplified through project activities, and some exemplars are detailed in the book. The draft of the book (and its associated units and activities) is of course in Chinese, and I can only apologise if the translation results in some strange-sounding activities.

The central new feature of all these activities is the demands they make on the critical and creative powers of pupils. It is no longer good enough simply to make products in *craft* mode. They now need to be designed and manufactured and the surrounding technology needs to be understood. Whilst design and technology teachers in the UK might be somewhat shocked at the outdated nature of current industrial arts courses in Taiwan, they

Figure 9.5 (a) Exploring powered transport.

(b) 2D into 3D

Table 9.1 The study units for living technology in years 7–9

Grade	Unit	Activity
7	Information and communication	'It's foolish but you are smart'
	Blueprint for design	'Recover your appearance'
	Computer applications	'A drawing says more than a thousand words'
	Construction and life	'A lighthouse in the huge sea'
8	Graphics and communication	'Red plum flowers never fall'
	Introduction to manufacturing	'The century war'
	Manufacturing and life	'Covering everything'
	Designing and making	'Musical sounds everywhere'
9	Exploring energy and transportation	'Make it move'
	Energy and power	'Electrical vehicle'
	Electronics and communication	'Back to the future'
	The world of transportation	'Loveboat'

would be far more comfortable with the textbook Dr Lee's development group are working on.

It is important to emphasise that this living technology curriculum is not yet in place in Taiwan. The new curriculum standard has been approved by the Ministry of Education, but its implementation is in the very early stages of development and it is not due for general distribution until September 1997. The development of the textbooks and other teaching materials is currently taking place around the few centres of excellence that exist in the schools and are being stage-managed by the institutions of teacher education.

At the Hualien Teachers College, for example, which specialises in training teachers for elementary schools, I saw some very interesting examples of how the planned curriculum will 'backwash' into elementary schools. Student teachers were developing projects for pupils in grades 5 and 6, and there was some excellent work (for example) with windmills and kites (Figure 9.6).

In the context of these projects, the really noteworthy feature of the work is the approach the college is taking in developing the pedagogy of its student teachers. The teachers' lesson plans and resources for pupils take the form of Chinese banners, like beautifully ornamented flip-charts. In the kite project, successive layers of the banner reveal the *history* of kites, the *science* of kites, the *materials* for kites and so on (Figure 9.7). There is also a layer concerned with helping pupils with the procedure for designing and making their own kite. And at the end there is a layer the requires the children to undertake a thorough evaluation of the kite they have designed and made. I shall examine this assessment aspect in more detail later in the chapter.

So the technology curriculum of the junior high school and the senior high school is gradually coming of age in Taiwan. Craft work is passing into

Figure 9.6 Windmills and kites.

history and being replaced by a more appropriate and a more demanding programme of living technology. But what of the second strand of technology curriculum – the vocational?

Vocational Technology

If one asks to see technology in schools in Taiwan, one is not automatically taken to junior and senior high schools: one is taken to the vocational high schools. In fact, I had to work quite hard to get into a junior and senior high school because my hosts assumed that the most interesting technology in Taiwan was in the vocational high schools. And it is true that these are awe-inspiring places with phenomenal facilities and prodigious budgets. And their principals and teaching staff – as well as ministry and city officials – are immensely proud of what they have achieved.

In the last twenty years, Taiwan has spent billions of dollars on these schools. As one indication of this, a single vocational high school in the city of Taipei – with 3000 students – has an annual budget of £12 million; and the city has another six of these schools. The government and the city education authorities spend far more money on these schools than they do on their senior high schools – by a factor of about 3 : 1. This illustrates the priority that Taiwan has placed on vocational education, and its commitment to it. The 'brightest' students – in the senior high schools – have far less money spent on them: all they need is desks, chairs and some basic facilities. By contrast, the vocational schools have to operate at an industry standard of equipment and training.

Of the seven vocational high schools in Taipei, five are 'industrial vocational' (predominantly boys); and two are 'commercial vocational' (predominantly girls). In other parts of Taiwan one also comes across 'agricultural vocational' schools and even 'marine vocational' schools. All vocational high schools are for those aged 15–18, and hence are beyond the formal leaving age. Students therefore pay tuition fees – typically about £100 per semester.

It is one of the oddities of the Taiwanese system of education that progression from one level to the next – from junior high to senior high or from senior high to college – does not depend on pupil performance in the school programmes. It depends entirely upon examination performance, and everyone takes the same examinations. To 'graduate' from junior high school pupils have satisfactorily to complete their courses, but their graduation certificate is of no importance at all if they want to proceed to a senior high school. The Joint Entrance Exam (JEE) holds the key to advancement, and – as we shall see – there is no technology component in the JEE so there is no telling whether students have any technological ability.

The curriculum of these vocational schools is quite different from the dated industrial arts of the junior and senior high schools (Figure 9.8). It is designed to take in pupils who have just graduated from junior high school, but without any serious understanding or skill in technical areas.

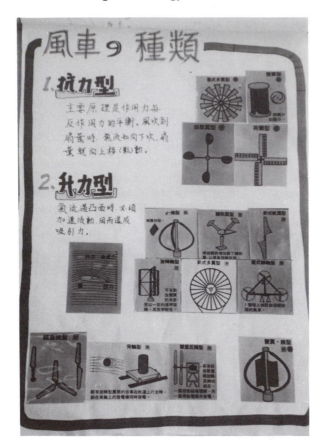

Figure 9.7 (a) The science of windmills.

And in the course of their three years they become sufficiently skilled and knowledgeable in a vocational area that industry will employ them.

In vocational high schools, the curriculum is half vocational and half general. The general components comprise courses in Chinese, English, maths, social studies and science, and these are the basic subjects of the JEE which enabled pupils to get their place in vocational or senior high school (see below). The other half of the curriculum is vocational, and students identify – at the outset – what vocational field they will enter. All their courses are then concentrated in this field. Students study 14 courses each semester for two or three hours per week each. Seven of their courses are vocational and seven general.

When a student enters vocational high school, s/he opts for one of the many vocational departments in which s/he might specialise. At Ta-An vocational high school in Taipei the choice was between:

mechanical technique
automobile technique

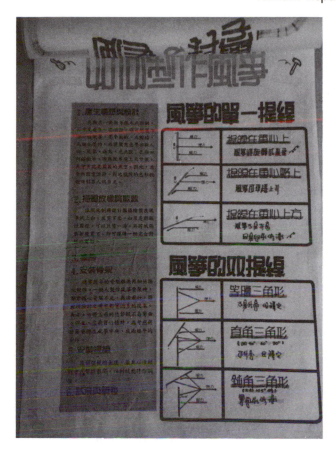

(b) The science of kites.

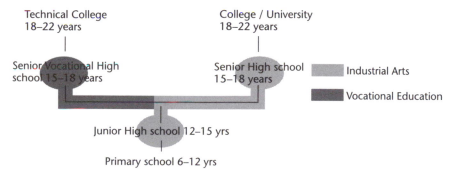

Figure 9.8 The two strands of technology in Taiwanese schools.

sheet metal technique
electrical technique
electronic technique
air conditioning and refrigeration
computer technique
control technique
architecture
printing

At Taichung vocational high school, the curriculum was divided into four clusters: electrical, mechanical, construction and chemical.

The choice of department is not a straightforward option, however, but is rather based on a priority option system: those with the highest marks in the JEE get first choice; and so on down to those with the lowest marks. Some departments (such as computer technology) have high prestige and serious academic requirements and hence attract the highest-fliers. This department had an average JEE score (1995) of 627 out of a maximum 700. By contrast, the sheet metal department had an average JEE score of 555.

Once in a vocational department, students stay within it for the whole three years. They enter as novices with nothing but the experience of industrial arts in junior high school, and they emerge, potentially, as certificated, industry-standard technicians. The technical/vocational half of the curriculum is therefore highly focused from the outset. In the first-year programme all courses (both in general education and in the specialism) are compulsory; in the second year 10 per cent may be optional and in the final year 30 per cent are optional. At the end of three years, the graduation certificate, in association with the industry certification that they can acquire at the same time, would get these students immediately into industrially related employment.

As an illustration of the kinds of courses that students would study in these vocational areas, the mechanical technique department at Ta-An vocational high school provides the following menu of courses:

	Theoretical courses	Workshop courses
Year 1	Manufacturing processes Mechanical materials Introduction to electricity Mechanical drawing	Basic machine (fitting, turning, sheet metal, casting etc.)
Year 2	Machine elements Industrial safety Introduction to pneumatics/hydraulics Jigs and fixtures Mechanical measurement Mechanical drawing	Machine practice (lathe, mill, shaping, grinding)

Year 3	Mechanics	Operation of machine tools
	Shop management	Automated machines
	Numerical control	Heat treatment
	Introduction to machine design	Assembly and testing
	Mechanical drawing	Maintenance

The circumstances in which these courses run are remarkable to the eye of someone brought up in English schools. Theoretical courses are taught in groups of 40, with each pupil assigned a desk; desks are arranged in neat rows and face the board from where the teacher conducts the instruction. The course of instruction comes straight from 'the book', which is one of the approved textbooks for teaching the approved 'standard' course. The teacher works through the book systematically and the instruction is rein-forced (I use the word advisedly) by regular testing (multiple-choice, true–false, fill-in-the-blank testing). None of this testing requires pupils to think or make judgments for themselves, and neither does the instruction. It is pure input by the book/instructor and pure output in the tests.

When it comes to the workshop sessions, it is even more astonishing – for here you see the level of investment that the government has poured into vocational high schools. The student group of 40 is divided in half, so the workshops are designed for 20. But in the mechanical technique workshop courses this means that there is a workshop with (for example) 20 identical, industry-standard, computer numerically controlled universal milling machines (Figure 9.9). And these are not toys – they are the real thing, standing 2.5 m tall and capable of real industrial production. Next door is a similar workshop with 20 of the latest centre lathes. The point is that all students experience the same work, on the same machines, from the same instruction book.

The electrical technique courses are exactly the same in terms of their organisation, though the content of course is different. In this case, the workshops will be equipped with 20 electronic control consoles, or 20 sets of circuits linked to 20 oscilloscopes (Figure 9.10). Sometimes the work-shop activities involve students working in pairs, but this will only be a sub-set of the lesson and they soon return to their own stations and their own equipment. The computer technique workshops would make a UK teacher salivate. They are equipped to just the same level of excellence, with 20 of the most recent high-specification multimedia machines.

The pedagogy in the vocational high schools is frighteningly simple. The teachers instruct, and it is up to the students to learn. All students get the same chance, because they are all taught the same thing in the same way. They also have to demonstrate their learning in the same standardised tests that are all marked by machine. The Taiwanese are proud of the efficiency of their vocational high schools, which are truly production lines to service the industry that has created the wealth of Taiwan.

But it is interesting that the Taiwanese education authorities are begin-ning to draw back from these programmes. They recognise only too well

Figure 9.9 (a) A mechanical technique workshop;

(b) a typical product.

that whilst they produce very efficient operatives, they do not produce imaginative, creative and exciting youngsters who are good at thinking for themselves. And increasingly these are the qualities that the authorities believe post-industrial Taiwan needs to foster in its youngsters.

Pupil assessment in Taiwan

The formal assessment of pupil performance in Taiwan is based around the transition points from one school to another (Figure 9.11). This takes the form of 'graduation', not unlike the situation in the USA. This graduation

Figure 9.10 (a) An electrical technique workshop;

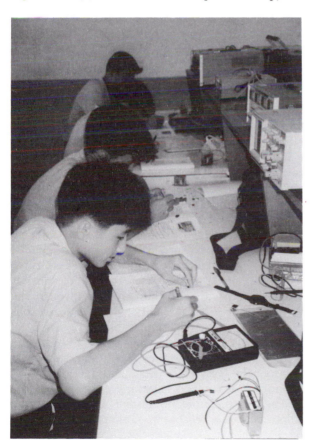

(b) students working from the manual.

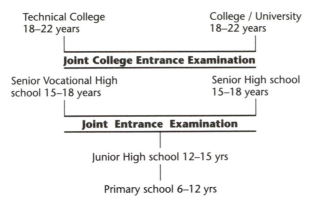

Figure 9.11 The examinations system in Taiwan.

exists in a very simple form at the end of primary school, and is more formalised and developed at the end of junior high school and senior high school. However, the high assessment stakes are quite remote from this process of graduation and centre on 'objective' testing which first occurs at the transition point into senior high school, and subsequently at the transition point into university.

Graduation from junior high school

All students from elementary schools progress automatically into their local junior high school at age 12 and most graduate from it at age 15. This graduation is based on marks from all subjects studied in the school. However, whilst the curriculum is centrally mandated by the ministry, the assessment arrangements are very flexible and are based on the preferred practice of teachers in the schools.

In technology in Darzen junior high school in Kaohsiung, all projects (which were all very craft-like and under the formal banner of industrial arts) were marked by the teacher out of 100, based on three marks accumulated during the pupil's progress through the project. The assessments covered the following broad areas of work: the early stages (marking out, etc.); the middle (making); and the final stages (finishing). These three assessments are aggregated into a single mark out of 100 for the project and this mark is further aggregated with all other projects through the year. The pupil then ends up with a percetage mark which is again converted into a 'year mark' on a five-point scale and subsequently into an overall mark for the three years work in industrial arts. This mark is then aggregated with the pupil's marks from other subjects and she ends up with a single 'graduation grade' between 5 (best) and 1 (worst).

There is no formal moderation of teachers' marking either within the school or across schools. There is therefore no system for checking the specifics of the marks allocated by a teacher to any particular pupil.

However, there is a system of annual inspections and these are used to help teachers to orientate their standards to an 'inspector' standard. These inspections are based on a selection of work and are therefore inspections of the *teachers*, not of the pupils. Any misassessment identified within the sample by the inspectors does not result in changed grades for pupils, but in advice and possibly further training for the teacher.

One has to say that the assessment system in Taiwan schools is somewhat relaxed. One teacher and school may be doing things very differently from the next teacher and school. And this relaxed and idiosyncratic system is explained only when one realises that it is largely irrelevant for a majority of pupils. Pupils' graduation marks count for nothing of any great significance except for those who leave school at the end of junior high school. For this minority, low-ability group, the graduation marks might affect the view taken by potential employers.

But for the vast majority of pupils, who aspire to a place in senior high school, vocational high school, or junior college, the only thing that counts is the JEE. Everyone knows that a graduation certificate (even an excellent one) from junior high school will not get you into these establishments, and that good marks in the JEE will. This is so much the case, that pupils at the upper end of the junior high school will routinely ignore the formal requirements of the curriculum – e.g. in physical education and industrial arts – since these do not figure in the JEE and are therefore not important. Everything depends on getting a good mark in the JEE, so there is much cramming and practising of examinations, and publishers get rich selling books full of exam papers from the previous ten years.

Joint Entrance Examination

This examination, at the end of junior high school, is the first formal assessment of pupil performance in Taiwan. The examinations are run by the city authorities for all their junior high schools and the results will determine which pupils go to senior high schools, which go to senior vocational high schools, which go to junior college, and which leave school.

The examination is broadly based in five subjects: Chinese; English; maths; social studies; and natural science. The examinations are described as 'objective', by which is meant that the questions are closed (always with a correct answer) and pupils respond in one of several modes, typically:

- by identifying true or false assertions
- by filling in the blanks in a statement from a menu of possibilities
- by identifying the 'right' response to a question when given multiple choices.

I am indebted to the Kaohsiung supplementary school (a 'crammer' for extra work at night for those who want to pass the exams) for the following samples from the English exam paper:

Fill in the blank.
1 Jean: ....? Sue: I am going home.
   a. What are you doing
   b. When will you go
   c. Where are you going
   d. How often are you going home

Which is the nearest in meaning?
2 If I had some money I could buy a boat.
   a. I have some money so I can buy a boat
   b. I bought a boat because I had some money
   c. I didn't have money, so I couldn't buy a boat
   d. I have no money, so I can't buy boat

Both these questions are intended to be unambiguous and have a single right answer. For the record, the answers are (c) and (d), respectively.

The pupils' marks are aggregated across all five subjects in the JEE, though the subjects are not of equal weighting for the final overall performance. The final aggregated score is composed out of a possible

200	for Chinese
100	for English
120	for maths
140	for social science
<u>140</u>	for science
700	

A very high level of performance – say, 625 out of 700 – would enable a pupil to take the pick of schools and courses at senior high school. Students who score around 570 out of 700 will probably not get into senior high school but might expect to get a place in a vocational high school. Those who score 520 might just get into vocational high school, but only if they opt for an unpopular or non-prestigious department. As one example of the significance of these scores, the Ta-An Vocational High School has ten departments, and the following represent the average scores of their students in the JEE for 1995:

Mechanical	593
Electrical	619
Sheet metal	555
Computer	627
Automotive	572

One of the ironies of the JEE system is that it controls access into all forms of technical/vocational study at high school and yet it does not even pretend to offer any measure of performance or aptitude in technical matters. It is a purely academic set of written examinations, or perhaps one should rather call them 'tick-box' examinations. The examinations are totally devoid of questions or activities that challenge the judgment or critical thinking processes of students.

Surprisingly, the lack of any technical dimension to the tests is not seen as a problem by the principals or the department heads in the vocational high schools. They accept the examination for what it is, and believe that it is fair because it is 'the same for everyone'. Their courses are self-standing and pupils can start from scratch.

Senior high school graduation

At the end of the three year high-school programme (years 10–12) pupils 'graduate', and the process is similar to graduation from junior high school. The pupils will accumulate course-work and test marks for all their courses throughout a semester and will thereby generate a 'semester average' which will be aggregated into a 'six-semester' final grade. This will be supplemented with marks for 'attitude', 'group work', PE and 'military training'. The whole profile is presented on a graduation certificate and amounts to a descriptive account of pupils' performance in high school.

In the vocational high school, this graduation certificate can be supplemented by a form of industry certification that allows pupils to gain immediate entry to industry on the basis of certificated skill levels. The award of these certificates is operated by industry itself and not by the schools, though the schools facilitate the taking of the necessary skill tests. These tests exist at three levels – A, B and C – and most pupils take and achieve level C (the lowest). Somewhat fewer achieve level B, and very few achieve level A certification during high school.

This industrial certification – along with the graduation certificates – has real credibility with employers. But it cuts no ice with colleges or universities, and the vast majority of high school graduates desire a place at university or technical college. To get into these institutions students have (once again) to go through the mill of academic testing for the Joint College Entrance Examination. Their graduation certificates and industrial training certificates are useful only if they do not go to college or university.

Joint College Entrance Examination (JCEE)

This is the sole means through which all students are selected for higher education. In 1995, 125,000 students took the examinations, competing for 60,000 places. The examination is divided broadly into two classes; one for entry to liberal arts/humanities courses and one for entry to science courses. The components of the examination are as follows:

Group 1   Chinese, English, Three Principles,[6] history, geography, maths
Group 2   Chinese, English, Three Principles, physics, chemistry, maths.

The examinations take place on the same three days in July all over Taiwan and the format of the examinations is very similar to the JEE: multiple-choice tests, true–false tests, and fill-in-the-blank tests. The examination is highly competitive, and once again students often engage the services of 'crammer' institutions to prepare them with hundreds of hours of practice at these tests.

Once the examinations have been sat and marked (largely by machine), the students are informed of their final aggregate score and are then asked to list a series of options for the university/college they would like to attend and the course they would like to take in it. Thereafter the computer software takes over. It places the students with the best results first, giving them their first choice, and it works down the list until all the university and college departments have filled their allocated numbers. Once this point is reached, the rest of the students are informed that they have not gained a place this year. One of the obvious consequences of this system is that a university department has no idea which students it is to receive until the computer has done its work. No one is interviewed. Another consequence is that a student who did badly (for example) in history in the JCEE could end up studying history at university. If his aggregate score was good enough and if history was one of his options (perhaps option 33) then the computer could make that selection.

On the other hand, one of the obvious benefits of the Taiwan system is that it is completely non-discriminatory. Selections are based solely on test scores and student options. Because there is no interview – and no direct contact with the potential students – there is no chance of gender, race or other forms of discrimination muddying the water. The Taiwanese would be very unhappy with the UK system, which they see as highly discriminatory.

Nevertheless, since 1995, the Taiwanese education authorities have become increasingly doubtful about this mode of selecting students for higher education, and they have established a research centre, the College Entrance Examinations Centre (CEEC), in Taipei to conduct research into the issue. In a recent paper on the matter, one of their principal research officers comments as follows on the problems created by the JCEE system:

1. The JCEE has totally distorted the goals of high school education, overemphasizing the importance of intellectual development whilst neglecting other aspects of development such as moral, physical, social and aesthetic development. . . .
4. Because of its characteristics of emphasis on standardised answers, memorization of bits of information, techniques of answering questions, and because of its characteristic neglect of the cultivation of and training in important abilities and skills such as data collection, comprehension, synthesis, analysis and creativity, expression and actual operations, the JCEE has deprived the student of the opportunity to develop wholesome attitudes and habits toward learning.
(Huang 1995, pp. 3–4)

This is strong stuff for a Taiwanese research centre to be saying about a system of assessment that underpins just about everything that happens in Taiwan's schools and universities. And Taiwan has begun to reform its university entrance system. It is, for example, building in alternative routes involving recommendations from high schools and reference to graduation certificates.[7] But it is not as yet undertaking any serious reform of the testing system that controls the transition from junior to senior high schools – which, in my opinion, suffers from the identical weaknesses outlined above by Huang.

Given the total domination of the JEE (for entry to high school) and JCEE (for entrance to university) in schools in Taiwan, and the fact that technology does not appear in either of them, it can readily be seen that there is no formal assessment of technology at all for these levels of study. The best that can be said is that teachers and schools have developed individual (and unregulated) approaches to assessing pupil performance in class-work, and that these assessments count towards students' graduation. In the absence therefore of any other technology assessment materials from Taiwan, it is worth briefly outlining some of the informal practices of classroom-based assessment. I have chosen three examples, one each from elementary, junior high and senior high schools.

Informal classroom assessment

The limited amount of design and technology activity that goes on in elementary schools does so under the banner of art and craft or sometimes manual arts. The windmill project mentioned earlier was one such piece of work in an elementary school in Hualien, and its assessment was remarkably sophisticated. It fell broadly into three categories as outlined in the following schedule:

(i) **Design**

Overall concept of the windmill	25%
Design of the rotor	25%
Structural design of the whole	10%

(ii) **Making**

Precision of manufacture (edges etc.)	10%
Cleanness/neatness	10%

(iii) **Function**

The rotor must spin well	10%
How well the energy is transferred	10%

At the end of the project the teacher made a series of judgments against these categories, and pupils ended up with a mark (a percentage) for the project which was then carried forward through the semester and contributed to an overall, aggregate percentage for all their work on the course. This was converted into marks on a five-point scale, and this in turn went forward as part of a kind of record of achievement from all areas of curriculum in the elementary school.

I have already outlined some of the classroom assessment arrangements in junior high school that lead to graduation. In one school, all projects (which were dominantly craft projects) were marked three times: at the outset (marking out, etc.), in the middle (making) and towards the end of the project (finishing). These marks were judgments out of 100, and they were aggregated into a single mark out of 100 for the whole project. There were no formal criteria published for the assessment, and no formal cross-marking or moderation procedures, though the teacher was firmly of the view that she could recognise excellence when she saw it.

At the Ta-An vocational senior high school the assessments were based on courses (rather than individual projects) that tended to last one semester, and these course assessments fell into two categories: performance skills (in drawing, machining, etc., including 'attitude to work'); and theoretical test scores (typically science-related). The first of these (amounting to 40 per cent) was based on pupil performance in everyday class-work as exemplified through the final product. The second (amounting to 60 per cent) was an amalgamation of three test scores (all multiple-choice) spaced approximately evenly through the 20 weeks of the semester and representing respectively 15 per cent, 15 per cent and 30 per cent of the marks.

There were no formal criteria identified for performance skills, and teachers were using their judgment to allocate marks to various elements of performance including the product itself, the pupils' technical report of it, and their attitude to their work throughout the project. The marks were unmoderated. In the theoretical domain, the teachers were responsible for generating the tests in the first instance, and they typically did this by reference to the 'ministry-approved' textbooks for the courses. These typically include extensive 'item banks' of questions for pupils to practise. Part of the value of these regular tests lies in preparing pupils – one might even say conditioning them – for the techniques of multiple-choice testing that will be needed in the JCEE. There are a multitude of test-taking techniques that are systematically taught in high school and ruthlessly drilled at the 'crammer' schools. This test acclimatisation is of course somewhat less valuable in technology, since there is no technology component in the JCEE, but the generalised (transferable) skills of test-taking feature strongly in the minds of teachers, pupils and (according to the teachers to whom I spoke) parents. The scoring for these tests is a simple matter, and some departments even had optical mark reading (OMR) facilities to automate the process.

School inspection and improvement

As I have pointed out above, the school system in Taiwan is highly cen-tralised. All courses are commissioned from expert groups appointed by the Ministry of Education, and the deliberations of the groups are then subject to approval by the Ministry of Education. The courses are defined in a *curriculum and equipment standard* for each subject that details the structure, content and week-by-week units of work that make up the course. Head teachers are responsible for ensuring that their schools work to these standards, and heads of department have this responsibility devolved to them.

It is recognised that the standard will need supplementary materials (such as textbooks) for teaching purposes, but even these are standardised and approved. All textbooks that all teachers use in the classroom have to be stamped with the approval of the Bureau of Textbooks of the Ministry of Education. The examination system is also under the direct authority of the ministry. It is perhaps just as well that Taiwan is a very conformist state. There is very little evidence of a desire for radical individualism. In the UK it is recognised that 'managing' academics is 'like herding cats' – very difficult, because individualism and academic autonomy are an important tradition in the UK. But it seems to be entirely absent in Taiwan. Teachers like to be told what to do and how to do it, and they seem happy to get on and do as they are told.

There is also, however, an enforcement arm to the centralised curriculum, in the form of school inspection by 'supervisors' from the ministry. These supervisors are in fact not employed by the ministry, but rather are academics from the teacher training colleges who perform advisory and inspection functions on behalf of the ministry. And these inspections typically happen each semester, or at least each year. The functions of these inspections appear to be very broad-ranging, covering management and organisation, school fabric and resources, classroom activity and pupil standards. In the context of assessment, one of the critical functions of the inspectors is to study a sample of pupils' work that has been marked and retained by the teacher of each course. This will be remarked by the inspector to check on the standards that the teacher is applying in the assessment of their pupils' work.

In two cities I also found a fascinating example of further liaison between the teacher training colleges and the schools, in the form of Wednesday afternoon support sessions. These were offered by the college staff (who were also the ministry-licensed inspectors) and were devoted to the professional development of teachers and curriculum in local schools. For example, every primary school in Hualien had a session from a college professor at least twice each semester – supporting innovation in the school. And this innovation – or development – was typically targeted at weaknesses identified in the inspections.

Whilst the curriculum is completely centralised, the key to developing standards in Taiwanese schools appears therefore to lie in the integration of the inspection function, the professional development function and the activities of the expert staff at the teacher training colleges. The whole thing is organised and licensed by ministry officials, but they do not get involved with the professional activity. This is left to the experts in the colleges. In the next few years it will be very interesting to observe how this arrangement facilitates the emergence of the new 'living technology' curriculum in schools – particularly as it will require such a major transformation of pedagogy.

Notes

1 This compares to approx 5 per cent in the UK.
2 A teacher with five years' experience might expect to be paid approximately £1000 per month, but with the interesting quirk that there are 15 monthly payments in the year: the ordinary 12, plus one as a bonus for the Chinese new year; half for the Dragon Boat festival; half for the Moon festival; and one as a 'merit' bonus that is almost universally awarded by the principals of schools. This award is not linked to any formal appraisal system.
3 While I was in Taiwan, Ofsted's Chief Inspector of Schools pronounced on the desirability of importing Taiwanese-style school practices: quietly sitting in rows, listening attentively to the teacher. As I pointed out at the time (Kimbell 1996), there are two problems with this. First, he is cherry-picking those features of the Taiwan system that he happens to approve of without mentioning the others (such as that teaching is in mixed-ability classes and is completely undifferentiated – which is not something that Ofsted has been known to support in the past). Second, the idea that we can import the surface practices of another school system without first importing the social, cultural and personal value systems that created these practices is unbelievably simplistic.
4 One of the notable features of education policy in Taiwan is that – just as in New York State – policy is being created by experts in education. The current Commissioner has taught for some years in junior high school and senior high school, has been a university professor and a university chancellor before taking up his present appointment. With a doctorate in educational psychology, he has a particular interest in special education. A further notable political fact is that about 80 per cent of the ruling cabinet in Taiwan are educated to PhD level, including the current Prime Minister, and the ministers of Law, Interior, Labour, Education, Foreign Affairs, and Traffic. The vast majority of the rest have master's degrees. People may not agree with their policies, but they respect their intellect.
5 In the UK we are moving towards 30 per cent by 2000.
6 The 'Three Principles of the People' is an examination in Chinese political philosophy.
7 The process by which CEEC is revising university entrance procedures is impressive. It has studied systems from around the world, and identified 12 criteria for the system to meet, including:

- the exam must not distort high school education;
- admission must be based on multiple information (high school grades, test scores, etc.);
- no discrimination on grounds of sex or cultural background;
- the exam must involve high school teachers' participation;
- the system must be fair, just and open;
- the system must not be disadvantageous to test-takers who have left school for some time;
- admission must correctly reflect the achievement of students' learning.

The CEEC has scored the systems of six other nations (including the UK, USA and Taiwan) against all 12 criteria and are using this as a means to evaluate their next steps. It is thorough research.

ten
———

Australia

Australia is composed of seven semi-autonomous states and territories, each with a state capital: Western Australia (Perth), South Australia (Adelaide), Northern Territory (Darwin), Queensland (Brisbane), Victoria (Melbourne), New South Wales (Sydney), and Tasmania (Hobart). The population is approximately 18 million and the national capital is Canberra.

Australia has a national curriculum framework that the states are empowered to interpret in their own ways, and in this chapter I shall highlight two contrasted interpretations, from Western Australia and from New South Wales (Figure 10.1). The two states are themselves highly contrasted. Western Australia is vast and largely unpopulated and contains huge areas of bush and desert. New South Wales – especially the coastal region around Sydney – is relatively developed and populated.

Western Australia

Western Australia (WA) comprises about one-third of the entire land mass of Australia, but its population is only 2 million. It is therefore a state in some isolation from the rest of the country. Distances from Perth to the other state capitals are enormous. It takes about four days of continuous driving (at 110 kph along arrow-straight roads) to cross the country from Perth in the west to Sydney in the east. Within WA the population is concentrated in the coastal region within about 300 km of Perth. There are huge mining operations and sheep stations in the interior, but the interior population represents a tiny proportion of the whole.

The wealth of WA derives from its resource-rich geology. There is gold, iron, aluminium, coal, oil, gas, and much more besides. The state is immensely rich in natural resources, but the conditions in which these resources are recovered are fierce. Temperatures in the interior goldfields routinely rise above 45°C and whole communities live underground in artificially constructed and maintained environments. There is also a serious

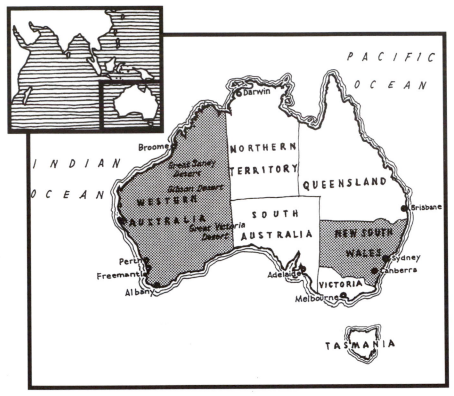

Figure 10.1 Australia.

shortage of water in much of the state, which contains the bulk of the Gibson, Great Victoria, and Great Sandy deserts.

In the more fertile south-west corner of the state, timber extraction has been a staple industry since it was established by the British in the nineteenth century. The huge natural forests of karri and jarrah (a kind of mahogany) have been repeatedly harvested in the face of seemingly endless demand from the UK and elsewhere. At one point in the late nineteenth century, many of the streets of London were literally paved with jarrah from WA. Within 150 years of occupation – the first British settlements were in the 1830s – the vast majority of the original (old-growth) forest had been felled and a lot of it had also been cleared for farming. Latterly, CALM, the body reponsible for conservation and land management, has protected the forests and transformed them into sustainable-yield resources.

New South Wales

New South Wales (NSW) is arguably the most developed of the states in Australia. Situated in the south-eastern quadrant of the country, it is more than three times the size of the whole of the UK. It has a population of approx 8 million, 3 million of whom live in and around Sydney, which is the commercial centre of Australia. It is difficult to keep a sense of scale in relation to the size and population of Australia. Whilst the UK has about 600 people per square mile, NSW has about 25 per square mile and WA has 2 per square mile, though much of the land in WA is uninhabitable to all but its indigenous people. The population of Sydney alone is one and a half times as big as the population of the whole of WA. One of the obvious consequences of this distribution of population is that outside the major cities, the thinly spread population creates a serious challenge to those charged with developing an education service.

Agriculture, including the burgeoning wine industry, is rich in NSW where the climate is gentle. There is a wide variety of industry and commerce, and NSW also surrounds the 'Capital Territory' around Canberra, which is the national capital and the centre of political decision-making for the federal government. At the risk of dangerous generalisation, the socio-political climate in NSW would be described as more 'liberal' than WA, which is regarded as more traditional and 'conservative'.

As I have alraedy mentioned, there is an Australian national curriculum which has been agreed by the federal government and subsequently passed back to the individual states for implementation in their own ways. However, before we can usefully explore these state interpretations, it might be helpful to outline the form of the national curriculum created by the Australian federal government.

The Australian National Curriculum

As early as 1987, the Australian Education Council (AEC) had begun a series of initiatives that were to lead to the establishment in 1994 of an Australian national curriculum. In 1987, the AEC produced a working paper for a national approach to monitoring student achievement, and a statement of 'national goals and purposes of education' in Australia. In 1989 it endorsed the ten 'Common and Agreed Goals for Schooling in Australia' and began the process of drawing up National Statements in eight broad areas of learning. In 1991 the task of linking assessment profiles to curriculum statements was taken over by the new Curriculum and Assessment Committee (CURASS) and in 1994 comprehensive national curriculum statements were issued for the eight identified learning areas:

the arts
English
health and physical education
languages other than English (LOTE)
mathematics
science
studies in society and environment
technology.[1]

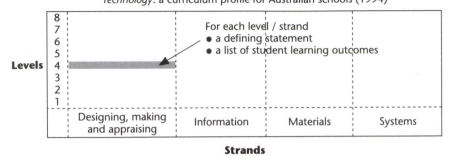

Figure 10.2 The framework for the Australian national curriculum for technology.

These national statements consisted of *subjects*, divided into *strands* (attainment targets by another name), structured into four *bands* (key stages by another name), presented at eight *levels* covering years 1–12; each level defined in a *statement* and a table of *learning outcomes* (statements of attainment by another name) and exemplified through *work samples*. The pattern of the national can therefore be illustrated through the example of technology, as shown in Figure 10.2.

The parallels with the National Curriculum of England and Wales are very apparent, as are some of the differences.

- **Similarities:** The whole structure of the curriculum is very similar, with equivalents of key stages, subjects, ATs, levels and SoA. Also, specifically within the 'Designing, making and appraising' strand further similarities appear, for it is divided into four sub-strands: investigating; devising; producing; evaluating. These appear to have been heavily influenced by the first four ATs in the original UK technology Order and many of the Australian learning outcome statements seem to have been taken almost verbatim from it. The 'Information' strand is also very parallel to our original AT5.
- **Differences:** The Australian profile includes years 11 and 12 and only has eight levels. It therefore provides a somewhat coarser scale of progression. Additionally, the subject has strands for two further content areas (materials and systems), and there are two parts to each of these other strands: one describing its nature, and one outlining the techniques that are appropriate within it.

As an illustration of the kinds of outcome statements in the Australian technology profile, I include here some samples from level 4:

Designing, making and appraising
- Investigating – the student determines the appropriateness of products and processes for communities and environments
- Devising – the student creates and prepares design proposals that include options considered and reasons for the choices made

- Producing – the student organises and implements production processes to own specification, recognising hazards and adopting safe work practices
- Evaluating – the student assesses the effectiveness of own designs, products and processes in relation to design requirements, including social and environmental criteria.

Information
- Nature – the student describes how processing and transmitting information have evolved and are continuing to change
- Techniques – the student selects and uses recognised procedures, conventions and languages to process information and create information products

Materials
- Nature – the student identifies the characteristics of materials and relates them to the functional and aesthetic requirements of own designs
- Techniques – the student applies a range of techniques for safely working materials to the functional and aesthetic requirements of own designs

Systems
- Nature – the student identifies the relationships between elements in systems (people and components) and some of the sequences through which the elements work
- Techniques – the student selects and uses techniques to organise, assemble and disassemble systems to manage control and assess performance.

(Curriculum Corporation 1994, p. 63)

The Australian statements and profiles were originally intended to provide a national framework for curriculum development, but shortly after their ratification there was a change of national government (from socialist to conservative) and it was decided that this framework would be returned to the individual states for interpretation and implementation. This political compromise effectively diluted the impact of the national curriculum, and was a source of considerable regret to many educators who had a vision of a national curriculum drawing the nation together. It did, however, allow the states to adopt it into their separate education systems with rather less upheaval.

I have chosen to examine this process of adaptation in WA and NSW, since they have adopted dramatically different approaches and are consequently encountering quite different kinds of problems.

An interpretation from Western Australia

The structure of the school system in WA is very similar to that in the UK, probably the biggest difference being that the transition from primary to

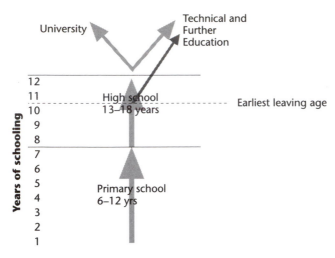

Figure 10.3 The school system in Western Australia.

secondary schooling takes place after year 7 (Figure 10.3). The school year is divided into two semesters with the long summer holiday over Christmas, and each semester is subdivided in half, producing a year of four terms of ten weeks each.

Unit-based curriculum

Since 1985 the high school curriculum in WA has been dominated by what is known as the 'unit curriculum'. This is a system in which schools offer course 'units' that are typically one semester or one year in length and which pupils opt into. The first year of study in year 8 is largely compulsory, but thereafter the curriculum is menu-driven and heavily influenced by the preferences of students and parents.

A typical pupil curriculum in year 8 would look as follows:

English	3 units
Mathematics	3 units
Social studies	3 units
Science	3 units
Art	2 units
Music	1 unit
Physical & health education	3 units
Industrial arts[2]	2 units
LOTE[3]	2 units
Study skills	1 unit

In years 9 and 10, the only compulsory study is in physical and health education, but most schools recommend a progression of units in English, mathematics, science and social studies. These are in effect the core curriculum. Other subjects are 'elective' much as they are in the USA, and students choose three electives each semester. The curriculum therefore looks as follows:

English	4 units
Maths	4 units
Science	4 units
Social studies	4 units
PE/health	3 units
Electives[4]	6 units

There are constraints operating on the choice system to encourage pupils to choose their electives from an appropriately wide range, but these constraints appear to be advisory and negotiable.

Technology curriculum units

There is a wide range of technology (industrial arts) units available in most high schools. The following list is available at one of the most advanced technology schools in Perth, and it speaks volumes about the current state of technology education in WA:

Materials technologies

Food and health	Creating with textiles
Food and technology	Technology and fashion
Caring for children	Jewellery
Clothing decisions	Woodwork
Food and fitness	Metalwork

Information and System technologies

Photography	Word processing
Technical drawing	Mechanical workshop
Information processing	Model making
Multimedia presentations	Technology studies
Money matters	Robotics mechanisms

The lineage of these technology units is clear. They draw from the traditional subjects of home economics, manual arts, information technology, technical drawing and business courses. Moreover, the titles of the courses suggest that – for the most part – these are traditional craft-based units; and that is the reality. The woodwork courses listed here for years 9 and 10 are based on traditional craft practice and they lead on in years 11 and 12 to units like 'Furniture – wood', which is more advanced craftwork. At the tail end, there are emergent signs of curriculum innovation emerging from the bulk of traditional practice. The units in 'robotics mechanisms' and 'technology studies' are in many ways parallel to elements of courses in design and technology in the UK (Figure 10.4). But these are very much

Figure 10.4 The technology studies unit is creating a focus for development:
(a) an electrical maze game;

(b) experiments with Lego;

(c) 'knock-down' furniture.

in the minority, and do not exist at all in most schools. This listing represents the course offering in a school at the leading edge of developments in WA where the teachers are experimenting with and developing technology. These teachers reflect on the literature they receive from the UK and estimate that the general state of development of the WA technology curriculum is 10–15 years behind practice in the UK.

The unit curriculum was designed to combine flexibility with central regulatory quality control by the Department of Education (DoEd).

- Creating the units is a rigorous process. A school seeking to generate a new unit must write it using a framework of objectives, skills, knowledge, activities and assessment. This would then be approved or not by the DoEd.
- Running units also involves a level of approval from the DoEd, since the school must make a return each semester to the DoEd listing all the units that it wishes to run. The DoEd may then inspect the school on a rolling programme to check that it is providing the resources as specified.
- Graded assessments are initially made at the school, but these are then moderated across schools by teachers taking a selection of work to a joint moderation meeting supervised by the DoEd.

For the last ten years in WA, the whole superstructure of the unit curriculum has therefore been supervised by, moderated by and approved by the DoEd. It was designed to allow flexible routes for learning and reflects many of the elements of practice found in the menu-driven elective course structures in the USA.

But it also has a major drawback that is widely acknowledged in schools, since it is impossible to ensure any continuity in elective programmes of study, including those in technology. Assuming that a pupil is taking a range of electives in the technology field in years 8–12; how does the technology teacher ensure that one year builds upon the experience of the last? Essentially, she cannot. The pupil might not do any technology course in year 9 and then do one in year 10. Or the other way round. Each unit therefore has to be designed to be free-standing and no progressive pathway can be required, or even hoped for. It might be supposed that one could overcome this problem by imposing prerequisites on course choices. But this idea collapses when confronted with the market economy of the high school curriculum. When departments put their elective course offering together, the primary requirement is to get bums on seats. If not enough children opt for the courses, then the department's full-time equivalent student load reduces and it will lose teachers. So there is a tendency for course offerings to exist in a 'beauty contest' environment that favours the trusted and familiar and penalises innovation. In technology, this appears to have had the effect of perpetuating the traditional, comfortable, craft courses well beyond their sell-by date.[5]

While most schools require a progression of units in English, maths, science, social studies and PE, there is no such framework for progression in elective units. Accordingly the situation for technology in WA can best be characterised as anarchic. Teachers are unable to plan a coherent developing curriculum over a period of years, partly because this curriculum needs to be written as a series of 'bite-sized' units and equally because pupils then have the choice to opt in and out of these units in ways that teachers are unable to control.[6]

This obvious down side of the unit curriculum makes many teachers (certainly the technology teachers) yearn for a less flexible, less menu-driven framework for the curriculum. In 1995, when the WA Department of Education accepted the challenge of implementing the national curriculum, the opportunity existed to think again about the how the curriculum might be structured.

Implementing the national curriculum in Western Australia

The first and most obvious manifestation of change brought about by the implementation of the national technology profile is that the informal grouping of technology-related subjects has crystallised into a single 'learning area' called *technology and enterprise*. The grouping is very much a reflection of the same thinking that linked home economics, CDT, art and design, business studies and information technology in the UK.

This is, however, a largely administrative and organisational matter, and does not address the central challenge that is contained in the fact that the national profile is significantly more based around designing and problem-solving than is currently the case in the vast majority of unit courses in WA. Accordingly the adoption of the national curriculum framework requires a major transformation from the prevailing pedagogy of craft-skill teaching.

The Department of Education in WA sees this curriculum development taking place alongside – and through the mechanism of – a further transformation that concerns assessment. One of the features of the national curriculum is the 'student outcome statements' that describe what students can achieve in technology at different levels as they progress through their schooling. These outcome statements have been somewhat customised by the DoEd but have basically remained intact. When the national curriculum is implemented (planned for 1998), these 'student outcome statements' will become the basis for all assessment in schools. Teachers who have for years been familiar with making graded assessments against unit-course objectives will now have to manage a completely different system of digital (yes/ no) assessment against a large number of outcome statements. Teachers in the UK will know the difficulties that this can create!

But this process of adaptation is rendered more difficult by the additional decision to use these *outcome* statements as the basis for designing the curriculum *input*. The National Curriculum of England and Wales had outcome statements (SoA) and also programmes of study – a description of what the curriculum should cover and that might reasonably be expected to generate the outcomes. In WA there are only outcome statements and the curriculum is left for teachers and schools to develop.

Building a technology national curriculum

A small number of innovative schools in WA are currently trialling national curriculum outcome statements as a means for framing the curriculum. And this in effect means that these schools are devising a whole new curriculum from scratch. Led by imaginative senior staff and using highly professional and innovative teachers, these schools are doing some great development work with the curriculum. In some, the whole concept of the curriculum as a body of 'subjects' has been challenged, and the schools are embracing quite new ways of organising learning. Cross-disciplinary and even cross-year learning teams are being developed and managed in ways that allow children to experience an individualised curriculum. These experiments in curriculum development are immensely effective in those schools and are highly stimulating for their pupils. But it is also a huge challenge involving immense workloads for the ablest teachers in the most supportive schools. And the DoEd openly admits that only a fraction of schools could cope with these levels of innovation with any degree of success.

In several schools that I visited in WA – that are thought to be at the leading edge of developments in technology – teachers are developing technology and enterprise courses from a basis in unit courses, restructuring them in line with the imperatives of the outcome statements. And it is a very difficult job: 'The Unit Curriculum ... was very rigid – you teach these 75 objectives in these 40 lessons. It was a breeze: you just sat there and did what they told you. Student Outcome Statements are a lot more dependent on me' (Bonser and Grundy 1995).

It has to be said that this is not strictly true, since the outcome statements are in fact decided already. The point that Bonser and Grundy are making is that it is very largely up to them what they do with them: how they convert them into a teachable curriculum. We learned in the UK how difficult it is to organise a curriculum on the basis of statements of attainment. They represent the assessments that are applied to measure the *results* of teaching: they are not the teaching itself. As Hicks[7] and others pointed out, it was the programmes of study that provided teachers with a coherent plan of action for what should be taught. As an illustration of this problem, it might (for example) be thought a good thing if one of the outcomes of schooling were to be that students are honest. But you cannot teach it, or at least not directly. As Tripp (1996, pp. 15–16), writing in WA, has pointed out:

> The essential point is that what makes an outcome statement into an outcome statement is not what is stated, but the way it is used. ... It is quite possible for a child to attain an outcome without ever having been taught it ... by the age of 6 most children have a vocabulary of several thousand words, but no one set out to teach them to attain a vocabulary of that size ... the student outcome statements towards which we are teaching will probably not appear in our proposed learning activities.

So what are the learning activities? From where do teachers in WA get a curriculum? This is the issue that is now confronting teachers in Western Australia, since neither the national statement in technology, nor the WA statement of 'technology and enterprise' contains a programme of study. That which is to be taught is therefore very elusive at this point.

Despite the ground-breaking work being done in a small number of trial schools, the great majority of technology teachers in the vast majority of schools in WA will need – or at least will greatly benefit from – a curriculum built for them. And the consensus of opinion is that it must start from the basis of the unit curriculum, since that is what everyone currently understands and uses. There is a clear and urgent need for curriculum guidance that empowers technology teachers in WA to cope with the two transformations that currently face them: that from a dominant tradition of craft practice to technology and enterprise; and that from sliding-scale assessment of unit-based objectives to assessment using student outcome statements. It is time to examine this matter of assessment rather more closely.

Assessment

Assessing the unit curriculum

The unit curriculum courses in technology (as in all other subjects) are all assessed on a simple five-point scale. To arrive at a grade, teachers typically amass a series of assessment grades for project work, for tests, for homework, or for whatever in their opinion is an important feature of the course. Assessments are initially internal to the school but thereafter a degree of levelling takes place through the moderation process that operates across schools at meetings conducted by DoEd supervisors. However, the teachers to whom I spoke were confident that they 'knew the standards' and had very few of their marks changed by this moderation process. Assessment is not seen as a big issue and does not take up much teacher effort or time. Most schools appear to allocate percentage marks to various pieces of work; aggregate these into a final mark for each pupil; and then convert the number into an A–F grade. At the end of year 10 – which is the earliest school-leaving point – a pupil could leave school with a record of his/her achievement in a range of units on this A–F scale.

However, some 75% of pupils choose not to leave school after year 10, but rather move on into years 11 and 12, and here the assessment regime is somewhat tighter and is regulated by the Secondary Education Authority (SEA).

Secondary Education Authority

The SEA operates in parallel with the Department of Education. It accredits courses (based on formal paper submissions), including their assessment arrangements; it monitors the teaching of them; it moderates teachers' assessments; and it certificates students. Only SEA-accredited courses are allowed to run in schools in years 11 and 12.

Until recent years, there have been very few technology-related courses in years 11 and 12, but as staying-on rates increase, more courses are beginning to emerge. There are now some interesting courses, for example, in applied technology and applied information technology that are currently being trialled in schools. The first of these is designed directly around the national statement for technology, as the introduction makes clear:

> This course caters for the individual who, through a core of design with strands of information, systems and materials, can apply broad design principles to areas of interest and specialisation. The course is designed to allow students to develop solutions through design processes and products that satisfy social and environmental needs.
>
> (SEA 1996, p. 29)

The 120-hour course is designed through ten 'outcome statements' that cover the general territory of graphics, research, designing, constructing, technological issues, and working with materials. Against each of the ten outcomes, the teacher is required to make a judgment about whether the student has achieved each one 'satisfactorily', to a 'high' level or to a 'very high' level. Portfolios are required to be submitted demonstrating these levels. The final mark from the course is once again presented on a five-point scale using a fascinating set of rules.[8]

A Very High in at least 50 per cent of outcomes and High or better in at least 50 per cent of the remainder
B High in at least 50 per cent of outcomes and Satisfactory or better in at least 50 per cent of the remainder
C Satisfactory or better in all outcomes
D Satisfactory in at least 50 per cent of outcomes
E Not meeting the requirments of D
Note: remainder includes Very Highs (V) which are in excess of the minimum required for a majority. In cases where students achieve an excess of Very Highs they may be combined with Satisfactories (S) using the following averaging procedure: 1V+1S=2H (2 Highs).

(SEA 1996, p. 35)

One of the interesting features of this assessment regime is that it requires the student to demonstrate these qualities in portfolios, but not on any one project. The design development work can be submitted from one project; the constructed product from another; and the evaluation from a third. The outcomes are assessed separately as 'assessment tasks' which might even (I suppose) be done as separate sub-tasks, but equally they might be extractions from whole projects.

My impression of this applied technology course is that it represents significantly updated thinking from the bulk of unit courses in years 8–10 and a natural progression from the more updated technology studies units in years 8–10. The level of course specification remains slight, with enormous scope for teachers to do as they choose. There is little specified conceptual matter (for instance, in material technology, ergonomics or electronics) and the assessment arrangements are less rigorous than would be required for A-level design and technology in the UK. However, we should remember that in years 11 and 12 in Australian schools (as in Germany, the USA and Taiwan, see Chapters 7–9) students study far more courses than British sixth-formers. Years 11 and 12 are not seen as specialist years, but as years of extended general education. Which brings me to the requirements for high school graduation.

Graduation from high school

At the end of year 12 students seek to qualify for the Western Australian Certificate of Education: Secondary Graduation. This carries a number of requirments as follows:

- a grade C or better in eight full SEA-accredited courses, with at least four in year 12;
- a grade C or better in year 12 SEA-accredited courses in English;
- a grade C or better in year 11 or 12 SEA-accredited courses in mathematics.

Those who fall at any of these hurdles will still get the WA Certificate of Education for the courses they successfully complete, but they will not 'graduate' from high school. The benefits of graduating are that it is a basic requirement for university entrance and also that many employers use it as a base line for job applicants. It is seen as a good level of general education, in much the same way as it is in USA and Taiwan. It is not a specialist preparation as are A levels in the UK. A significant majority of Australian, US and Taiwanese students succeed in graduating from high school, whereas British A-level courses are only designed for a minority (approx 30 per cent) of students.

Given this open arrangement for the curriculum in years 11 and 12 there would appear to be plenty of scope for the applied technology course to be taken by students with a variety of interests. It might, for example, be linked with maths and science by those interested in pursuing a university course in engineering, or it might equally be linked with arts and humanities courses. But unfortunately the reality of university entrance in WA is that it is controlled in a very traditional manner that eliminates these potentially exciting possibilities.

University entrance

If students have aspirations to university entrance, they must follow the rules for course selection, and less than half of SEA-accredited courses count for university entrance scores. These are the Tertiary Entrance Examination (TEE) courses, and they are listed in the SEA syllabus manual as 'TEE approved'. Unsurprisingly, this approval is given to traditional academic courses and not to upstarts like technology.

Students seeking university entrance must complete at least four TEE-approved courses in year 12 and the aggregated examination score from these is rendered out of 500. There are exensive moderation and scaling procedures to standardise these data from schools. Students who get a very high score (around 460) might get into the medicine department at the University of Western Australia (a very traditional academic institution). If they want to do engineering at Murdoch University they will need a lower score. Having stated their preferences (in a version of the UK UCAS system), the students simply wait to see if the course/university of their choice will accept their score. If they are above the cut-off they are in; if not they are out. There is no interviewing; no portfolios;[9] just a score.

This arrangement results in the anomalous situation in which a student who is interested in studying 'engineering design' at university could gain a place as a result of her TEE scores in music, geology, politics and art history, but not as a result of her studies in technology.

This and several other anomalies have increasingly been recognised by the SEA and others, and recently the Director of the SEA has produced a discussion paper with a series of options for the overhaul of the university entrance system (Partis 1996). Amongst these options is the following:

Expansion of the list of subjects which count for tertiary entrance purposes
The number of courses which count toward tertiary entrance has hardly changed in the last ten years. It is of some interest to look at the number of subjects which count towards university entrance in other states.

S Australia	152
New South Wales	149
Tasmania	75
Queensland	54
Victoria	44
W Australia	28

(Partis 1996, p. 7)

The issue has also been brought to light by the recognition that there is more to tertiary entrance in WA than just university entrance – there is also technical and further education (TAFE). Currently at the end of year 12 about 33 per cent of students go to university courses, 33 per cent go to TAFE courses and 33 per cent seek employment. TAFE entry is dependent on successful graduation and good performance in the prefered subjects for further study. The problem is that – often with parental pressure – students in years 11 and 12 feel obliged to take only the courses that have TEE approval so that later on they can choose whether to go for university entrance or for a TAFE course. This results in many students, particularly those in the middle-ability band who might reasonably go in either direction, being forced into inappropriate choices.[10]

Assessing the national curriculum

I have described earlier some of the issues being faced by teachers in developing the 'technology and enterprise' national curriculum and some of the curriculum trials that have been established in schools to blaze the trail. As far as possible I kept that discussion to curriculum matters, but it is important now to explore some of the assessment issues.

We should remember that most teachers and schools are not yet faced with implementing the national curriculum, or with assessment through outcome statements. The vast majority of teachers and schools continue with unit curriculum courses and will do so until the DoEd passes and enforces the mandate for the national curriculum. This is proposed to be in 1998. In the interim, the trials in selected schools are seeking to develop approaches that will help to get to grips with assessment in the new regime of the student outcome statement (whimsically abbreviated as SOS). These trials are being monitored and reported by the DoEd, which has recently encapsulated them into an executive summary report (Department of Education of Western Australia 1996).

The approach to assessment in these trial schools typically involved the teachers in rewriting the SOSs in their own words to relate them to the tasks in hand. This was a procedure that was frequently used in the UK and one that helps teachers to understand the SOSs in their own terms. It is also a process that – in the Australian context – is supported by the national curriculum statement, in which each of the SOSs is elaborated through a series of 'pointers', that is, things that pupils might do to demonstrate mastery of the SOS. The teachers are now in effect elaborating their own lists of 'pointers'.

The assessment forms that I observed in use no longer included the SOSs, but rather listed the teacher's personalised pointers to be 'checked off' for that project.[11] As an illustration, a year 7 'land yacht' project – which was part of a wider 'cross-curriculum learning team' topic – was assessed using the form based on 'pointers' for all the design, make and appraise substrands, for example:

Investigating pointers	'lists differences in sail design'
Devising pointers	'develops ideas with alternatives, e.g. round corners (for a simple part)'
Producing pointers	'does other tasks while waiting for equipment'
Evaluating pointers	'gives reasons for changing part of [his/her] plan'.

An assessment was required for 26 pointers, and teachers had refined the process from a simple yes/no into a three-level response of A (achieved), W (working towards) or N (no progress/evidence). All 26 pointers had to be checked, either as an A, a W or an N (a total of 78 options/boxes) for all 22 pupils in the group.

Having observed the process of assessment in operation, it is clear that the teachers are grappling with a number of interrelated problems.

- *The level of the pointers:* The four pointers listed above are taken from levels 1, 2 and 3 of the eight-level scale. However, when presented selectively in this text, it is difficult to see which pointer is supposed to be at which level. More importantly, however, as the class was of year 7 pupils I asked the teacher why he was not using pointers from levels 2/3/4 or 3/4/5. His response was interesting. 'I could have done that –

but we decided to start at the baseline.' In other words, he is imposing meaning on the SOSs through his own 'pointers'; he made them make sense in relation to his project. But equally, he could have made other levels make sense for the same project.

- *The reliability of pointers:* Because the pointers allow the teacher such a high level of interpretation of national levels, my next question to the teacher was obvious: 'Would a teacher in another school have similar pointers for levels 1/2/3?' 'Probably not' was the reply. I followed this with another obvious question: 'What chance is there that the pupil would be assessed as level 2 (as Dan had been) if the assessment was being done by another teacher in another school?' ' I would say – zip'. By which I think he meant 'very little'.

- *The time-consuming nature of this assessment:* Assessment using this process is very time-consuming as teachers in the UK will recall (see Chapters 5 and 6). The response to this in several departments I observed was to develop a process of *selective* assessment: we shall only assess 'investigating' in this project; next time we can assess 'devising'; and so on. This approach made the work burden manageable, but it is fraught with difficulties. Interestingly, it is not uncommon in WA, and the reader will recall that the SEA-accredited course in applied technology used the same selective approach to assessment.

- *Reporting the level:* The problem of ascribing meaning to pointers emerged in another form when teachers were faced with the problem of pupils being awarded level 1 in one sub-strand and level 3 or 4 in another. What should they report about the overall level? This difficulty was very clearly articulated in one school I observed, and they tackled it by rewriting the pointers to 'level' the pupils back to a more consistent spread. Once again it came down to the interpretation of the level in the pointers that were devised by the teacher.

I gained two overriding impressions of the implementation of SOSs in the trial schools in WA. There is no doubt that the trials have had a profound effect on teachers' understanding and articulation of technology in those schools. They have worked extremely hard to understand, modify and interconnect SOSs from a range of disciplines and it has therefore been a very positive experience of curriculum development. As an exercise in assessment, however, it has been no more successful than it was in the UK. Teacher judgments are not exactly arbitrary because they are tied to what teachers judge to be progressively demanding 'pointers'. But these have been personalised by the teacher – and normalised to the school – to such a degree that they only have meaning in the specific context of that school. There is an interesting paradox here. SOSs were designed to standardise assessment judgments across the nation. But they only really work when teachers have personalised them to their own projects and to the standards in their school.

The principals with whom I discussed this conclusion did not dispute it, but the surprise for me (brought up on the National Curriculum of England and Wales) was that whilst acknowledging this lack of reliability they were not in the least upset by it since the assessments are not to be reported publicly and do not form the basis of league tables. The UK system was designed around the idea of testing for accountability – and hence the publication of levels and thereafter the inevitable league tables of excellence – and the equally inevitable 'market' in high achieving schools. In WA, the system (at least at the moment) seems to be designed to enable teachers to build progressive curriculum demands on the basis of a personalised form of the national curriculum. And at that level it works as a curriculum development device.

However, when the Department of Education seeks to develop the accountability dimension of the SOSs, things might be expected to change. The executive summary of its report of the trials deals with this matter explicitly. It reports, for example, that there is now 'a common language in which to discuss student achievement and progress. This has ensured consistency of teacher interpretation and comparability of standards' (Department of Education WA 1996, p. 13). It must have been looking at different schools than I. Nevertheless, the accountability imperative is later made quite explicit: 'Student performance information gathered using the outcome statements framework has been used successfully in management information systems . . . the framework can be used at classroom, school and system level to demonstrate accountability' (Department of Education WA 1996, p. 14). This is true of course. The information can (and probably will at some point) be made public and used to measure the performance of schools. The questions are whether the data currently being collected have any meaning when used across schools in this systemic way, and what the effects will be upon teachers' assessments when they realise that their judgments are being used in this way. The teachers that I observed assessing pointers at levels 1, 2 and 3, will feel under considerable pressure to move up the scale and rewrite them for levels 3, 4 and 5, so that level 4 emerges as a year 7–8 norm rather than level 2. I have no doubt that they could do this, since the meaning of the SOS is all in the interpretation.

School improvement

There is a very small state inspectorate in WA, reflecting serious cutbacks in the education service in recent years. The handful of 'supervisors' in the Department of Education with specific subject responsibilities are therefore not used for inspecting schools so much as in maintaining and promoting alternative means for raising standards. And the principal means for this to happen operates through course unit approval and moderation. New unit courses have to be approved by the DoEd and there is a good deal of monitoring of standards across schools through the assessment of pupils' work in years 8–10. And in years 11 and 12, the SEA exerts a considerable grip on state standards in their approved courses. It runs regular regional moderation seminars in relation to all its approved courses and if schools wish to run one of the courses, they are required to attend the seminars.

Beyond these course-specific activities there is, however, a further arm of monitoring: monitoring of standards in schools (MSS). This is a WA version of what used to happen under the auspices of APU in the UK (see Chapter 3). On a rotating basis, subjects are selected for monitoring; standardised tests are developed; these are then administerred to a small, randomly selected sample of pupils; and results are compiled about the standards of work in the subject across the state. Whilst data are inevitably collected at the student level, it is not intended as a student assessment process. Aggregated data only are analysed and reported at school, region or state level. The tests are typically designed by the Australian Council for Educational Research (ACER) in Melbourne. For the first time ever, technology was chosen in 1996 as one of the subjects for monitoring.

An interpretation in New South Wales

On the opposite side of the country, NSW represents a serious contrast to the situation in WA. As I pointed out at the start of this chapter, the population of Sydney alone is one and a half times as great as the population of the whole of WA. With this concentration of population, NSW has been able and willing to invest in a more comprehensive curriculum support structure. The Board of Studies is the body responsible for writing and administering the curriculum in NSW, and for assessing and examining student achievements. It has curriculum teams in all specialist fields, and publishes courses and examination syllabuses, along with guidance materials for teachers and parents.

Technology Curriculum

Design and technology courses are far better established in NSW than they are in WA, and they operate right across the 5–18 age range of schooling. In the primary years (from kindergarten (year K) to year 6) technology is taught in a mandatory combined programme with science. In years 7–8 there is a mandatory design and technology programme, and in years 9–12 there are optional design and technology programmes in which pupils' performance can count towards university entrance qualifications.

The development of this portfolio of courses since the late 1980s has been fairly rapid, and has been significantly influenced by developments in the UK. There is, however, a distinctive flavour to it that was encapsulated for me in a response from one of the technology specialists who was presenting the NSW curriculum at a conference in 1994.[12] Following an excellent presentation about the curriculum, I asked about the assessment procedures that would be used, and received the answer: 'We haven't

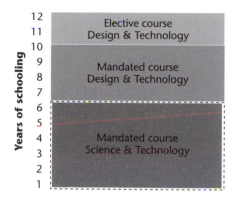

Figure 10.5 Technology courses in New South Wales.

written that chapter yet'. The answer was partly in jest, but equally it was partly serious and reflected the view that the first priority was to get a good curriculum up and running in classrooms and only then to pay more attention to the problems of assessment. This priority remains absolutely clear in all the literature that is currently emerging from the Board of Studies.

The work of the Board of Studies in developing design and technology courses over the last few years has been quite outstanding. The technology team has researched, developed, trialled and published a huge amount of material that has all been designed to support classroom developments in technology. Its syllabus statements provide clear rationales, statements of content, discussions of the strengths and weaknesses of different teaching strategies, planning frameworks, and an outline of desired learning outcomes; and it always contextualises the materials within a wider curriculum framework.

Critically, however, the documents also provide extensive descriptions of possible 'units of work' – projects that teachers can just pick up and run with to get themselves started. The units are presented as a series of tasks and activities elaborated with suggested content, teaching strategies, links to other curriculum areas, suggested resources, and potential outcomes. The following brief selection is taken from the science and technology programme for years K–6 and the design and technology programme for years 7–10.

Science and Technology, years K–6

Thirty-nine units of work have been developed, each designed at different levels of sophistication, reflecting the progression of demand that it is recommended teachers build into their projects. It is recommended that pupils study four of the science and technology topics in each year (one each half semester) throughout years K–6.

Unit of Work	Task	
Keep in touch	(T)	• designing and making a method for communicating news to other classes
	(Sc)	• investigate the variety of ways of communicating specific conditions
Sounds Great	(T)	• design and make a device that carries sound over a long distance
	(Sc)	• investigate that sound travels through a variety of materials
Moving pictures	(T)	• design and make a photo story exploring a theme/topic
	(Sc)	• investigate how pictures appear to move
Switched on	(T)	• design and make a device to test which materials will conduct electricity
	(Sc)	• investigate the conditions needed to make an electric circuit

(Board of Studies NSW 1993a)

Each unit is presented on a double-page spread. The book is 230 pages of high-quality presentation, and in total there are three pages devoted to assessment.

Design and Technology, years 7–10

This resource is presented somewhat differently – in three ring binders with ten units of study, each of which has a mass of copyable materials to support classroom activity. 'Flying high', for example, is a unit about kites and flight that contains 80 pages of material that it is suggested might spread over 40 lessons (typically ten weeks). It embraces exploring how kites and gliders fly; how their flight can be controlled; exploring air pressure and drag; making a wind tunnel; testing kite materials and frames; personalising kites; managing manufacture; testing performance and evaluating the final product. It is presented as a mix of individual and group activities. There is also a slide bank, a detailed reference and resource list and a proforma for teachers to evaluate and modify the activity for themselves. However, there is almost nothing that specifically addresses issues of assessment by the teacher – though there is plenty of material to help pupils to engage in critical reflection of their own work.

The planning framework for the year 7–10 curriculum is somewhat more complex since the secondary curriculum is (as in most countries) more subject-specific and involves the delineation of numerous statutory requirements. The formal requirement in NSW is that, within years 7–10, all pupils should follow a course of study in design and technology over 200 hours. This is typically placed in years 7 and 8 and involves 2.5 hours per week throughout the two-year period. Each unit of study is designed for about 10 weeks, and it is expected that four will be taught each year (one each half semester).

Beyond the mandatory course in design and technology (typically taught in years 7 and 8), the courses available in years 9 and 10 are a good deal less noteworthy (to say the least). They are the remains of old curriculum units from former days including for example 'technical drawing', 'sheep-husbandry', 'technics' and much other outdated material. They have survived as optional supplements to the mandatory design and technology programme.

Higher School Certificate in design and technology (years 11 and 12)

In years 11 and 12 pupils work towards the award of the Higher School Certificate (HSC), which apart from being a valuable school-leaving certificate is also designed to integrate with university entrance requirements. Typically a student would study six courses of two units each. The units must be chosen to reflect a balance of study across the curriculum, and in year 12 this means a minimum requirement as follows:

English   at least two units
Maths/science/technology   at least one unit
LOTE/creative arts/social studies   at least one unit.

The course leading to HSC in design and technology is made up of two components: the preliminary (year 11) course and the HSC course. Each counts for two units and is expected to involve 120 hours of study. The whole programme was first available for students in 1993. The programme is built around a core of design strategies: designing, producing, evaluating, researching, communicating and managing. It also delineates a range of knowledge, including

- design in the environment
- systems
- resources and their management
- health and safety
- communicating and marketing.

This core of procedures, knowledge and skills – supplemented by statements of the expected attitudinal developments – is fleshed out in a series of outcome statements that pupils will be expected 'to know, do and understand'.

The course requirements include many of the features that one would conventionally expect in a design and technology programme. And principally the teaching and learning revolve around design projects; a series of minor ones in the preliminary course and a major one in the HSC year. There is also, however, an interesting 'comparative study' that 'aims to assist students to understand how the structure of organisations is related

Figure 10.6 Student exhibits for the High School Certificate:
(a) wedding fashions;

to the design and technological activity and to the level of operation of the organisation' (Board of Studies NSW 1993b). Students are expected to select two organisations of contrasting scale and structure and study their technologies, resource use, policies and implementation modes, functions, and their impacts on people, society and the environment. This activity is reinforced in the year 12 HSC unit with additional studies of innovation in design (both successes and failures) and of the nature and management of entrepreneurial activity (including legal, moral and ecological issues).

The course of study seems very like a UK A-level programme, and the kinds of major projects that have emerged during 1996 (only the third year that the course has been operating) mirror exactly the kinds of innovative outcomes that one would be looking for in our programmes:

(b) remodelling the reception area of a hotel.

- the roller sail – a hand-held sail system to be used when roller-blading
- a veterinary surgeon's suit – meeting the needs of protection and implement storage
- the echidna caravan – challenging the traditional caravan concept
- artificial insemination – improving the efficiency of farmers using AI procedures.

Interestingly, following the mandatory programme in years 7–8, the HSC programme has taken off with great success and currently has in excess of 7000 students enrolled, which is approximately 14 per cent of the entire year 12 cohort.

Curriculum development in design and technology in NSW has undoubtedly been driven through the activities of the Board of Studies. Bob Staples, the head of the technology section, is at pains to point out the

Board's debt to the UK. It has watched closely our developments and has taken what it regards as the best of our practice and developed it for the NSW setting. Amongst the features that it sees as 'best practice' has been the coallescing of a core of design and technology that transcends the traditional disciplines in rigid materials, food, textiles and graphics.[13] The NSW curriculum has extended this integrating core (for example into management and entrepreneurial endeavour) and has downplayed the separate disciplines even more than did the original UK Order.

In schools, however, the adoption of design and technology practice remains patchy. Many schools are taking forward the syllabuses and producing excellent work right up to HSC level, but equally there remain a significant group of teachers and schools who cling to a more traditional view of technology and who – as far as possible – continue to operate within a comfort zone of 'industrial technology', 'home economics' and the like. However, given the relatively late start that NSW made with technology programmes (most of them have come on stream since 1992) it has made great progress in the last five years. And this appears to be due to the combined activities of the Board of Studies in developing and promoting the programmes, and the Department of Education in supporting them through the work of the specialist supervisor/inspector teams.

Assessing technology

I have already suggested that assessment does not feature strongly in the course developments of the last few years in NSW. It is all but absent from the year K–6 course, and just about evident in the year 7–8 course. It is present principally as advice on the kinds of things that might be done by teachers in order to make an assessment. For example, it suggests that one might:

- engage in conversation with pupils;
- establish and listen in to group discussions;
- encourage pupils to mount exhibitions of their work.

But advice is singularly lacking when it comes to what the teacher might actually *do* with these kinds of evidence. There is no advice on converting evidence into data. However, this criticism is less true with the HSC programme in years 11 and 12. In part because of the requirements of university entrance, the assessment arrangements are somewhat more defined here and involve written examinations and project assessment. The written examination contributes 40 marks and falls into three sections:

(i)   a series of compulsory multiple choice questions (max. 10 marks);
(ii) some structured but free-response questions (max. 20 marks);
(iii) some questions related to the 'comparative study' (max. 10 marks).

However, the bulk of the marks (60 per cent) derive from the major project, and this is subdivided into sections as follows;

- Project management (15 marks)
  - action, time, and finance plans
  - application of plans
  - identification and use of resources
- Project development and realisation (38 marks)
  - documentation of research
  - testing and experimentation
  - idea generation and development
  - communication and presentation
  - skills and quality
  - creativity and innovation
- Project evaluation (7 marks)
  - identification of appropriate criteria
  - analysis of functional and aesthetic requirements
  - final evaluation of original proposal.

The documentation of these subdivisions includes specific criteria that need to be met, and students 'need to show the relationship between the documented evidence of development recorded in the folio, and the project outcome' (Board of Studies NSW 1993b).

The process of project assessment requires the students to mount an exhibition of their work which is visited by two examiners from the Board of Studies who mark the work 'blind' and then compare and negotiate agreed marks. This procedure involved the Board in appointing and training 200 examiners from all over NSW. Strangely, however, no interaction is allowed between the examiners and the teacher responsible for the course in the school. All such contact must wait until after the results are published. In the interests of secrecy, NSW is thereby missing out on one of the most powerful devices of professional development for its teachers, since the process of agreeing project marks with an examiner is a very formative process that helps teachers to focus on the critical strengths and weaknesses of projects. However, at the end of each examining cycle, the Board of Studies produces a detailed 'Examination Report' on all facets of the examination, pointing out strengths and weaknesses and reproducing annotated samples of work (see, for example, Board of Studies NSW 1995).

The assessment procedures of the HSC design and technology course do undoubtedly reflect the principles of the course, but they are rather less developed than is the course itself. Whilst the course readily accepts the idea that outcomes may be of a variety of kinds – some with more of an investigative focus and some with more of a product focus – the framework of requirements for assessment is not permitted to reflect this differential. The mark allocations are fixed and non-negotiable. And the large blocks of marks result in some uncertainty between markers that probably reduces reliability.[14] Nevertheless, the examination is clearly gaining ground and is fully accepted as a university entrance qualification. It is worth underlining this point, since it is a matter of real significance in NSW and a point of major difference with WA.

University Entrance

The university entrance process is similar throughout Australia, but – as I pointed out earlier in this chapter – the different states credit student performance on different courses as part of the process. In WA only a limited number of courses (28) are allowed to count towards the Tertiary Entrance Examination (TEE), but in NSW 149 courses count towards the compilation of the Tertiary Entrance Rank (TER). But not all at the same level. Courses are graded in significance as A or B, or not counted at all. Interestingly, design and technology is graded as an A subject, whilst its predecessors (industrial technology, technical drawing, etc.) are typically B grade and hence of far less significance for the TER. It is recognised that the intellectual demands of the design and technology course represent a significant extension of the demand in former courses, and it is credited accordingly. This factor will have been significant in encouraging recruitment into the HSC course in design and technology and out of the former courses.

NSW and the national 'Student Outcome Statements'

It is also worth mentioning the relationships that exist between the current course assessment procedures in NSW and the national profile of SOSs in technology.

First, it is important to recognise that the technology personnel in the Board of Studies in NSW – significantly Bob Staples – were very influential in the drafting of the national SOS in technology. NSW was considered to be a leading state in the development of design and technology courses, and the Board of Studies team in NSW was therefore pivotal in the debates that sought to identify the national profiles.

However, once it became clear that the implementation of the SOSs was being devolved to the individual states, the NSW Board of Studies adopted the policy of translating the capabilities enshrined in the national SOSs into syllabus requirements for the year K–6, 7–10 and 11–12 courses in design and tchnology. Outcomes-based assessment was not explicitly adopted in NSW, so the outcomes were included in the course documents as part of the articulation of the syllabus. In the HSC programme, for example, a course objective would be elaborated as follows;

Course objective (i.e. students will . . .)	Outcome (i.e. students should be able to . . .)
• develop skills in managing	• establish priorities and goals for designing and producing
	• plan and implement a sequence of operations
	• investigate the management of two contrasting organisations

In this way, the essence of the national 'outcome' statements was absorbed into and expressed through the 'input' documents for a course of study.

The 'outcomes' became advice to teachers on what might be expected of the course. They did not become assessment boxes to be ticked.

Australia in retrospect

The state of development of design and technology curricula in Western Australia and New South Wales is very different. Unit courses in WA are still largely dominated by the craft traditions of some years ago. And where there are innovative technology units in WA they are the result of the individual initiatives of teachers and schools. By contrast, in NSW there has been significant central investment in curriculum development for design and technology through the Board of Studies, and this is gradually permeating into schools and developing practice across the state.

However, the differences in assessment practice are just as interesting – and they centre on the very different approaches being taken with respect to the national SOSs.

In WA the plan is that the SOSs will be used as an assessment device to help drive curriculum development. The unit courses are to be rewritten by schools to accommodate the SOSs, and this involves teachers tackling two quite different tasks: transforming their current traditional craft-centred courses into design-based courses under the generic flag of technology and enterprise; and transforming their current assessment practices (judgments on a sliding-scale) into a system of 'checking off' a series of student outcome statements.

In NSW, the first of these tasks has been supported from the centre by the Board of Studies curriculum development in design and technology. And the second task has effectively been side-stepped since the national 'outcome' statements have been reframed into 'input' course documents to support teachers, rather than to be used as an assessment instrument.

There is no doubt that there are innovative schools in WA that are tackling the whole business of outcomes-based education with vigour and with exciting consequences. The whole curriculum is being re-examined and reconstructed. But this is the minority of schools that will make the system fly. And even in these schools the teachers readily acknowledge that the benefits are in terms in curriculum development rather than assessment. The central problem, however, for the remaining majority of schools is that they are to be given all the new 'outcomes' to achieve with their pupils – but they will be given no curriculum through which to do it. It is difficult to see how they can reasonably be expected to manage the consequences.

One obvious solution (from an outsider's perspective) is that WA could readily absorb the curriculum development materials that have already been prepared in NSW. Why not adopt the latter's resources and courses? This would have at least three obvious effects: first, it would give WA teachers a teachable curriculum, one that would help them move towards design and technology; second, it would enable WA (like NSW) to address the national SOS through its course materials; and third, it would prevent teachers in WA from getting bogged down in assessment against uncountable SOSs. But it would also offend the principle of state autonomy, so sadly there is no chance of it happening.

Notes

1 It is fascinating that, whatever the basis of listing, technology always manages to get to the bottom!
2 Industrial Arts is the dominant form of studio/workshop activity in WA. It is traditional craft-based activity (see Chapter 8 for an account of industrial arts in the USA).
3 There is currently much debate about LOTE. The major languages are French and Japanese, with Indonesian picking up fast and some debate about the need for Chinese.
4 All technology (industrial arts) and LOTE units, are electives.
5 One of the consistent features in the development of design and technology courses in the UK is that they were initially developed against the tide of opinion. Such courses are challenging and initially uncomfortable for pupils and for teachers, and they are unfamiliar to and therefore mistrusted by parents. In this situation, such courses only developed where there was strong leadership in a department/school that was prepared to ride out this initial resistance. These became the centres of excellence upon which the whole development of the design and technology National Curriculum was founded. In WA, there are currently very few such centres.
6 Consistent exposure to the processes of design and technology has been a significant feature of technology developments in the UK, where annual timetables – rather than course units – shape the curriculum. This raises interesting questions about the relationship between flexibility and innovation.
7 Mr G Hicks was Staff Inspector for Design and Technology at the Department of Education and Science in the late 1980s when the UK was seeking to finalise and implement the original technology Order (DES 1990). His thinking had been very influential in the emergence of design and technology during the late 1970s and 1980s. In the early years of implementation of the National Curriculum (1990–92) he was alarmed that teachers were looking more to the SoA than to the PoS as the guiding light for curriculum, and he was very critical of the consequences.
8 I am reminded of the formulae that were initially used to calculate National Curriculum levels in England and Wales from a pattern of SoA 'hits'.
9 The exceptions to this are art courses and some 'performance' courses. Art history is a TEE-approved course for which portfolios can be considered by the receiving institution. And some performing arts courses involve interviews.
10 This is a problem that teachers in the UK will remember from pre-GCSE days when we had to advise pupils about GCE or CSE courses. Whenever two systems run in parallel, and one has prestige and tradition behind it whilst the other has different merits, teachers will be torn in their advice to students. I fear that the development of GNVQ as an 'alternative A level' (whilst real A levels remain alive and well) may be forcing us into the same trap.
11 I use the term 'checked off' deliberately, since it was used frequently by the teachers.

12 The conference of the Australian Council for Education through Technology (ACET), held in Hobart, Tasmania in January 1994.
13 The NSW technology team at the Board of Studies is critical of the successive revisions of design and technology in the UK which it sees as moving back from these integrating principles towards a more limited and disciplinary approach.
14 I had the opportunity to discuss the allocation of marks with several examiners, who readily admit to the difficulty of pitching a mark out of 38 for pupils' 'project development'.

part three

International reflections

eleven

Reflections

It has been a genuinely fascinating process putting together the four sketches of practice in technology curriculum and assessment from around the world. And it is very tempting at this point to leap into broad-brush comparisons between these highly contrasted arrangements. It would be interesting, for example, to analyse the effects on education systems of academic selection into separate kinds of schooling. In Germany there is a rigidly separated tripartite system (*Hauptschule*, *Realschule* and *Gymnasium*) and in Taiwan there is a twin-track system (senior high school and vocational high school) whilst in Australia and the USA there are comprehensive systems. Or it might be interesting to analyse the consequences for policy-making of having the highest education policy position held by an expert in education. The Commissioners of Education for Taiwan and for New York State were both teachers and experts in education before their appointments as policy supremos. But I shall resist this kind of broad-brush analysis, since I am not an expert in comparative education and it was never the purpose of this book to engage in such systemic analysis. I set out to examine how these four countries dealt with technology curricula and the associated assessment, and I have only included broader description of the education systems in order to contextualise this technological material.

As far as these system-wide features of education policy are concerned, therefore, I shall content myself with the somewhat anodyne observation that national education policies appear to be a reflection of the prevailing values of the societies they serve. In Taiwan, for example, far more effort, time and hence money are spent on the lower-ability vocational students than on the high-fliers in the belief that the future of the nation is dependent on all students being educated to the highest possible level. By contrast, in Germany, policy is far more selective: picking out high-fliers and throwing far more lavish facilities, opportunities, and hence life chances in their path. I am tempted to suggest that the UK sits somewhere between these two contrasted positions.

So, returning to my principal concern with technology, the study has demonstrated that technology is without doubt an idea whose time has now come. All the overseas case studies reveal significant action towards the development and formalisation of technology curricula, and it would be tempting to engage in some cherry-picking towards an idealised version of a technology curriculum and an associated assessment regime, drawing on what seem to me to be the best ideas in the examples from overseas. I might suggest, for example, that we should encourage more of the 'complex systems' activities that exist in Germany (see Chapter 7) that require pupils to take whole socio-technical systems (like a hospital or a super-market) and analyse and model them in relation to the human, financial and technical systems that they necessarily integrate. It is interesting that a very similar kind of activity (the 'comparative study') is promoted in New South Wales within the Higher School Certificate course in years 11 and 12 (see Chapter 10). But this kind of cherry-picking would result in a highly personal construct of my own, and accordingly I think it is more appropriate that readers should take what strikes them as important in the overseas examples I have presented and find their own ways of incorporating any new ideas into their own teaching.

I have therefore resisted all these tempting visions of what this final chapter might be like, and I shall hold to my original purpose, which was to take the strands that emerged in Part One of this book – crystallised in Chapter 6 as the 'lessons we should have learned' – and to see whether, or to what extent, these issues have been played out in the overseas examples described in Part Two. I shall therefore tackle this task by using the same analysis that I used in Chapter 6, briefly reminding the reader of the issue and how it arose in the UK and then drawing from the international comparisons to illuminate, enrich and/or adjust the account of the 'lessons we should have learned'.

The limits of law in the classroom

The essence of this issue is in the extent to which teachers are able to make professional judgments about what they will teach, how they will teach it, and about how they should assess the abilities of their students. To what extent is the practice of teaching controlled by policies imposed from elsewhere and – conversely – to what extent is it the professional responsibility of the teacher? Early versions of the National Curriculum for England and Wales were highly prescriptive and removed much of the professional autonomy of teachers – but in subsequent revisions this has been significantly lessened, allowing teachers far more freedom of action.

The international picture is clear on this point. Taiwan stands alone in operating a tightly controlled curriculum. The curriculum is drawn up by ministry-approved bodies and is supported by ministry-approved textbooks. The majority of teaching 'follows the book' and this is thought quite proper in what is undoubtedly a highly conformist culture. By contrast, in

New York State, teachers could compose for themselves a series of quite new curriculum activities, as could teachers in Germany and Australia.

There is a further major issue embedded in this matter, however, for in all countries the technology curriculum is struggling to establish itself by transforming existing traditions – typically craft traditions. So the issue of freedom of action for teachers cuts both ways. In New York State, in particular, I have shown how the 'free market' in curriculum units acts as a reactionary pressure, tending to maintain existing practice rather than encourage change. Exactly the same can be said of Western Australia. By contrast, when Taiwan completes its new curriculum standard in 'living technology' it is planned that it will be enforced from the centre as the new orthodoxy for all teachers.

Successful transformations to technology curricula appear to move through four stages of development, two of which are critically dependent upon the freedom of action of teachers, and the other two on central policy. Development invariably starts in individual classrooms where teachers have the autonomy to experiment with new ideas and practices. This has been the case in every country I have visited, though is far more the case in some than others. In Germany there is plenty of scope, but in Taiwan there is much more limited scope. These developments – often centred on individual teachers and schools – gradually enable individual schools (or local groups of schools) to emerge as centres of excellence that are the proving ground for subsequent developments.

Thereafter, in a second stage, successful development of new technology curricula appears to depend upon sufficient central direction to create and disseminate materials and support training regimes. The critical issue here is that centrally produced materials enable teachers to experiment with the new practices without having to take all the responsibility of developing them for themselves. This point was reached:

in the early 1980s in the UK, with developments towards GCSE;
in the late 1980s in New York State, with the mandated junior high school curriculum;
in the early 1990s in New South Wales, with the work of the Board of Studies;
it has just been reached in Taiwan, with the new 'living technology' curriculum;
and it has not happened at all in Germany.[1]

The third phase of adoption is reached when there is a sufficient head of steam behind the initiative to make it mandatory and enforce the requirement of a technology curriculum. This condition currently exists only in a much more patchy form: in the UK for ages 5–16 in the National Curriculum; in New South Wales for ages 5–14; in New York State only in the junior high schools (12–14 years); in Taiwan also in junior high schools (12–14 years) at some point in the near future when the 'living technology' curriculum becomes the standard; and in Germany not at all.

But in this process of adoption, there appears also to be a fourth condition for the successful development of a technology curriculum. There is a need for teachers to have the freedom of action to embed the new practice into their own existing practices in their own ways. This requires the mandatory framework to be sufficiently light and flexible to enable teachers to accommodate it within their own circumstances, and equally it requires that teachers have the right to be choosy about centrally developed materials – adopting, modifying, customising or rejecting them as is appropriate in their individual classrooms.

Developing curriculum and assessment practice is a highly complex process, and it is expecting a lot to have the right political and educational climate for this combination of conditions to be met. The conditions are even to an extent contradictory, since the important autonomy to innovate (stage 1) can so easily be overridden by the equally important need to legislate (stage 3), and the early days of National Curriculum implementation in England and Wales provide a classic example of this. The apparent contradiction can, however, be harmonised by having a light legislative framework, and explicit encouragement to teachers to innovate within it. And undoubtedly the smoothest development I have observed is in New South Wales, which was able to learn from experience in the UK and, in addition to legislating a framework of provision and providing some excellent curriculum materials, empowered teachers to pick and choose and modify the materials in their own ways and for their own purposes. And as a result it now has an established and respected technology curriculum. The USA will almost always fall at the third (central legislation) hurdle, being very reluctant to mandate any technology in schools. Whilst two of the 50 states have a small bridge-head of mandated technology courses, the devolved nature of US decision-making in schools makes it a very uphill battle. Taiwan's late development in technology is easily explained by the lack of initiating centres of innovation. Schools were all following the former 'standard' of industrial arts. But – informed by pressure from overseas – the *living technology* curriculum has been approved and is being resourced centrally. It will be interesting over the next few years to see how the final adoption stage in individual classrooms is managed and encouraged. And in Germany, in all but one of the 16 *Länder*, policy-makers do not take technology sufficiently seriously to sponsor central developments – believing it to be an industrial, vocational issue of limited relevance to general education. So whilst there are isolated examples of innovative practice in schools and in teacher education, there is very little cohesive development.

These examples provide some helpful guidelines for what are the appropriate limits of law-makers in the classroom. Law-makers have a very limited role at the start of the process of development. They will seldom initiate a new curriculum development; rather they respond to the innovations of others. And neither (at the other end of the process of development) can law-makers force teachers to do things in their individual classrooms.

But law-makers are critical in the middle stages of the process, sponsoring the development and dissemination of materials and training and ultimately creating the mandatory framework that transforms the optional, innovative development into a formal requirement. I shall return to this point at the end of this chapter.

The separation of assessment functions

One of the guiding ambitions for National Curriculum assessment in England and Wales was that it would unite all the multiple forms of school-based assessment into a single system. Formative classroom assessment, summative awards and certification, and evaluative system monitoring were all to be accomplished in a single unified system of assessment. And, as I attempted to illustrate in Chapters 5 and 6, it failed.

In none of the countries I have examined for this book is there such a single unified system of assessment. New York State gets closest with its attachment to testing (typically standardised multiple-choice testing) which enables it to link summative with evaluative functions.[2] Newspapers (for example) produce a version of league tables that list the graduation rates of individual schools – which are standardised because of the state tests. But none of the teachers I spoke to would claim that such tests fulfil a formative function, except in so far as they help to condition the pupils into the techniques of test-taking. In Taiwan, the JEE and JCEE test results (see Chapter 9) are not published, and league tables of schools are therefore not produced. This is partly because the information is thought to be confidential, and partly because – up to senior high school – pupils attend their local schools and a 'market' in schools (with 'successful' schools attracting more applicants) would not be permitted.

In most countries, the evidence suggests that two of the three functions can be unified, but not the third. In Germany, Australia and Taiwan, formative classroom assessment is successfully linked to summative awards and certification of various kinds, but nowhere has this been linked to the formal evaluation of schools. This system-wide monitoring function is typically conducted either by some version of APU testing using small representative samples of pupils (see Chapter 3), or by inspection procedures, or both.

The limitations of atomised assessment

This issue arose in the National Curriculum of England and Wales when teachers were faced with hundreds of 'statements of attainment' and had to tick 'yes' or 'no' for each pupil. The assessment forms became enormous, with ever smaller boxes to be ticked, and the procedures became increasingly unmanageable and meaningless to the point where it all collapsed and has now been completely redesigned.

In Western Australia there are signs that this same precipice is looming. Western Australia is currently developing and trialling 'Student Outcome Statements' (SOS!) – similar to those used in the early days of the National Curriculum – as a means for assessment and reporting student performance. And even in the advanced and supportive trial schools, teachers are experimenting with dubious ways to reduce the immense labour and the burden of paper that result. The Department of Education officers in technology have no expectation that the system will be generally workable in all schools across the state. It is therefore unclear at this point quite what will happen, but I predict that something will intervene to transform the initiative before 1998 when it is scheduled for implementation.

None of the other countries or states that I have examined for this book has developed anything like our still-born SoA (or Western Australia's SOS) as a means for assessing and reporting pupil performance in technology. I sincerely hope that this message will not be lost on the National Council for Vocation Qualifications in the context of GNVQ assessment in the UK, which in its preliminary pilot phase is experimenting with dangerously atomised approaches to assessment (see Chapter 2).

The universal message from technology assessment practice overseas is that using a plethora of outcome statements as performance criteria for assessment can be used effectively to support other mechanisms of assessment, but they are not of themselves a complete system of assessment. They are – at the same time – too atomised and too imprecise and they rely on the dangerously simplistic belief that pupils can be categorised yes or no; black or white, sheep or goats. None of the countries I visited is using such a system.

The false dichotomy of norms and criteria

The assessment trend of the last 20 years has been away from norm-referenced assessment towards criterion-referenced assessment. I have argued (in Chapters 5 and 6) that neither is a complete solution and I used the metaphor of the battlefield to illustrate the point. If we want to hit a target, the bearing (the direction in which we should be aiming) is provided by the criterion; but the range (how far we go in that direction) is provided by the norms of the target group we are seeking to make judgments about. Criteria alone are inadequate for reliable assessment, since their level of difficulty needs to be calibrated before the criterion has any meaning (see Chapter 6).

This point is beautifully illustrated in the German six-point scale of assessment (see Chapter 7). There are criteria for assessment in each subject that define performance from *Note* 1 (excellent) down to *Note* 6 (unacceptable) and these criteria stay the same throughout years 6, 7, 8, 9 and 10. How can this be? Surely its unfair since if the criteria are supposed to be unchanging stamps of quality, how can they reflect the fact

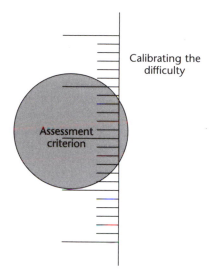

Figure 11.1 Teachers need additional information to calibrate the difficulty of criteria.

that the pupils become more competent and knowledgeable as they grow up through these years? The point is that the criteria are quite explicitly 'normed' by a further addition to each group of criteria in the assessment regime that says 'the level of performance, commitment and effort was appropriate to the potential of a pupil of his age'. So *Note* 1 means something at year 6 and something more sophisticated at year 7, 8 and so on. The criteria exist on a sliding scale of interpretation.

In Taiwan and New York State, this debate might appear irrelevant since the vast majority of the high-stakes assessment procedures are based on multiple-choice tests that can be 'marked' by machines. In both systems there is some classroom-based assessment of course-work that is informed by criteria, and which lead to marks that count towards graduation. But there is no requirement for teachers to justify the criteria they use or the marks they derive from them. The exercise is non-critical and therefore the use of criteria (and the interplay of norms with criteria) has not been seriously debated. The critical debates surround the high-status test data, and here the issue of the relationship of norms and criteria is significantly illuminated by the process of test development. I describe this process in Chapter 8, and illustrate how the tests themselves – the supposedly pure, objective discriminators – are in fact normed to the test population. Trial questions are pre-tested to derive a 'facility index' (the proportion of the population that can get the right answer) and questions will only be used in the real test if their 'facility' is within given tolerances. Criteria and norms are therefore quite explicitly embedded side by side in these supposedly objective tests.

Western Australia is trying to get to grips with Student Outcome Statements as a means for assessing and reporting performance. And it is beginning to experience precisely the same difficulties that emerged in the
UK when we tried to do assessments against the 150 SoA in the original
technology Order. The SOSs in the WA curriculum are just as imprecise
and malleable as were our SoA. Their meaning lies entirely in interpretation, and as I pointed out in Chapter 10, once the SOSs become part of the
Western Australian state monitoring procedures for schools, teachers assessing pointers at levels 1–3, will feel under considerable pressure to move
up the scale and rewrite them for levels 3–5, so that level 4 emerges as a
year 7–8 norm rather than level 2. I have no doubt that they could do
this, since the meaning of the SOS is all in the interpretation. The SOSs
(like UK SoA) are not – and can never be – precise criteria of excellence
that (in themselves) enable teachers to make reliable judgments. They will
always rely on interpretation, and teachers' interpretation will always be
in relation to performance norms derived from their experience. There is
absolutely nothing wrong with this. It is quite proper and indeed quite
inevitable. But we do need to acknowledge that it is what happens.

The challenge of national standards

The issue here concerns how we move progressively to a position in which
the judgments made by teachers are the same nation-wide. I made the point
in Chapter 6 that whilst judgments must start with individual teachers
holding standards derived from their own experience, we must also have
a system for enabling teachers to share these standards more widely –
across the school, the region and ultimately the state or country – to
ensure that standards are consistently applied.

I was surprised to find that this is not a matter that receives much
attention in Germany. School-leaving examinations in technology are
devised locally in the school and marked in the school, with no requirement for moderation or adjustment in relation to a regional or national
standard. Standards are thought to reside quite properly with teachers, and
when I challenged this idea it was seen almost as though I was challenging
teachers' honesty or integrity. There is the *Fachberater* system of advisory
teachers who are available as consultants to the school and who will visit
to discuss and help to develop the curriculum or the assessment procedures. But the process is advisory and their duties are not formally related
to any examination and assessment system. It is a very relaxed regime.

As I have outlined above, the Taiwanese and New York State systems
place great faith in the reliability of their relentless testing regimes. And
with good cause. The limitations of the testing is all in the validity arena
– whether the tests provide anything like a valid way of measuring performance. The focus is on bald 'facts' and the idea that an examination
might involve activities as complex as composing an argument, performing
an experiment or analysing a problem would not be given too much house

room. However, if one is prepared to be ignore this validity problem, there is no doubt that their tests provide highly reliable data in the sense that they measure pupils right across the state/country by exactly the same standards. Such is the blind certainty of the right/wrong answers to these multiple-choice tests that student scripts are frequently machine-marked. Taiwan in particular sees this as a real strength since it removes any possibility of racial, gender, or any other kind of improper discrimination. Beyond this centralised testing, and in the more personalised domain of assessed course-work in Taiwan and New York State, there appears to be no requirement of moderation within or across schools – let alone across the state/country – so there is no system to develop or enforce a national standard.[3]

New South Wales has quite deliberately downplayed the importance of assessment in the early years of developing a technology curriculum, but the success of that curriculum development has been such that the state is now faced with large numbers of students taking technology as part of the High School Certificate, which has university entrance significance. Consequently, it is now seen as very important that assessments are reliable as well as valid, and New South Wales has appointed 200 examiners who assess exhibitions of work mounted by candidates in schools all around the state. Every candidate's work is seen by two examiners (separately) and marks have then to be agreed between them. There is a system for cross-moderating the examiners, and for reporting back to teachers the strengths and weaknesses of the year's work. In the interests of dispassionate assessment, the teacher in the school does not speak to the examiners, but receives a full report at the end of the process.

In short, New South Wales has invested in a state moderation system that is similar in many ways to some of our UK course-work assessment systems for technology, with roving examiners moderating students course-work exhibitions.[4] The systems are expensive to operate – especially in New South Wales where they require two external examiners – but they achieve much more than just a reliable assessment. The state HSC examination – and the roving external examiners – act as a powerful means for disseminating understanding about the curriculum and for sharing standards of excellence.

However, I do recognise the considerable expense involved in visiting examiner systems, and it seems to me that it would be possible (for New South Wales and for UK course-work examining) to improve the system and make it cheaper at the same time. The development of small regional centres (based in a school or in a college or university) would make it possible for teachers to take their candidates' exhibitions and agree marks across the schools – in much the same way as happened in the CSE days of project assessment (see Chapter 1). These agreed marks could then be presented to a visiting examiner for sampling at the grade boundaries. This would have two benefits: it would reduce the burden and hence the cost of visiting examiners; and it would reinstate the cross-school role of teachers in negotiating and agreeing standards. In the process, it would reassert the professional role of teachers and combine it with a powerful learning and dissemination benefit.

Progression and the value of sliding scales

This issue is related to the initial requirement for teachers to tick or cross statements of attainment for assessment purposes in the UK National Curriculum. The argument is linked to the points above about atomised assessment and norms and criteria, since I argue in Chapters 5 and 6 that even atomised nit-picking criteria are never the black and white things they purport to be.

Teachers' concern is with improving the performance of their students and the concept of improvement is far more manageably and appropriately discussed when using sliding scales of excellence. Bald 'yes' or 'no' judgments are supremely unhelpful in this kind of debate. Moreover, they are based on a dangerous assumption that improvement requires pupils to do something different, rather than doing the same thing to a higher level of quality.

None of the countries I examined is currently using any form of absolutist yes/no assessment against pre-specified performance statements. They are all using some form of sliding scale – generally informed by criteria. Typically the criteria are specified, and then blocks of marks are allocated to each so that performance against the criterion can be debated at different levels of quality (see below).

As I have described above, Western Australia is the only state where student outcome statements are being debated for the future; but in its trial schools teachers are already constructing their own sliding scales for each SOS and there seems very little likelihood that the system will be implemented on schedule, if at all (see Chapter 10). There are so many educational and management failings in these systems of assessment, that it is encouraging to see that they are also very rare. They are a fragile and (hopefully) an increasingly endangered species of assessment.

Uniting scales with criteria

A mixture of principle and pragmatism therefore brings us to the logical end-point of these arguments. Criteria are useful both in identifying the targets towards which pupils should be working and in giving form to the measures of excellence used by teachers. But criteria alone are not enough since they are enacted by teachers largely through a process of interpretation that is capable of adjusting their difficulty. Sliding scales of excellence are important to teachers in two ways. At the pupil level, they help teachers to have purposeful discussions about improvement; but at the assessment level, they help teachers to develop and hold in their minds a sense of quality. And they do this by enabling teachers to relate the performance of

Figure 11.2 Criteria, performance descriptors and sliding scales of excellence.

their pupils one to another; the best 'modellers' or 'researchers' or 'makers' can be examined alongside the less good and the differences between them help to inform the debate about what we might mean by quality. Norms and criteria therefore interact in constructive ways.

In Chapter 6 I illustrated the Oxford A level assessment form, which had arrived at this position in the late 1970s. But modifications on this system have since become the standard means for assessing technological activity. Criteria are identified, and for each one a block of marks is allocated to it that reflect its perceived importance. A scale of excellence is then attached to each that places a number of performance descriptors on a quality scale. In identifying the appropriate level for any pupil's work, the teacher is informed both by the descriptors themselves and by the judgments s/he has made of the equivalent performance of other pupils in the same activity. The judgment is then rendered into a mark allocation.

There is a natural hierarchy of importance here that enables us to discriminate between criteria and performance descriptors. The criteria are significant features of the activity, whilst the performance descriptors are merely examples (at different levels of quality) of how the criterion might manifest itself in pupils' work. Some schemes invite teachers to supplement the performance descriptors with their own examples to aid the process of teachers' 'owning' the system. And other schemes invite teachers to customise the system to individual projects so that whilst the criteria stay the same in all projects, the performance descriptors are written to be relevant to the particular activity. And yet other schemes (as with the Oxford Delegacy nearly two decades ago) allow teachers to supplement the core criteria with additional ones – along with appropriate supporting performance descriptors – up to a certain proportion of marks.

Some variant of this arrangement was at work in most of the countries I visited. In New York State, the project assessment process for the junior high school 'introduction to technology' course and the senior high school 'principles of engineering' course used this approach (see Chapter 8). In Taiwan the trial schools working on the 'living technology' course are using criteria with associated mark allocations and sliding scales of excellence, but have not developed it to the point of performance descriptors. In New South Wales in the Higher School Certificate course a similar position has been reached, though in this case, whilst the assessment mechanism itself does not formulate performance descriptors, the syllabus incorporates the national student outcome statements. They are not specifically assessed, but they exist in the planning framework for the course. In Germany, technology as a vehicle of general education is not taken seriously, and certainly technology project assessment does not feature significantly in school examination systems. However, where project work exists for example, in 'materials handling' in years 6–9 in the *Hauptschule* – the six-point assessment systems use a combinaton of a sliding scale illuminated by criteria. And the criteria are of two kinds; the generic ones that define the six-point scale for the whole of the years 6–9 inclusive, and the task-specific ones that are used to tune the generic criteria to the immediate project (see Chapter 7).

The assessment process therefore involves criteria, and performance descriptors on a sliding scale, and (typically) mark allocations to reflect and subsequently to compute the judgment into a final score. The act of assessment is then a two-stage process: the pitch (in which the teacher makes an initial judgment about where on the scale a piece of work should best be located); and the check (in which the teacher compares the work with adjacent examples of other pupils' work to confirm the quality rating (see Chapter 3). All the features of the assessment scheme have an important role to play in this process, and none of them, on their own, could be a complete system.

The naivety of early norm-referenced systems of assessment (that had few – if any – criteria to guide the marking) is matched only by the naivety of recent criterion-referenced systems that assume there is no role for scales and flexible quality ratings. Teachers need both to make good assessments.

Teachers as professional curriculum developers

The final lesson to which I drew attention in Chapter 6 relates to the issue of raising standards of pupil performance. When the UK government took on this slogan in the late 1980s it resulted in a massive transfer of authority to the centre – and equally a massive reduction in the freedom of action of teachers in the classroom. Huge quantities of 'bumf' were produced as directive after directive was dreamed up in the ministry (and its associated quangos) and weeks later thumped weightily on to the doormats of schools. The rhetoric was that this was all done in the interests of raising standards, but in technology the evidence was that it lowered them. But it could have been handled differently and policy has now evolved to a more intelligent position.

The problem was that the National Curriculum was seen in government circles as a complete prescription for all rather than as a minimum (baseline) statutory requirement. By presenting is as a complete prescription, our best and most innovative schools were stopped in their tracks – and even went backwards. Instead of providing a base line below which it was unacceptable to fall, the National Curriculum technology Order was presented as a straitjacket into which everyone had to fit.

From its very inception in the late 1960s, the growth of the technology curriculum has been dependent upon pioneering developments emerging from schools. These pioneering centres provided models of curriculum and developed standards of practice that were gradually disseminated and subsequently became the rocks upon which was built the idea of a National Curriculum entitlement in technology. It is ironic indeed that the debt that was owed to these centres was repaid by removing from them the right to go on developing their curriculum. It is as though we were saying: 'Thanks for developing the curriculum for us up to now, but we know all the answers now so you must just do as we tell you'.

The well-being of the technology curriculum is, was and always will be dependent upon the imagination and enterprise of teachers. And such teachers are dependent upon having the right to continue developing their curriculum and their practice. As I trust I have shown in Chapters 7–10, this right of teachers is well established in Germany, in New York State, in New South Wales and in Western Australia. It is far less common in Taiwan, where conformist cultural traditions result in curriculum development being initiated every ten years or so from the centre. But interestingly (as I have shown in Chapter 9) this centrally inspired curriculum change has been significantly influenced by international developments in technology curricula, not least the New York State junior high school 'introduction to technology' course, which was in its turn a development of some of the UK strands of technology curriculum.

I suggested above that technology curricula have emerged, and continue to emerge, through a four-stage process:

- Development invariably starts in individual classrooms, where teachers experiment with new ideas and practices.
- Thereafter, in a second stage, successful development depends upon sufficient central direction to create and disseminate materials and support training regimes to enable teachers to experiment with these new practices without having to take all the responsibility for developing them for themselves.
- The third phase of adoption is reached when there is a sufficient head of steam behind the initiative to make it mandatory and enforce the requirement of a technology curriculum at some (or all) stages of schooling – backed up by some form of assessment and testing.
- The final stage of adoption is where teachers embed the new practice into their own existing practices in their own ways, being choosy about centrally developed materials, and adopting, modifying, customising or rejecting them as appropriate in their individual classrooms.

This is the nature of curriculum development as we have experienced it in technology. And any nation that seeks to embark on nationalising its curriculum must have a strategy for ensuring the conditions that enable the first and last of these stages to happen. It is (relatively) easy to legislate a curriculum. It is far harder to create the conditions that allow it to become a reality in every classroom and ensure that the curriculum continues to develop and avoids becoming a fossilised dinosaur.

In 1985 I was asked to write the 'guide for teachers' that introduced the 16+ GCSE examination in CDT.[5] In the four-stage process outline above, it represented a major move within the second stage: a national consolidation of developments, but not at that time a compulsory national curriculum. But even at that time I was conscious of the dangers implicit in such a consolidation, and in the concluding section of the guide, I wrote as follows

> The National Criteria for CDT represent a timely consolidation of current thinking. However if the steady growth and development of CDT over the last twenty years has taught us anything at all, it is that to advance our thinking we must rely on the innovation and creative endeavour of teachers in the classroom. The National Criteria are not carved in tablets of stone and the provisions exist to modify and extend them in the light of further curriculum developments. Without this possibility of innovation, CDT will wither and die and our common aim should be to look back in twenty years time and note how far we have progressed . . .
>
> (Kimbell 1986)

The first half of those twenty years has now passed, and we have had a real white-knuckle roller-coaster of a ride, alternately crashing forwards and lurching backwards amidst much excited screaming and desperate clinging on. But hopefully we are now emerging into calmer waters, where the assurance of national standards can coexist with the creative development of the curriculum.

I truly hope we have learned that the quality of our technology curriculum, and the quality of pupils' work within it, depends critically upon our ability and willingness to develop and support teachers as autonomous creative professionals.

Notes

1 Germany's reluctance is probably accounted for by its deeply embedded belief that technology is industry-related and vocational. It is therefore not the concern of the high-status *Gymnasium*, and hence not worthy of a centrally directed effort in curriculum development.

2 I believe that the idea of national testing – with results aggregated up from the individual child to the school, region, state and country to create various kinds of league tables – was imported by Secretary of State Kenneth Baker as a result of his numerous transatlantic trips to Reagan's America. Short, sharp testing was never previously part of the UK landscape, but it no doubt seemed obvious and simple. It all fell apart when test developers in the UK insisted on tests that had educational significance in the classroom.

3 It remains to be seen whether New York State will develop and enforce the state test for maths science and technology (MST) outlined in Chapter 8. If it does,

then it will raise interesting issues of who does the marking and how these marks are to be ratified.

4 It is a matter of great regret to me that the Oxford A-level examination in design, that was for years a pioneer of sophisticated project assessment techniques, has recently eliminated the visiting examiner system on grounds of cost.

5 CDT in the 1980s was one of the most influential stages through which we developed the technology curriculum in the UK.

Bibliography

Assessment of Performance Unit (1981) *Understanding Design and Technology.* London: DES.

Assessment of Performance Unit (1989) *Science at Age 13.* London: HMSO.

Atkinson, E.S. (1995) Approaches to designing at Key Stage 4. In J. Smith (ed.) *Proceedings of IDATER 95: International Conference on Design and Technology Educational Research and Curriculum Development,* Loughborough University.

Becker, G.E. (1988) *Assessment and Evaluation of Lessons: Performance Oriented Didactics.* Basel: Beltz Verlag.

Ball, S. (1994) *Education Reform.* Buckingham: Open University Press.

Black, P. (1993) The shifting scenery. In P. O'Hear and J. White (eds) *Assessing the National Curriculum.* London: Paul Chapman.

Board of Studies, New South Wales (1992) *Design and Technology Years 7–10: A Teaching Kit.* Sydney: Board of Studies, New South Wales.

Board of Studies, New South Wales (1993a) *Science and Technology K–6.* Sydney: Board of Studies, New South Wales.

Board of Studies, New South Wales (1993b) *Design and Technology for the High School Certificate.* Sydney: Board of Studies, New South Wales.

Board of Studies, New South Wales (1995) *High School Certificate 1995 Examination Report: Design and Technology.* Sydney: Board of Studies, New South Wales.

Bonser, S. and Grundy, S. (1995) *Using Student Outcomes in the Restructured School – Dangarsleigh (Phase 1).* Perth: Department of Education of Western Australia.

Bowen, R. (1996) Quality teaching in primary school design and technology. *Journal of Design and Technology Education,* 1: 1.

Bruner, J. (1964) The course of cognitive growth. *American Psychologist,* 19: 1–15 January.

Bruner, J. (1968) *Towards a Theory of Instruction.* New York: Norton.

Consortium for Assessment and Teaching in Schools (1990) *Design and Technology: Trial 1990 – Interim Report.* London: CATS/Hodder & Stoughton.

Consortium for Assessment and Teaching in Schools (1991) *Technology KS3: Pilot 1991 – Report.* London: CATS/Hodder & Stoughton.

Curriculum Corporation (1994) *Technology – A Curriculum Profile for Australian Schools*. Carlton, Vic.: Curriculum Corporation.

Curriculum Council for Wales (1989) *National Curriculum Technology, CCW Advisory Paper 5*. Cardiff: Curriculum Council for Wales.

Dearing, R. (1993a) *The National Curriculum and its Assessment, Final Report*. London: SCAA.

Dearing, R. (1993b) *The National Curriculum and its Assessment, an Interim Report*. London: NCC/SEAC.

Department for Education (1995) *Design and Technology: Characteristics of Good Practice in Secondary Schools*. London: HMSO.

Department of Education and Science (1981) *Understanding Design and Technology*. London: DES.

Department of Education and Science (1987a) *The National Curriculum – A Consultative Document*. London: DES.

Department of Education and Science (1987b) *Craft Design and Technology 5–16, Curriculum Matters 9*. London: HMSO.

Department of Education and Science (1988a) *Interim Report of the Design and Technology Working Group*. London: HMSO.

Department of Education and Science (1988b) *Task Group on Assessment and Testing – A Report*. London: DES.

Department of Education and Science (1989a) *National Curriculum: From Policy to Practice*. London: DES.

Department of Education and Science (1989b) *Design and Technology for Ages 5–16*. London: DES.

Department of Education and Science (1990) *Technology in the National Curriculum*. London: HMSO.

Department of Education and Science (1992) *Technology – Key Stages 1, 2 and 3. A Report by HM Inspectorate on the First Year, 1990–91*. London: HMSO.

Department of Education of Western Australia (1996) *Report of the Trial of the Student Outcome Statements: Working Edition 1994; Executive Summary*. Perth: DoEd.

Eggleston, J. (1996) Back to a worn-out drawing board. *The Times Educational Supplement*, 8 March.

Gipps, C. (1993) The structure of assessment and recording. In P. O'Hear and J. White (eds) *Assessing the National Curriculum*. London: Paul Chapman.

Goodson, I. (ed.) (1985) *Social Histories of the Secondary Curriculum*. Lewes: Falmer Press.

Gunstone, R. (1991) Reconstructing theory from practical experience. In B. Woolnough (ed.) *Practical Science*. Buckingham: Open University Press.

Hicks, G. (1983) Another step forward for design and technology. *APU Newsletter*, 4. DES.

Huang, P.H. (1995) Current reform of the Joint College Entrance Examination System in Taiwan ROC. Paper presented to the *International Symposium of College Entrance Examinations*, Tokyo, 4 June.

Hutton, W. (1995) *The State We're In*. London: Vintage.

International Technology Education Association (1996) *Technology for All Americans*. Blacksburg, VA: ITEA.

Kelly, V., Kimbell, R., Patterson, J., Saxton, J. and Stables, K. (1987) *Design and Technology Activity – A Framework for Assessment*. London: HMSO.

Kimbell, R. (1982) *Design Education: The Foundation Years*. London: Routledge & Kegan Paul.

Kimbell, R. (ed.) (1986) *GCSE Craft Design and Technology. A Guide for Teachers.* Milton Keynes: Secondary Examinations Council and Open University.

Kimbell, R. (1988) The Assessment of Performance Unit project in design and technology. In J. Smith (ed.) *Proceedings of the First National Conference in Design and Technology Education Research and Curriculum Development, Loughborough University.* Loughborough University of Technology.

Kimbell, R. (1991) Tackling technological tasks. In B. Woolnough (ed.) *Practical Science.* Buckingham: Open University Press.

Kimbell, R. (1992) Assessing technological capability. In D. Blandow and M. Dyrenfurth (eds) *Proceedings of INCOTE 92,* Weimar, Germany.

Kimbell, R. (1994a) Progression in learning and the assessment of children's attainment. In D. Layton (ed.) *Innovations in Science and Technology Education.* Paris: Unesco.

Kimbell, R. (1994b) Not so much a workshop manual – more a professional guide. *Design and Technology Times,* May.

Kimbell, R. (1996) Lessons from Taiwan. *Independent,* 15 June.

Kimbell, R., Stables, K., Saxton, J., Wheeler, T. and Wozniak, A. (1989) A response from the APU team to the interim report of the National Curriculum Design and Technology Working Group. *DESTECH Series 2,* January.

Kimbell, R., Stables, K., Wheeler, T., Wozniak, A. and Kelly, V. (1991) *The Assessment of Performance in Design and Technology – The Final Report of the APU Design and Technology Project.* London: SEAC/COI.

Kimbell, R., Stables, K. and Green, R. (1996) *Understanding Practice in Design and Technology.* Buckingham: Open University Press.

Kommunales Technikzentrum (1996) *Kommunales Bildungseinrichtung für Arbeit, Wirtschaft und Technik.* Erfurt: Kommunales Technikzentrum.

Kultusminister Nordrhein-Westfalen (ed.) (1981) *Richtlinien für die Gymnasiale Oberstufe in Nordrhein-Westfalen – Technik.* Cologne: Kultusministerium Nordrhein-Westfalen.

Layton, D. (1981) *Aspects of National Curriculum Design and Technology.* York: National Curriculum Council.

Liao, T. (1983) Using engineering case studies to integrate the study of math, science and technology. In *Principles of Engineering: An MST Approach to Technology Education.* Albany: New York State Education Department.

Lockley, P. (1995) Who'd be a teacher. *Independent,* 28 December.

McCormick, R. and Murphy, P. (1994) 'Learning the processes in technology'. Paper presented to the British Educational Research Association annual conference, Oxford University, 8–11 September.

National Center for Education Statistics, US Department of Education (1991) *Digest of Educational Statistics 1990.* Washington, DC: US Government Printing Office.

National Council for Vocational Qualifications (1994) *Grading Foundation and Intermediate GNVQs: Revised Criteria and Guidance.* London: NCVQ.

National Council for Vocational Qualifications and School Curriculum and Assessment Authority (1996) What are the assessment requirements for Part One GNVQ? In conference pack for Part One GNVQ Pilot 1996 Summer Support Conference, London.

National Curriculum Council (1992) *Starting out with the National Curriculum.* York: NCC.

New York State Education Department (1993) *Technology Education: Introduction to Technology.* Albany: New York State Education Department.

New York State Education Department (1996) *Learning Standards for Mathematics, Science and Technology*. Albany: New York State Education Department.

Northern Examination Association (1986) *CDT: Design and Communication. A Syllabus for the General Certificate of Secondary Education*. Manchester: Northern Examination Association.

North Western Secondary School Examination Board (1970) *A Course of Studies in Design*. Manchester: NWSEB.

Office of Technology Assessment of the US Congress (1992) *Testing in American Schools – Asking the Right Questions*. Washington, DC: United States Government Printing Office.

Page, R. (1983) The Schools Council's 'Modular Courses in Technology' Project. In *The Stanley Link in Craft Design and Technology*. Sheffield: Stanley Tools.

Partis, M.T. (1996) *University Entrance in Western Australia with Particular Reference to the Tertiary Entrance Examinations*. Perth, WA: Secondary Education Authority.

Penfold, J. (1988) *Craft Design and Technology: Past Present and Future*. Stoke on Trent: Trentham Books.

Peterson, J. (1983) *The Iowa Testing Program*. Ames: University of Iowa Press.

Samuelson, F. (1987) Was early mental testing (a) racist inspired, (b) objective science, (c) a technology for democracy, (d) the origin of multiple choice exams, (e) none of the above? Mark the RIGHT answer. In M.M. Sokal (ed.) *Psychological Testing and American Society 1890–1930*. New Brunswick, NJ: Rutgers University Press.

Satterly, D. (1989) *Assessment in Schools*. Oxford: Blackwell.

School Curriculum and Assessment Authority (1996) *Exemplification of Standards: Key Stage 3*. London: SCAA.

School Examinations and Assessment Council (1989) *A Guide to Teacher Assessment (Pack C). A Source Book of Teacher Assessment*. London: Heinemann Educational/SEAC.

School Examinations and Assessment Council (1991a) *Profiles and Progression in Science Explorations*, *Assessment Matters 5*. London: SEAC/Central Office of Information (COI).

School Examinations and Assessment Council (1991b) *National Curriculum Assessment at Key Stage 3: A Review of the 1991 Pilots with Implications for 1992*. London: SEAC.

School Examinations and Assessment Council (1991c) *National Curriculum Assessment – Assessment Arrangements for Core and Foundations Subjects – Responsibility of LEAs in 1991–2*. London: SEAC.

School Technology Forum (1974) The essence of school technology. In *Technology Interface, School and Teacher Training*. Standing Conference on School Science and Technology. Nottingham: National Centre for School Technology, Trent Polytechnic.

Schools Council (1970) *The Next Two Years*. Nottingham: National Centre for School Technology, Trent.

Schools Council (1975) *Education through Design and Craft*. London: Edward Arnold.

Schroeder, H. (1990) *Performance at School*. Basel: Verlag Michael Arndt.

Secondary Education Authority (1996) Applied technology (year 11). In *Syllabus Manual Years 11 and 12 Accredited Courses*. Perth, WA: Secondary Education Authority.

Secondary Examinations Council (1985) *The National Criteria: Craft Design and Technology.* London: HMSO.

Stables, K. (1992) Issues surrounding the development of technological capability in children in their first years of school (ages 5–7). In D. Blandow and M. Dyrenfurth (eds) *Proceedings of INCOTE 92,* Weimar, Germany.

Sutherland, S., Dearing, Sir Ron and James, R. (1993) *Recording pupils' achievement – a letter to CEOs and schools.* London: SCAA/Ofsted and Office of Her Majesty's Chief Inspector of Schools.

Taylor, R. (1993) The future of assessment and testing in schools. Lecture to MA students, Goldsmiths College, London.

Terdiman, A. (1996) Education without expenses. In V. Schaffner (ed.) *Empire State Report: Politics, Policy and the Business of Government.* New York: Floyd Weintraub.

Theuerkauf, W. (1995) Technology education in Germany's Gymnasia. In K. Langer, M. Metzing and D. Wahl (eds) *Technology Education Innovation and Management.* Berlin: Springer-Verlag.

Thüringer Kultusministerium (1996) *Thüringer Oberstufe: Thüringens neuer Weg zur Abitur.* Erfurt: Thüringer Kultusministerium.

Tripp, D. (1996) Eight fundamentals of student outcome statements. In D. Tripp (ed.) *SCOPE: A Manual for Teachers.* Murdoch University, Perth.

Williams, R. (1965) *The Long Revolution.* Harmondsworth: Penguin.

Index